Hitler's U-Boat Fortresses

HITLER'S U-BOAT FORTRESSES

Randolph Bradham

THE LYONS PRESS
Guilford, Connecticut
An imprint of The Globe Pequot Press

Copyright © 2003 by Randolph Bradham

First Lyons Press paperback edition, 2005

Hitler's U-Boat Fortresses by Randolph Bradham, originally published by Praeger, an imprint of Greenwood Press. Copyright © 2003 by Michael Gordon. Published in paperback by arrangement with Greenwood Publishing Group, Inc., Westport, CT. All rights reserved.

ALL RIGHTS RESERVED. No part of this book may be reproduced or transmitted in any form by any means, electronic or mechanical, including photocopying and recording, or by any information storage and retrieval system, except as may be expressly permitted in writing from the publisher. Requests for permission should be addressed to Greenwood Publishing Group, Inc., Attn: Rights and Permissions Department, 88 Post Road West, Westport, CT 06881.

The Lyons Press is an imprint of The Globe Pequot Press.

10 9 8 7 6 5 4 3 2 1

Printed in the United States of America

Library of Congress Cataloging-in-Publication Data

Bradham, Randolph.
    Hitler's U-boat fortresses / Randolph Bradham.
        p. cm.
    Originally published: Westport, Conn. : Praeger, 2003.
    Includes bibliographical references and index.
    ISBN 1-59228-680-1 (pbk.)
    1. World War, 1939-1945—Naval operations, German. 2. World War, 1939-1945—Naval operations—Submarine. 3. Navy-yards and naval stations—France—Lorient—History—20th century. 4. Navy-yards and naval stations—France—Saint Nazaire—History—20th century. 5. Lorient (France)—History, Military—20th century. 6. Saint-Nazaire (France)—History, Military—20th century. I. Title.

D781.B68 2005
940.54'51—dc22

                                     2005045133

*This book is dedicated to the families
of the soldiers killed in this campaign*

CONTENTS

PREFACE

During this campaign, I was a 20-year-old staff sergeant and squad leader of the third squad, third platoon, Company E, 262nd Regiment, 66th Infantry Division. Many questions arose in our minds, although there was little time to seek answers. There were basic priority needs that had to come first. After the war and discharge from the army, most of us "hit the ground running," as we were anxious to put the war behind us and to get on with education and life itself. It was "catch-up" time.

For me, however, questions about the war and curiosity about its massiveness persisted. After retiring in 1995, I began a diligent search into the battle focused on St. Nazaire and Lorient and realized that the war there lasted for five years in devastating sequences of bombardment, reprisals, and an intense ground war that laid waste to the entire area. Hitler had ordered his troops to defend these U-boat fortresses until the bitter end, and this they did.

There will not be many more books on WWII from veterans, as our ranks are fading. Those of us who look back on our experiences have no complaints and feel privileged to have done our part.

ACKNOWLEDGMENTS

I wish to thank the following for their time and effort in helping bring this book to fruition.

My daughter, Elizabeth Bradham, for her review and constructive criticism of the manuscript throughout its development, as well as aiding in the quest for a proper publishing company.

Jack Parker, for helping in the beginning to locate the proper military museums and archives for material pertinent to this subject.

Brent Hepburn, for much translation from French to English and for tutoring me at least to a survival level in French.

Robert Fleury, former member of the French Navy in WWII, for his personal account of the occupation of the French naval station in Lorient the day the Germans arrived and for his help in getting material from friends and military organizations in France.

Lucien Le Francois of Toulon, France, for the personal account of living in Lorient during the German occupation and the Allied bombardments as well as maps and other pertinent material.

Ray Roberts, former member of the 66th Division and author of four books, three on the sinking of the *Leopoldville* and one on soldier stories of the time. His encouragement and advice during the preparation of the manuscript have been most helpful.

Carol Coffee, former member of the 66th Division and author of *From Tragedy to Triumph,* for his help, guidance, and continued encouragement.

French General Dumas-Delage of Lyon, for the detailed history of the beginning of the French Resistance and the Free French of the Interior (FFI) and for the eloquent history of the 8th Cuirassiers, the oldest of the French cavalry units.

Francois Kauffman Tardivel of Cannes, France, for much information on the Battle of Saint-Marcel, in which a relative participated.

Luc and Marc Braeuer, owners and curators of The Grand Blockhaus Museum at Batz-sur-Mer, France, and authors of multiple books on the campaign in and around St. Nazaire, for opening their files to me and for graciously sharing photos and documents germane to this subject.

Rachel Lopin, administrator of International Affairs in the Hotel de Ville, Lorient, for furnishing so many excellent photos from the city archives and having them re-photographed for improved clarity. Rachel, who speaks English and French fluently, has been invaluable as a translator in helping acquire more material in Lorient.

James Dorian, author of *Storming Saint-Nazaire,* for his guidance in preparation of the segment on Operation Chariot and for reviewing this segment of the book.

Patrick Andersen Bo, curator of Musée de la Resistance Bretonne at Saint Marcel, for opening his files and sharing photos, maps, and books.

A special thanks to all of the 66th Division veterans who responded so quickly and with so much accuracy to my request for their remembrances of the sinking of the *Leopoldville* and combat against the Germans.

Dr. Heather Ruland Staines, senior editor, History and Military Studies, Greenwood Publishing Group, for her help, advice, and guidance in the process of developing the manuscript into a worthy publication.

INTRODUCTION

Until 1939, Lorient and St. Nazaire, two seaports on the coast of Brittany, were happy towns. France and Great Britain had declared war on Germany following Germany's invasion of Poland, but essentially no fighting had begun and these early months after the declaration of war were called the "Phony War." Life went on as usual. Lorient was known for its fishing industry, in which many of the men in town were involved. Winemaking and other agricultural activities contributed greatly to the economy of the town. St. Nazaire was known for its shipbuilding, which created a very positive economy for St. Nazaire and the surrounding communities.

Both towns were beautifully situated on the Bay of Biscay, with the Loire River coursing through St. Nazaire and the Blavet, Scorf, and Laita rivers running through Lorient. Magnificent churches and colorful gardens were prevalent throughout the towns and surrounding villages. The people were steeped in tradition, and each holiday was a major event with many people turning out in attire of historic tradition.

Lorient had the picturesque islands of Belle Isle and Ile de Groix in close association with its coast. These islands were sources of dairy products, fruits, and vegetables for the city. The Quiberon Peninsula jutted out into the Bay of Biscay between the two ports. People flocked to Quiberon during the summer to enjoy the beaches and the great fishing that it offered.

St. Nazaire was flanked to the west by La Baule, a magnificent resort beach where crowds gathered during vacation times to enjoy the weather, the long wide sandy beaches, swimming, boating, and fishing. Good hotels, restaurants, and shops were plentiful. The large grand homes there were similar to those seen at Palm Beach.

All of this was to change drastically in the months to come. St. Nazaire and Lorient would be built into the two most formidable fortresses of Hitler's Atlantic Wall, so constructed as to give complete protection to the extensive submarine bases to be built by the Todt organization with prisoner of war and slave labor. These two cities and their surroundings were to become the focal point of an ongoing, devastating five-year war, and though both cities would be destroyed, the submarine bases—targets of bombardment by land and air—would remain intact and continuously functional until the end of the war in Europe. There was no other area in Europe that suffered as long and as continuously as this area in Brittany.

Peripheral villages such as Hennebont, Caudan, Bouvron, Etel, Port Louis, and many others would also be reduced to rubble from the wayward bombs and the ground war that followed the invasion of the French coast by the Allies. St. Nazaire and Lorient were never taken by the Allies. The Germans finally surrendered them to the Allies in May 1945, when the German army capitulated. Hitler had ordered his commanders to hold these two forts to the last man. There was to be no surrender. His U-boats were to be protected at all cost, because they were essential to the destruction of Allied ships bringing supplies across the Atlantic to support the advance from Normandy to Berlin.

Eventually, during this five-year battle, all of the destructive machines of war would be involved, leaving many civilians and soldiers dead or wounded. The civilians, especially, suffered tragically. Bombardment by air was intense until the invasion of France, and then the ground war began. This campaign was not an exciting battle with dramatic beach landings, tank assaults, and wholesale carnage as in other battles. It was a day-by-day methodical infantry-and-artillery war of containment, both sides capable of preventing their adversary from major advance. Having sustained significant casualties taking Brest, the Allied command was reluctant to attempt to take these two fortresses while supporting the thrust of war toward Germany. The original Allied plan was to take all the ports on the west coast of France so as to utilize them for the supply line necessary to proceed to Germany and to deny Hitler bases for his U-boats.

After occupation by the Germans, St. Nazaire and Lorient became the two most active submarine bases in the world. From his headquarters in Lorient, Admiral Karl Donitz, commander of the German submarine force of the German navy, controlled the whole marauding pack of German U-boats and maintained personal contact with each one.

There was then the long occupation by the Germans from June 1940 to their capitulation May 10 and 11, 1945, an occupation punctuated by numerous reprisals against the population. During this time, Lorient and St. Nazaire were battlefields. The British began bombing them in 1940 and were joined by the American air force in 1942. The bombing tapered off in 1943 as the Allies prepared for the invasion of France. The breakthrough from the beaches occurred in July 1944. This was the beginning of the ground war at St. Nazaire and Lorient, where many of the retreating Germans gathered to strengthen the defenses of this segment of the Atlantic Wall, which had already been fortified with generous quantities of food and ammunition.

In the meantime, on March 28, 1942, St. Nazaire was attacked by British naval personnel and commandos in a daring raid to destroy the only dry dock that could service Hitler's prize battleship, the *Tirpitz*. The next day the destroyer *Campbeltown* was rammed into the Normandie dock and exploded with timed fuses, killing many Germans. Following this raid, dubbed "Operation Chariot," which left most of the British dead or captured, the civilian homes were ransacked as the Germans searched for hidden commandos. The ports remained Hitler's two jewels, as they were home base for his marauding "gray wolves," which were organized in "wolf packs" to attack Allied shipping. These U-boats, in final analysis, were the most destructive weapon in Hitler's arsenal. One need only to gain some knowledge of the sinking of hundreds of Allied ships bringing supplies to Europe and Russia to understand the value of the two bases, main home ports for the German submarine force that almost "brought England to its knees" in 1940, 1941, and 1942. The German submariners called this period of success "the happy times." One can see why Hitler would not allow them to surrender.

The devastating effects of the U-boats were brought home to the soldiers of the 66th Infantry Division on Christmas Eve 1944, when U-486 sank the *Leopoldville* in the English Channel at a loss of 802 young men. There wasn't a GI in the 66th Division who did not suffer the pain of losing so many comrades. They were intent on getting revenge and did so.

The plight of the civilians was the most horrifying aspect of this war. Most villages, towns, and cities in Europe, which were caught in the path of the war, had some bad days or weeks, but in very few areas was the killing and destruction as constant and prolonged as it was in St. Nazaire, Lorient, and the surrounding villages. These citizens were caught in a combat zone from the beginning to the end. Like a front-line soldier, they had to endure bombing and artillery barrages on a near daily basis for five years. Food and water were hard to come by, and electricity, clothing, and other necessary supplies were almost nonexistent.

The horrors of war affected the Germans too. In addition to the ground combat that took many lives and maimed many more, the submarine service lost 75 percent of its submarines and submariners. The dreadful fear and suffering that accompanied each submariner to his death made it a cruel and painful way to die. Unless killed instantly, their last moments were spent drowning at sea, suffocating in a downed submarine or burning to death either on the surface of the ocean or in one of the compartments of the submarine. Even Admiral Donitz lost his son, a submariner in the Atlantic.

The tentacles of war reached out from the center and destroyed so many areas, such as Hennebont, which is a small village, representative of hundreds, where so much carnage took place. All of these small villages suffered the wrath of the bombardments and artillery barrages. The townspeople had to endure seeing friends and village folk murdered at the hands of the Germans as reprisal for an act of resistance or suspicion of one.

The 4th Armored Division, which had a most outstanding record in WWII, was stopped abruptly at Pont Scorf by German artillery in the Lorient pocket after blasting its way there from the beachhead in several days. General John Wood, the 4th Armored Division commander, was relieved to get the order to contain, rather than persist, in his previously assigned mission to take Lorient, because he realized that it would require much more of a force than his armored division to neutralize this port. Naturally, it would have been much better strategically if the Allies could have taken Lorient and St. Nazaire. Neutralizing them would have eliminated strong military forces in the rear of the advancing Allied armies and greatly lessened the advantage of the U-boats in being so near the shipping lanes in the Atlantic Ocean when supplies were being shipped to Europe for the invasion. However, containment, although an alternative, did eliminate the strong German forces from the major battle in the east.

The French troops fought courageously against the Germans who had overrun them in 1940. They were out for revenge and to restore their honor. The members of the Resistance maintained a smoldering fire under the Germans, thus generating an element of fear and uneasiness. They fought the Germans openly in a vicious battle at St. Marcel, just north of St. Nazaire, thus sensitizing the Germans to their strength and intent. Even civilians in the pockets furnished the Allies with much useful information at the risk of losing their lives if caught. The Free French of the Interior (FFI), mostly made up of patriotic young men from farms and villages, answered the call to fight for their country following the Allied invasion. Their numbers grew to 30,000–40,000 in Brittany and they became well organized into proper units. With the help of the Americans, they were trained enough to control the Germans south of the Loire River and in the eastern section of Lorient. Eventually, the FFI was absorbed into the regular French army.

Although St. Nazaire and Lorient were fortresses, the Germans met their match with each of the armored and infantry units. In spite of exceptionally long lines to defend for a single division, the soldiers of the 4th and 6th Armored Divisions and the 83rd, 94th, and 66th Infantry Divisions with their attached units and supported by the FFI and French regular army units, held their ground and allowed no trespassing into Allied territory. The nature of the warfare required planning, intelligence, stealth, aggressiveness, and courage—all of which these units had "in spades."

The Army Specialized Training Program (ASTP) soldiers and former air force cadets, who joined these units after having been tucked away in college for three to nine months, "came out swinging" and turned out to be one of the finest groups of front-line soldiers as has ever been present in our armed forces. Their intelligence combined with seasoning as front-line soldiers made a great contribution to our fighting efficiency during the last months of the war. Had the war lasted a little longer, many of them would have received battlefield commissions.

France showed her appreciation by erecting beautiful monuments in Bouvron, Caudan, and Pont Scorf in honor of the American and French soldiers who fought there. Monuments at Forts Benning, Rucker, and Blanding are dedicated to the hundreds of young soldiers of the 66th Division who lost their lives in the English Channel and in combat.

In summary, this book, *Hitler's U-Boat Fortresses,* graphically describes the history of death and destruction associated with war in Brittany, an area that has been given very little attention relative to its importance. Hopefully, it conveys not only the horrors of battle, but also the cruelty, devastation, and punishment of war to everyone and everything under its dark and threatening cloud.

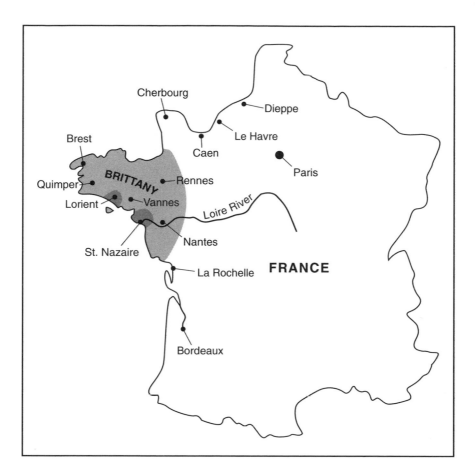

France.

Brittany.

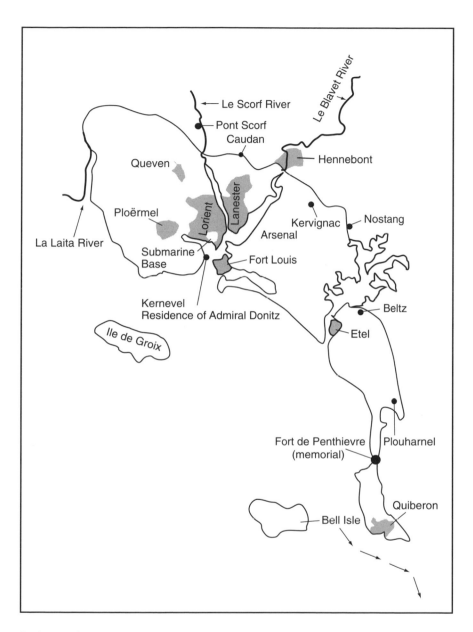

Lorient pocket.

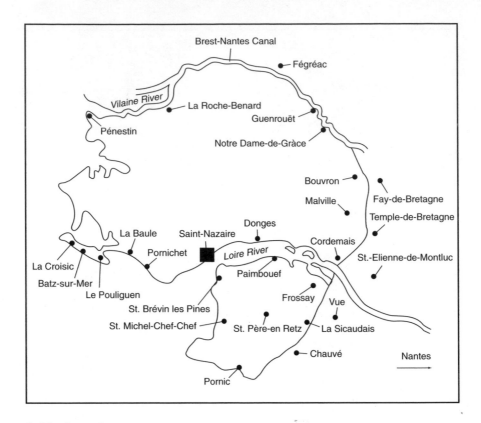

St. Nazaire pocket.

Chapter 1

1940

THE BEGINNING

In May 1940, Germany began its campaign against France with tanks and planes in a mobile attack against the static Maginot Line. This was a fast moving new kind of warfare perfected by the Germans during the interim between WWI and WWII. The Maginot Line was simply bypassed and the victory secured with the German air force and the rapidly advancing panzer divisions sweeping across France. Three-fifths of the country became occupied overnight, and the remainder would be occupied in November 1942. This tragic defeat of France shocked the world. Who was to blame?

Total rejection of the occupiers was bound to be no more than marginal. A few Frenchmen departed to England to join General Charles de Gaulle, who opposed any agreement with the Germans. Others moved clandestinely to the Free Zone, where a new government was being formed. This government was a product of defeat and occupation, but it would impose the law. For the vast majority, there seemed no alternative but to submit, bow before the triumphant force, and adjust their behavior accordingly. Despite their secret defiance, even those determined to resist had to appear to compromise so as not to expose their underground activities.

The German attack began May 10, 1940, and in one month, France had to make a decision between continuation of a war against seemingly insurmountable odds or capitulation. Paul Reynaud, leader of the government, called on Marshal Henri Phillipe Pétain to serve as vice-president of the

Council of Ministers on May 18, 1940. He dismissed Paul Gamelin, commander in chief of the French armed forces, and replaced him with Louis Maxime Weygand. Pétain was a hero of WWI, notably for saving France at Verdun in 1916. He had remained in the government more or less since that time and was popular with the people.

Paul Reynaud then took Edouard Deladier's place in the Department of Defense and brought in General de Gaulle as well as Paul Baudoin and Yves Bouthillier. Weygand began to recommend that France sign an armistice and on June 13, 1940, at a meeting of the Council of Ministers, Pétain agreed. The government was moved from Paris to Bordeaux to escape the oncoming Germans.

On June 16, 1940, the Council of Ministers met in Bordeaux and antagonistic positions were presented. Reynaud withdrew and Pétain was appointed by the president to run the government. He appointed Baudoin to head foreign affairs, Weygand to head national defense, and Admiral Jean Francois Darlan to head the navy. On June 17, 1940, Pétain called for an end to hostilities and approached the Germans for an armistice.

In the meantime, the first tragedy to beset St. Nazaire in this five-year conflict was about to unfold. Large numbers of the Allied Expeditionary Force—driven across France by the onrushing Germans—arrived at St. Nazaire with the hope of being evacuated to England in one of the French and British ships waiting there. At 3:35 P.M., a heavy air attack on the *Lancastria,* which had embarked 5,800 troops, resulted in damage so great that she sank within 15 minutes, with the loss of nearly 3,000 men. The crew of the *Cambridgeshire* saw the attack and went immediately to the *Lancastria's* aid, rescuing 900 to 1,000 men. It is still unclear why so many men perished in an area with so many small craft present. It is thought that there was an inadequate number of life belts available, and the waters were covered by burning fuel. Prime Minister Winston Churchill withheld this information from the public, fearing it would badly discourage an already depressed nation. He later said, "I had intended to release the news a few days later, but events crowded upon us so black and so quickly, that I forgot to lift the ban, and it was some time before the knowledge of this horror became public." Six weeks later, the news reached the United States.

A similar tragedy occurred at Lorient, when evacuating ships leaving the harbor were blown up by magnetic mines dropped into the bay by German planes. The day after this tragedy, on June 18, 1940, de Gaulle made his famous broadcast from London. He had broken from Pétain's government and was appealing to the French to continue the struggle and not compromise their country by signing an armistice. His was truly a voice in the wilderness, as the great majority of the French people remained loyal to Pétain, convinced that he was acting in their best interest. Pétain maintained vehemently to his dying day that this was true. However, de Gaulle was joined in London by other state and government leaders who had chosen exile so that they could carry on the struggle against the Germans.

De Gaulle appealed to the military, engineers, and armament workers in England, and Pétain spoke to the army, former combatants, and the people of France.

A break with the Third Republic occurred July 10, 1940, and an armistice was presented to the French statesmen at Rethondes in the same railway car in which the Germans had signed the surrender papers in 1918. Even Hitler was present. The French, in vain, sought modifications to the armistice but were denied them.

Three-fifths of the territory of metropolitan France would be occupied. The dividing line ran obliquely from the Spanish frontier up as far as Tours, then sloped east toward Geneva. Germany thus appropriated the richest and most populated part of France. The French government had to pledge collaboration of its administration, and France's fleet and air force were to be disarmed. (Hitler promised not to use them.) France was then forced to sign an armistice with Italy. These armistices came into effect on June 25, 1940. Immediately thereafter, the British pounded the French fleet at Mers-el-Kéber near Oran in Algeria. Thirteen hundred French sailors were killed, several ships were sunk, and many others were damaged. Churchill was taking no chances. He trusted neither Hitler nor Darlan and made it clear to Hitler that the British were there to stay.

Soon thereafter, Pétain brought Pierre Laval, a former premier of France, into the government. The French government moved to Vichy, which was located in the unoccupied or Free Zone of France, and became known as the Vichy Government. New laws were invoked that gave Pétain and the council autocratic control. Francois Blancho, mayor of St. Nazaire, and his council resigned a few months later and were replaced by Vichy-appointed officials.

Under the autocratic rule of Pétain, prefects were empowered to arrest, without charge, anyone suspicious of imperiling the security of the state. Many innocent people were arrested, sometimes at the suggestion of a neighbor. Two years later, 80,000 were in prisons or concentration camps, and anti-Semitism was growing.

Pierre Laval was named as Pétain's successor in the event that Pétain left office. Laval was a former prime minister of France and found no fault in collaborating with the Germans, but his staff was divided. Some agreed with Laval that they should make the best deal possible with the Germans, while others felt they should remain loyal to Great Britain and that Great Britain would defeat Germany.

Under Laval's direction, France became a police state. He was instrumental in providing the Germans with 641,000 Frenchmen for German labor camps. Deportation of Jews would begin later in 1942. Because of the increasing presence of resistance groups, the government ruled that all male relatives of a resister over 18 years of age would be candidates for the death penalty. His female relatives would be delegated to forced labor and the younger relatives would be sent to reformatories.

Public opinion began to manifest itself against the Vichy government, and local officials, police, and magistrates began to ignore orders from Vichy when they disagreed with its policies. National movement began soon, albeit subtly at first. Local groups of resistance formed and met clandestinely. A group in one village or community would reach out to a similar group in the neighboring community until gradually a loose network began to form. This type of cooperation was invaluable in returning downed Allied aviators to England. Valuable information about the enemy was passed on to the Allies. This network proved to be an invaluable source of information for the Allies throughout the war.

De Gaulle appealed to remnants of the army and overseas French loyalists to create a new French regime. He knew that this authority would be accepted by the French people who were resisting the Germans; by the French Resistance; and by the American, British, and Russian governments.

In the beginning of the war, de Gaulle was not well known. Initially, all that he could offer was faith and action. He firmly believed that France was not through and should continue to fight. Defeating Vichy was as important to him as defeating the Germans, as he did not want Vichy in place at war's end.

He also began to build a military organization to combat the Germans and gain a voice in the postwar government. The Americans and, to a lesser extent, the British, underrated de Gaulle's and the value of the Resistance and refused initially to consider a de Gaulle government postwar. Therefore, de Gaulle, in exile, had a long uphill fight to win the American's favor and could depend on no one but himself. Churchill recognized de Gaulle August 7, 1940, but the United States did not officially recognize him as leader of France until 1944.

Fortunately for de Gaulle, an event occurred that began to give him some status. St. Pierre-et-Miguelon was part of a French colony of islands off the south coast of Newfoundland. It lay at the mouth of the St. Lawrence River and had strategic importance because it could harbor German U-boats and report the exit of convoys or individual ships from the St. Lawrence River. Agents there reported to Vichy by radio. Canada, Great Britain, and the United States met to consider the best way to neutralize this island of communication. While they "dragged their feet" in deliberation, de Gaulle sent Admiral Emile Muselier with three corvettes and a submarine to take the islands, which he did.

AERIAL BOMBARDMENT

While all of this was going on, the cruel brutality of war began to make itself known in Brittany, especially around St. Nazaire and Lorient, which were to become prime military targets.

No one suffers more in war than the civilians in its path. They are injured or killed. They are displaced from their homes and separated from loved ones and friends. Children are shipped to other towns or countries with name tags pinned to their jackets, many of them never to see their parents again. Homes are destroyed and looted. Gardens wither and die. To flee the ravages of war is a desperate hardship. Finding food, water, and shelter is a constant ordeal. The sick and elderly become depleted, many succumbing to life on the run as a refugee. This was the fate of the inhabitants of St. Nazaire and Lorient once the British began bombing their cities. They were unlucky enough to have prime military targets—the submarine bases—in their midst. Robert Fleury, now living in Moncks Corner, South Carolina, was a 16-year-old naval cadet in Lorient when the Germans occupied the city. He was an eyewitness to their entrance and the frenzied activity in the port just before they arrived. His account is as follows:

> When the German tanks were near Rennes, at the beginning of the Brittany peninsula, there were no defense lines or French forces all the way to Brest, except the naval defense of the two navy bases of Lorient and Brest. The admiralty had only a short period of time to evacuate 159 ships of all styles: 83 French war ships, 48 French merchant ships, 10 English, 18 Dutch and Norwegian ships. They all left for England for North Africa or West Africa. In that short time on June 16, 1940, orders came to evacuate all the gold of the French treasury of the Bank of France, including the gold reserve at the banks of Belgium and Poland. All that gold left Lorient and Brest for West Africa and Martinique. In all, 1,000 tons of gold were evacuated to different French colonies without losing a penny. Also evacuated from Lorient and Brest were

all senior classes of different training schools including the midshipmen of the French Naval Academy, aboard the unfinished battleship *Richilieu.*

A newly promoted General Charles de Gaulle received orders to reach England for a mission to obtain ships from the British to evacuate as many French troops as possible to Africa. That is how de Gaulle got stuck in England and started his patriotic movement to refuse to recognize the defeat and broadcast his appeal on June 18, 1940, on BBC London.

For 10 days, it was hell between the bombs falling all over the city and the navy base. We saw many ships packed like sardines with either military personnel or civilians with children being blown to bits in the bay without anybody being able to do anything to rescue them. Then, day and night, there were continuous explosions to destroy military equipment and the navy fuel tank farm. Flames shot a hundred feet into the air, creating thick smoke, which blocked the sun and rained clumps of soot on everything.

All of the waterways on the river Scorf and the bay were on fire with burning ships that could not leave. The *La Martiniere* was suddenly surrounded by flames and I could see men jumping overboard, trapped in thick flaming oil, and again we could not do anything about it. All military and merchant ships and fishing boats left the port between June 15 and 21, even under the threat of German planes coming from the north, flying close to the roofs of our barracks, and dropping magnetic mines into the channel.

At 2:00 P.M., those of us students remaining were called to the parade yard near the flagpole. A column of German panzers entered the school gate. A group of our officers met the German leader and gave their ceremonial swords as a protocol of surrender. Next was the worst I ever felt in my life, a feeling I would never wish on anyone else who loves his country. A cadet was given the order to bring down the French flag from the staff, and we all sang the "Marseillaise" with all the verses. A German soldier then raised the nightmarish swastika. The Germans saluted; we did not.

The base was under the command of French Admiral de Penfentenyo de Kervereguen, who was afraid that he would not have time to evacuate the port of all ships and destroy the entire arsenal. The admiral himself and General Mussat, his assistant, all in full dress uniform, were at the front line to stall the advance at "Les Cinq Chemins." General Mussat, who was standing near the admiral, was wounded; also the navy doctor Labbe, who was taking care of the general, was hit and wounded. Two other officers nearby, Captain Gandinien and Captain Doctor Menlette, were killed on this June 21.[1]

Another eyewitness to the occupation of Lorient by the Germans was Lucien Le Francois, who now lives in Toulon, France. He was an 11-year-old boy at the time, and his family remained in Lorient most of the five years that the Germans were there, despite the hardships.[2] He describes the plight of the inhabitants:

In mid-June 1940, enemy planes bombard and drop magnetic mines in the harbor entrance. Then we hear of the presence of German troops in Rennes. All ships in Lorient receive orders to leave and to board important material, military personnel, and civilians. Armored trains came to Lorient and Brest with tons of gold from treasuries from Poland, Holland, Belgium, and France to be evacuated on navy ships. In the shipyard they organize the blowing up of all shops, stocks, ships under construction, radio towers, the burning of sensitive records, and destruction of the fleet fuel tank farm. One of the last ships to leave the harbor was the steam trawler *La Tanche* with 200 people on board and blew up in the afternoon on a mine in the channel. For over a month entire families with children 4–15 years of age were found washed up on beaches. There were only 18 survivors. One hundred and seventeen bodies were recovered.

When the Germans entered Lorient, I was with my maternal grandfather about 15 minutes from home visiting a scrap dealer. A plane came over with black crosses on its wings, flying low. When we got home my grandmother was furious and kept talking loudly about the "Boches" were coming.

The armistice was signed officially on June 15, 1940. People were at first satisfied because the war was over and the prisoners would be back. Disappointment was painful. All French military were confined awaiting shipment to Germany. Some were already doing forced labor.

Food became a problem. To trash leftovers was unthinkable. School brunch at 4:00 P.M. was one slice of bread spread with pork fat and two lumps of sugar. Teachers began distributing vitamined cookies. Hygiene difficulties began because of a lack of soap. All transportation for civilians ceased, as there was no gasoline. The Germans looted stocks of food and equipment wherever they found them. The fishing industry was reduced by lack of fuel and confiscation of fishing boats. Bombardment by the Royal Air Force took its toll also. What was left of the fishing boats moved west to Concarneau.

We traveled to the countryside by bicycle once a week for food and to try and find scraps of wood in the forest for fuel. We made charcoal-like balls by using old newspapers and sawdust, wetting them and making them into patties and let them dry. We tied rubber from old tires to our shoe soles. Rationing of meat, bread, and butter became severe.

School became a problem. Because of the British air raids at night, children often did not get enough sleep. A child who had a bad night either did not come or came late. On the way to school, we collected shrapnel, which had fallen from the German antiaircraft firing.

Acts of resistance were prevalent and some arrests took place. The German crews of the Todt organization continued to pour tons of concrete for their submarine base. The first Nazi submarine came to re-supply on July 7, 1940.

Pierre Picaud was a 13-year-old teenager in 1939, living near St. Nazaire. His recently recorded memoirs add interesting insight into the lives of the French people at that time.

I have written these memoirs for my 14 grandchildren as I think they have learnt truly very little about this historical period, which was very troubled. In 1939, I was 13 years old. The war broke out. All of our neighbors left for the war. I stopped going to school to help the women on the farms. It was miserable work. My first job was to try and remove silt from the Slyl River. I worked with an 80-year-old illiterate, Thomas de Bouke, who taught me very much. In 1940, ration tickets appeared. We were lucky in the country to have food. Feeding people became a problem as there was no harvest. Things were quiet at first. We were confident of our Maginot Line.

In May 1940, Hitler launched his attack with Stukas. The tanks followed and rapidly crossed Belgium. Our only significant resistance was by Colonel de Gaulle and his armor. We had one tank and one plane against 20. My father, who fought in WWI, said, "We are 50 years behind. What do we have to stop the Boche?" The government was set up at Bordeaux and Marshal Pétain, conqueror of Verdun during WWI, was made chief of state. He brought in Pierre Laval to run the new government and this marked the end of the Third Republic. Pétain signed the armistice with Hitler and this was shame for France and the beginning of collaboration.

On June 18, 1940, General de Gaulle made his appeal on the BBC radio from London, which I heard at a neighbor's home. I went back home and told everyone of hearing de Gaulle and he said that we had lost the battle but not the war. Most were skeptical. Ninety percent of the people supported Pétain. What can you do when you are 14 years old and most disagree with you? I was vexed. My parents were informed by my uncle, who was a colonel, not to listen to de Gaulle or to the English. I threw this letter into the fire.[3]

The occupation itself changed the lives of the inhabitants completely. A Colonel Welcher took command of St. Nazaire and established a curfew from 11:00 P.M. to 6:00 A.M. The city officials, through posters placed around the city, requested that people remain calm and cooperative. Thousands of people were put out of work because the defense projects in the shipyards were no longer active. On July 8, Francois Blancho, the mayor of St. Nazaire, tried to negotiate work programs for the people and, finally, on July 31, was given an appointment with Admiral Darlan, secretary of the navy in the Vichy regime. However, bombardments by the British air force began, making further work projects in the port untenable.

When German soldiers were fired upon in early August, the curfew was changed to 9:00 P.M. to 6:00 A.M. Five hostages were taken and were to be executed if there was further trouble. Francois Blancho and the parish priest presented themselves to replace the hostages, but the Germans declined and soon released the hostages.

French war prisoners were used to build defensive structures on the beaches. French civilians slipped them food and cigarettes until they were shipped to Germany in September. Magnetic mines were dropped in the harbor by the British as an antisubmarine measure. The Germans had previously dropped magnetic mines into the harbor to damage ships evacuating soldiers after the fall of France.

U-BOAT MENACE

There would have been no battle in Brittany of any magnitude or significant duration had it not been for the importance of the submarine bases at Lorient and St. Nazaire. As two of Hitler's primary sources of destruction to Allied ships and supplies, the bases were prime targets.

After the war, Prime Minister Winston Churchill said, "The only thing that frightened me during the war was the U-boat menace." If one reviews the Battle of the Atlantic in WWII, it is easy to understand why Hitler placed so much emphasis on St. Nazaire and Lorient and made them fortresses to protect the U-boats, his most destructive weapon. During WWI, a small German submarine force had "brought England to its knees" and was repeating the performance in 1940. During WWI and at the beginning of WWII, Allied defense against the U-boats was not well developed, and Allied ships were easy prey. By the end of WWII, 8,000 Allied ships and 890,000 men had been sent to the bottom of the Atlantic Ocean.

Early in the war, Britain's lifeline of supply ships from the United States was devastated. In this first year, with an average of only six U-boats operating in the Atlantic at any one time, at least 1,000 merchant ships were sunk with their essential cargoes of fuel, armaments, ammunition, tanks, and planes. By mid-July 1940, the Royal Navy was down to a two-month supply of oil. By September 1941, 25 percent of the entire British Fleet had been lost. Sir Dudley Pound, the British First Sea Lord said, "If we lose the war at sea, we lose the war."

How did this happen? Although the Treaty of Versailles forbade Germany to build submarines, the Germans secretly had a civilian group designing submarines for a Dutch firm, which was probably a front. An Anglo-German treaty was signed in 1935, giving Germany parity in submarine production. Shortly thereafter, Germany launched a small U-boat, *V-1*.

During 1935, Admiral Erich Raeder, commander of the German navy, placed Admiral Karl Donitz in command of the submarine force. Admiral Donitz had entered the German navy in 1916 and had been captured by the British in 1918. After being released at war's end, he remained in the German navy but was forced to spend his time on surface ships because of the sanctions on submarines. His mind, even when he was in prison, remained loyal to U-boat design and combat strategy, and he formulated many new ideas and tactics. One was the concept of the "wolf pack." While a young submariner in WWI, he sank an Allied vessel and realized that he could have taken more from the convoy had there been other submarines to help. It was this incident that started him thinking about U-boats traveling near enough to each other so that all could respond when a convoy was sighted. Donitz was convinced that he could win the war if he had enough U-boats in the Atlantic.

But he had a hard, uphill fight with his superiors to gain proper recognition for the submarine force. Since the large surface ships were favored by the navy and considered the principle menace to Allied merchant ships, this left the submarine force confined to coastal waters to prey on the "leftovers." At the beginning of the war, Donitz had only 26 serviceable submarines and made it known to Hitler that he needed a minimum of 300. However, with the small fleet and in spite of his assignment to coastal waters, Donitz's success soon became so apparent that Hitler began to pour money and attention toward the buildup of the U-boat fleet and its defenses. By war's end, approximately 1,000 had been built and utilized.

The real break for Donitz and the U-boat fleet came when the German army overran France and occupied the Brittany ports of St. Nazaire and Lorient, Brest, La Pallice, and Bordeaux. St. Nazaire and Lorient, already submarine bases, were selected to be rebuilt by the Todt organization (a large German construction company that built much of the Atlantic Wall) to withstand any type of Allied attack. For example, when the Royal Air Force dropped 146 tons of bombs on the U-boat pens at Lorient, there was little damage. Donitz first visited these ports on June 21, 1940, and personally supervised the plans and construction of the new submarine pens.

The U-boats moved to the new bases from those in the Baltic, such as Bergen and Tronheim, thus shortening the distance to the Atlantic Ocean

German U-boat entering harbor St. Nazaire after combat tour in the Atlantic.
Courtesy: The Grand Blockhaus Museum, Batz sur Mer, France.

hunting grounds by 450 miles. This change produced immediate results in
Allied tonnage sunk. The first submarine to enter Lorient arrived July 7,
1940. It was the *U 30,* commanded by Kapitan-Lieutenant Fritz-Julius
Lemp. The *U 334, U 52,* and *U 99* Type IX submarines arrived in August.
Others followed, and Lorient became a bristling U-boat port and the head-
quarters for the Atlantic Fleet.

  Shortly after Admiral Donitz established Lorient as his headquarters,
Lieutenant Commander Otto Kretschmer, Germany's top U-boat ace,
radioed Donitz's headquarters on July 5, 1940, that he was in position in
the Atlantic, having traveled from a Baltic port. On the way there, he had
sunk a Swedish and a Canadian vessel. He was now attacking a convoy
and had sunk one vessel, but because of some faulty torpedoes, he failed
to strike again. A small escort vessel found him and pinned him to the
ocean floor for 18 hours. While down and with depth charges exploding
around them, Kretschmer lay down, picked up a book, and began to read

in order to reflect calmness to the crew. One astute submariner noticed, however, that the book was upside down. They were finally able to slip away and sank three more vessels before heading to Lorient.

Kretschmer, operating alone, had already sunk a quarter million tons of supplies. When he arrived in Lorient, Admiral Raeder was there to present him the Knights Cross to the Iron Cross. *U-99* was one of the first U-boats serviced in Lorient. Because of his recent experience, Kretschmer saw the wisdom of the "wolf pack" system and enthusiastically supported it.

The U-boats operated at night because they could surface. Darkness gave them protection from observation. This allowed for faster speed and greater maneuverability to station themselves. The Allies had a device named for the Allied Submarine Detection Investigating Committee (ASDIC) since WWI. The American version, sonar, consisted of a transmitter receiver placed in a dome under a plane or ship. Sound impulses were reflected on submerged objects, giving the well known "ping." But the device could not pick up a surfaced submarine, which was another reason for night attacks.

Donitz once said, "The greater the number of U-boats brought into the attack, the more favorable would become the opportunities for each individual attacker." His strategy was to have one-third in transit between ocean and port, one-third in port for supplies and repairs, and one-third in the battle zone. When a U-boat spotted a convoy, a message was sent to Donitz's headquarters. (He also received information from the crypt analysis section on convoy routes, size of convoy, and number of escort vessels.) He would dispatch U-boats to the area of the convoy and set up the plan of attack.

On October 16, 1940, Lieutenant-Commander Heinrich Bleichrodt in *U-48* spotted Convoy SC-7-30 ships with only three escort vessels. He radioed Lorient of position, speed, course, and number of ships and escorts. He then sank two ships and withdrew as dawn was approaching. An escort vessel found him and kept *U-48* down for eight hours with depth charges. The following U-boats responded to the first notice of the convoy and banded together for a "wolf pack" attack: Heinrich Liebe in *U-38,* Fritz Frauenheim in *U-101,* Karl-Heinze Moehle in *U-123,* and Engelbert Endrass in *U-46.*

The attack on the convoy began at 8:45 P.M., October 18, 1940. The U-boat crews were jubilant, as only 15 of the 35 ships in the convoy reached port and no U-boats were lost. Kretschmer sank six ships and Moehle sank four. As some of the U-boats headed into Lorient for fuel and repairs, those remaining received the message that a convoy of 49 vessels was approaching on the same route. Gunther Prien, U-boat ace, joined the pack. The attack of the previous night was repeated and Convoy HX-79 lost 12 ships. The menace called the "wolf pack" had begun.

From September 1939, to June 1940, 2,300,000 tons of Allied shipping were sunk. From July 1940, through December 1940, 2,500,000 tons of ships and supplies were sunk. The Germans lost only two U-boats between July and October 1940. The U-boat crews called this "The Happy Times."

The terror that the U-boats spread was not only measured in ships and men lost, but those who died at sea experienced horrific pain and suffering before death finally closed out their misery. The ones who died outright from the explosions were the most fortunate, as death was instant. Others were trapped in darkness with no way out and water rising in their prison. There were those who jumped into the sea to be overcome by burning oil on the surface. Others were sucked down when the ship sank and died gasping for breath. Some escaped the ship to float around in that tremendous expanse of ocean—all alone, left lost to endure the suffering of thirst, delusion, cold, sea sickness, and fear. A few were lucky enough to get into a lifeboat or raft. It was an ugly war in which very few prisoners were taken. At war's end, Admiral Donitz was convicted as a war criminal for his "no prisoner" policy and given a 10-year prison sentence by the Tribunal at Nuremburg.

Duty on a German U-boat was one of the most hazardous in WWII. Germany lost 28,592 of its 41,300 submariners and 753 of its 863 operational U-boats. U-boats were often submerged at 300–600 feet with depth charges exploding near them for hours. Going deeper risked destruction by water pressure and ascending increased the risk of triggering the depth charges.

The following is a list of some of the aces and their records.

	Tonnage sunk	Ships sunk
Otto Kretschmer	266,629	44
Wolfgang Luth	223,712	43
Enrich Tapp	193,684	34
Karl Ericjrich Nertin	186,064	29
Victor Schutz	171,164	34
Hebert Schultze	171,122	26
Georg Lassen	167,601	28
Heinrich Willenbrock	166,596	22
Heinrich Liebe	162,333	30
Gunther Prien	160,939	28

Two U-boats docked in St. Nazaire. Note damage
to tower, probably from depth charges. Courtesy:
The Grand Blockhaus Museum, Batz-sur-Mer,
France.

German planes could fly 1,000 miles over the Atlantic to look for convoys. The Allies could only protect the convoy by air from 300 miles off
each Atlantic Coast. The Germans also had the advantage of having broken the Allied code, so they had all of the information on each convoy and
could track them. A "wolf pack" would stretch out at right angles to the
path of the convoy. The U-boat first detecting the convoy would radio the
others to converge. They would infiltrate the convoy and attack up and
down the aisles. Escort vessels were insufficiently constructed and armed,
and crews were poorly trained and inexperienced.

The British had other disadvantages. Their navigational aids were rus-
tic. There was a lack of aircraft, trained pilots, and equipment. It was not

U-boat heading into pen at St. Nazaire. Courtesy: The Grand Blockhaus Museum, Batz-sur-Mer, France.

unusual that a plane sent to protect a convoy could not find it due to navigational errors and to convoys being off course. In addition, limited numbers of planes could be allocated to this phase of the war.

Early on, there were quarrels between the British admiralty and the Royal Air Force, but eventual cooperation enhanced Britain's submarine defenses. Another break came when Britain's code breakers began to break the German codes.

THOSE WHO WOULD RESIST

When Germany occupied France, the French reacted toward the Germans in three basic ways. First, there were those who collaborated with the Germans for personal gain and to have a better life during the occupation. Then there were those, by far the largest group, who maintained indifference to the Germans but were not aggressive toward them. The last group, small in number, were very brave people who tried to do as much harm to the Germans as possible. These acts ranged from harassment to overt murder. These were members of the Resistance.

When the members of the Resistance acted in some destructive manner toward the Germans, there was always the aftermath to deal with. At times this could be circumvented and at times it could not. The German reprisals were usually severe, which always raised the question, Were the acts worth the reprisals?

Boris Vilde, Anatole Lewitsky, and Yvonne Oddon often met at the Musée de l'Homme in Paris—a hangout and meeting place for the Resistance. They became a small group dedicated to carrying out acts of resistance against the Germans and gathering pertinent information for the Allies. An additional member, René Creston, was recruited and the group began collecting information on German military installations and sabotaging German operations.

The men recruited friends in St. Nazaire who had access to the German submarine base and prepared plans and maps of the port with emphasis on potential targets for British bombardment. Creston passed these documents to the Musée de l'Homme and Vilde sent them to British agents via Frenchmen traveling to London. Some of the couriers were intercepted by the Germans and the Gestapo traced them back to Oddon, Lewitsky, and Vilde. They had been betrayed.

The three of them were sentenced to death, but Oddon's sentence was changed to life imprisonment. She survived a concentration camp and returned to Paris when it was liberated. Anatole Lewitsky and Boris Vilde were executed with five other men by firing squad on the top of a hill outside of Paris. All were singing "La Marseillaise" when they were killed.

In Pau, there was a Resistance group led by Marie-Madeleine Fourcade, the only woman to head a major Resistance organization. Antoine Hugon, an agent from Paris, appeared one day in Pau proudly wearing Germany's Iron Cross, which he had been awarded in the First World War for saving a drowning German soldier. He stood in front of his friends, took off his clothes, and produced a huge map of all the U-boat pens in St. Nazaire. These drawings were made to scale down to the last inch by an engineer named Henri Mouren. London was very excited to receive these drawings, which, no doubt, played an important role in planning the British Commando raid on St. Nazaire in March 1942.

The Resistance movement continued to grow stronger, and by war's end involved thousands. One of its greatest contributions was helping to organize the Free French of the Interior (FFI), which became a large, well-organized force of front-line combat soldiers who came forth following

the Invasion to help the Allies finish the war. They were especially prevalent in the campaigns around St. Nazaire and Lorient.

NOTES

1. After Robert and three other cadets quietly slipped out of the gate one
stormy night in July, he traveled for four days to his home in Honfleur on the
Channel. He lived in this occupied zone for five months and then crossed the bor-
der to the unoccupied zone under Vichy control. He finished his training at Toulon
Naval Base and graduated from Saint-Mandrier Military School in December
1941. Following graduation, he volunteered for service in Dakar (Senegal),
Africa, and was assigned to the destroyer *Le Terrible*. After the Allied landing in
North Africa, the French joined the fight against Germany, Italy, and Japan.
Robert participated in many subsequent campaigns and was decorated numerous
times. This is another example of Frenchmen returning to the war for the honor of
France.

2. A continuation of Lucien's experience as an inhabitant of Lorient will follow in the next chapter.

3. Marshal Pétain was such a national hero that many of the French people
remained loyal to him, feeling that he honestly thought he was making the right
choice for France. He maintained that until his dying day. It was hard for them to
believe that he had become a collaborator.

Chapter 2

1941

EXPANSION OF THE U-BOAT BASES

As soon as the Germans moved into the ports of St. Nazaire and Lorient, they immediately began making plans to create huge submarine facilities with cement walls so thick as to make them impervious to Allied bombing.

At St. Nazaire, the Todt organization prepared to build 14 submarine pens in the port during January 1941. This construction was to be completed in 1943. These 14 pens would house 20 submarines. By direct contact with the sea through the old entrance, the base of the building would be 295 meters long, 130 meters wide, and 18 meters high. It would cover a surface of 39,000 square meters. The construction required 480,000 cubic meters of concrete. In addition to the submarine compartments; there were workshops, dormitories, and other support facilities.

Some of the hangars were protected from the outside by armed doors. Numbers one through eight (east to west) were dry docks with pumping stations and submersible caissons. Numbers 9 through 14 were longer and always filled with water and could house two submarines. The hangars were separated from the workshops by a corridor five meters wide that housed a railway.

The Germans also were not satisfied with the moorings and supporting facilities in Lorient and immediately began constructing similar U-boat pens with ceilings three meters thick. Two "cathedral bunkers" were constructed with the steep roof designed to deflect the bombs so they would explode on the sides rather than on the roof. These were 84 meters long, 16

Submarine pens at St. Nazaire facing Basin of St. Nazaire. Author's photo.

meters wide, and 25 meters high. Another bunker was built on the Scorf River to house four U-boats. Its roof was 3.5 meters thick. The new facility would be on the Keroman peninsula, just on the edge of Lorient, and would be composed of three separate units: Keroman I, Keroman II, and Keroman III. Keroman I began in February 1941, and Keroman II three months later. Keroman III followed some months after that. In spite of 200 workers being killed by British bombs, the work advanced rapidly and accommodated the first U-boat in August 1941. The pens contained repair and maintenance facilities as well as accommodations for one thousand men.

In summary, at St. Nazaire, the submarine base contained 14 covered wet moorings and was located in an outer basin of the harbor. It was accessible at all stages of the tide by means of a bomb-proof entrance lock adjacent to the Normandie dock.

By contrast, 12 of the 20 pens in the Lorient base were dry, served by an ingenious system of docking that is still unique. The submarines were winced out of the water inside a bomb-proof slipway, mounted on cradles traveling on a transverse track, then pushed into the covered pen. An electric locomotive pulled the trolley up the track and transferred the submarine in its cradle onto the tracked platform.

To defend Lorient, approximately 400 defense units formed a ring around the fingers of land that enclosed the three major inlets of the harbor. The principal coastal batteries covered the western passage while the sea approaches were within the range of the heavy batteries on Ile de Groix, Grognon, and Quiberon. Numerous other strong points lined the beaches, and the roads leading into the town were heavily defended. Over 30,000 mines protected the land perimeter. The antiaircraft artillery at Lorient comprised 20 navy batteries in four groups, mainly composed of heavy caliber guns between 10.5 centimeters (cm) and 12.8 cm, all well equipped with radar. There were five other antiaircraft batteries around the post.

Quiberon peninsula and Bell Ile, positioned between St. Nazaire and Lorient, both held heavy seacoast batteries that dominated the shoreline. Four 34 cm guns at Quiberon could keep open a sea link between the two ports. A chain of strong points protected Quiberon and the Gulf of Morbihan, and these stretched as far as the Vilaine River, and together with the Nantes-Brest Canal, formed two sides of the outer defenses on the fortress of St. Nazaire.

The antiaircraft defenses of St. Nazaire were even more formidable than those at Lorient. There was an entire naval brigade of four groups comprising 73 guns of 10.5 cm in addition to the standard 8.8 cm guns and

Openings of U-boat pens at Keroman, Lorient. Courtesy: Hotel de Ville, Lorient, France.

more than 100 light automatic weapons. The coastal artillery covered the seaward approaches with batteries at Pointe de Chemoulin and Forte de Leve, overlooking the northern side of the Loire estuary, with three batteries at St. Brevin opposite. The heavy naval battery of three 24 cm guns at Batz, west of La Baule, covered the northern channel. These defenses at Lorient and St. Nazaire are examples of the extent to which the Germans protected a strategic center.

As headquarters, Lorient was visited by almost all of the aces and even referred to as "the base of the aces." *U-47,* commanded by Kapitan Lieutenant Gunther Prien; *U-99,* commanded by Kapitan Lieutenant Otto Kretschmer; and *U-100,* commanded by Joachin Schepke, all left Lorient after a service visit in February 1941 for what were to be their last voyages. Prien's *U-47* was sunk March 7 by the destroyer HMS *Wolverine.* The *U-100* was sunk March 17, 1941, by the destroyers HMS *Vance* and HMS *Walker.* The *U-99* was lost that same night. Prien and Schepke disappeared with their vessels. Most of their crew were lost (81 lost on *U-47* and 36 lost on *U-100.*) *U-99* lost only three sailors; its commander, Otto Kretschmer, was taken prisoner. *U-48* had the greatest hunting record in WWII and *U-99* was second. *U-103, U-123, U-124, U-107,* and *U-37* fol-

Admiral Donitz and staff reviewing naval personnel. Courtesy: Unknown
French veteran.

lowed in that order according to tonnage and ships sunk. These seven submarines sank 320 ships while operating out of Lorient and Baltic ports.

Submarines of the Japanese Imperial Navy visited Lorient. The Japanese submarine *I-30* arrived in Lorient on August 5, 1942. It returned to
Denang in Malaysia in October and was sunk four days later.

During 1941, the production of U-boats was increased and more were
added to the Atlantic Fleet. With the short run to home base for supplies
and fuel, the efficiency of the submarine force greatly improved. In 1941,
2,900,000 tons of Allied shipping were lost. The U-boat menace was at its
peak. During the last half of the year, Hitler began keeping the majority of
his U-boats close to home to protect the convoys of German supplies. This
angered Donitz, particularly in view of his recent successes. He felt
strongly that concentrating the U-boats in the Atlantic would help win the
war.

The United States entered the war in December 1941, and Donitz
shifted some of his submarines to the United States's East Coast. Early on,
places like Miami, New York, and Atlantic City resisted the recommend
blackout and enabled the U-boats to see the ships coming out of their
ports. Soon, it was not unusual to see ships burning off the coast.

A very important advance in escort protection was introduced by "Johnnie" Walker early in 1941. At the time, its importance was not recognized, but his contribution to antisubmarine warfare would become a major factor in the eventual defeat of the U-boats. Walker was a proficient antisubmarine tactician and designed ways to bring a maximum number of escort vessels and firepower against the U-boats during their night attacks. He coordinated the escort vessels into a team under the escort commander's direction. When a submarine was detected, his plan was to force it to dive by concentrating depth charges around the area. Submerged and traveling at a slower speed, the U-boat was more vulnerable.

The idea was proven early in 1941 when Walker's group was escorting Convoy H-G 76. When a sub was sighted, Walker sent five escort vessels in pursuit. Contact was made, depth charges were deployed, and *U-311* surfaced. Walker's men fired upon it extensively. Another boat, *U-574,* was sighted and Walker rammed it. It sank soon thereafter. There are other examples: The British lost the escort carrier *Audacity.* Engelbert Endrass's sub was sunk. A Liberator (B-24) appeared and chased off a German Kondor, then attacked two U-boats on the surface; one was damaged and the other scuttled. Donitz's U-boats abandoned the attack.

With port-to-port cover and the kind of offensive escort that "Johnnie" Walker had developed, convoys were proving to be a formidable adversary to the "wolf pack." Although this was early in the campaign, and it took time to build up sufficient escort vessels, these tactics eventually prevailed.

BOMBARDMENT CONTINUES

Bombardment of St. Nazaire and Lorient began to increase toward the end of 1941 and progressively became more intense as 1942 approached. In November 1941, Lorient was subjected to 15 days of intense bombing. In spite of these attacks, Germans launched the *Sans-Souci* and the *Sans Pareil,* two aviation supply vessels. These were followed quickly by the tankers *Cataracte* and *Quad.*

On November 4, 1941, English planes appeared and hit the shipyards of St. Nazaire, greatly damaging the sheet and metal supply. La Baule was included in this bombardment.

Bombardment was not the only hardship heaped upon the populace of St. Nazaire. Pierre Picaud tells us that animals were requisitioned by the Germans and the Travail Obligatoire en Allemagne (S.T.B.) began. (The S.T.B. was a compulsory workforce for young adults.) Collaboration began and black marketers became rich.

THE RESISTANCE

At the beginning of 1941, the Resistance was still very much under cover with small units working together and planning their own activities against the Germans. General de Gaulle was not well informed about the Resistance at this time but was beginning to get more information and gain respect for this brave, small group of volunteers who were scattered around occupied France.

At the end of 1941, de Gaulle sent one of his principal lieutenants, Jean Moulin, back into France. Moulin united the movements in the south, an important stroke toward eliminating Vichy as a force for the future. He then combined the northern and southern Resistance groups and acquainted them with Gaullism. De Gaulle soon became recognized as the unrivaled leader of all forces *Francais*.

Now that the Resistance groups had established some communication with the Allied forces through de Gaulle, they tried to get the Allies to stop bombing cities and killing civilians. From their observations, they found much more damage done to civilian areas than to military targets. They volunteered to sabotage the military targets and thought with proper explosives they could be much more effective. They were probably right. In spite of hundreds of bombardments by the Royal Air Force and the United States Air Force, the submarine pens remained virtually undamaged.

The unfortunate destruction of so many nonmilitary areas in and around St. Nazaire was due to several factors. One was the weather. During the fall and winter months, Brittany is rainy and overcast much of the time. The targets were often obscured by the weather. Another factor was probably the heavy concentration of flak that Allied pilots encountered when flying over St. Nazaire and Lorient. St. Nazaire was known as "Flak City." Also, many of the pilots were young and inexperienced and probably released bombs prematurely when the weather and flak became significantly obstructive. These factors resulted in so many of the surrounding towns and villages sustaining intensive bombardment.

On October 20, 1941, an event occurred that was attributed to the Resistance. The German commandant in Nantes, Field Commandant Hotz, and his ordnance officer were shot and killed by assailants while walking to work. This was done by members of the Communist Youth, and they were not apprehended. In reprisal, the commander of the German Forces in France, General Von Stulpelnagel, ordered 50 hostages shot and another group held and shot if the assailants were not identified by October 23. A reward of 15 million francs was offered for their capture. Fifty political prisoners from a camp in Chateaubriand were selected. Twenty seven belonged to the Communist party; the youngest was 17 years old. The 27 shot included 3 Nazairiens. Of the 16 shot at Nantes, there were 2 Nazairiens, ages 17 and 35.

Five more were shot at Valerien and 50 more at Bordeaux (for other causes at the same time). The Germans began collecting 50 more hostages, including Francois Blancho, the mayor of St. Nazaire. This created such commotion that the Germans backed down and released them.

One of the bravest accounts of subterfuge was told by Ray Roberts from Bridgman, Michigan. Ray was a member of the 766th Ordnance Company, which was part of the 66th Infantry Division. When the 66th Division entered the campaign in Brittany, Ray and his company were stationed in Messac, a small, beautiful town northeast of St. Nazaire. He became acquainted with Alyette Fras, who was a music student and spoke fluent English. He and a friend, Tommy Mitchell, were invited by the Fras's to their house for dinner and music, an invitation they gladly accepted. Dr. Stephen Fras, the father, was a medical doctor for the village. There were nine Fras children; the oldest was Stephen, age 20. They had a wonderful time and were invited again, usually once a month and were given a farewell dinner when the division departed.

Ray and his wife returned in September 1984, and visited the Fras family. Dr. Fras was deceased and Mrs. Fras was 90 years old. Lyonel Fras, who was 10 during the last year of the war, was now the village doctor. After refreshments, Lyonel took Ray and his wife, Lucille, to a large family room in one end of the house and explained that this was the room where his father took care of the sick and injured American airmen when Germans occupied their country. At times, he would have as many as 12 patients in the room. This went on even while two German officers were living in second-floor bedrooms at the other end of the house. When the German soldiers found out that Dr. Fras had fought in World War I and been wounded, they asked him to have a drink with them. He declined, saying, "I will drink later," which he did on VE Day.[1]

The maquis brought the airmen to the Fras home. (Maquis is a common name for undercover fighters and comes from the word for "brushwood-covered heath," in which it was easy to hide.) The family got them civilian clothes, and when they could leave, Stephen took them to a small port where a French fishing boat would take them to safety.

Dr. Fras never gave the soldiers his name or address for security reasons, so he never received any thanks. Neither have the American or French governments honored him or his brave family. But they never wanted honor. They are just proud to have helped their American friends who had come to help them. Many of the older French people feel that way about the Americans.

NOTE

1. I visited the Fras family in May 2000, and Lyonel gave me a tour of their large home. The arrangement of the rooms is such that one can see how Dr. Fras kept his secret from the Germans.

Chapter 3

1942

U-BOAT DESTRUCTION

The United States had just entered the war and had little or no experience defending against this formidable submarine force. At the time, the U-boat destruction of Allied ships was at its peak. In early 1942, Admiral Donitz had 22 U-boats in the Atlantic. The remainder of his ninety submarines were being repaired or were in the Mediterranean. The United States had few escort vessels. Captains of merchant vessels had not been given pertinent instructions. Crews were inexperienced. Radios were used too frequently. Miami refused to cut off its miles of neon lights for fear of scaring the tourists away. Americans did not benefit from the lessons already learned by the British and repeated their mistakes. A lot of time and effort was wasted sending out hunting patrols, as the subs stayed submerged during the day. Convoys were not used at first. Eventually Britain convinced the United States of their value. When the United States began to use the convoy system, the losses to the U-boats dropped off dramatically. Suffice it to say that the United States was at the beginning of a learning curve but was destined to learn quickly and effectively, as results would soon begin to verify.

At the beginning of 1942, the United States Air Force joined the British in the bombardment of St. Nazaire and Lorient. With the losses in the Atlantic increasing, more focus was placed on destroying these ports. The British bombed at night and the United States bombed during the day.

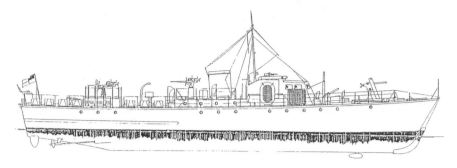

Fairmile Motor Launch (similar to those used in "Operation Chariot").

One heavy bombardment of St. Nazaire took place on January 7, 1942—an attack that accounted for 19 deaths and 19 wounded. During a major bombardment on February 15, 18 people were killed and 50 houses were destroyed with 50 more severely damaged. The bombers returned to St. Nazaire on March 8 and 9, and 8 civilians were killed and 10 were wounded. The shipyard was greatly damaged. A workshop, power works, and numerous houses were destroyed. Lancaster and Wellington bombers saturated the city with tons of bombs on March 25, 1942, leaving casualties.

Another prime military target existed at St. Nazaire. A large dock, which had been built to house the prewar luxury liner the *Normandie*, was the only dock on the west coast of France that could receive and service the prized German battleship, *Tirpitz*. It was 350 meters long, 50 meters wide,

Normandie dock. Author's photo.

and 16 meters deep. It could be used as a wet or dry dock by means of giant hollow gates called "caissons," one in the front and one in the back. The caissons, which were nine meters wide, could be rolled into "cambers" on the dock's west side by machinery contained in "winding huts" placed at the end of each camber. The impressive pumping house was also on the west side. The lock could be drained or filled in 14 hours.

The following is the story of a group of very brave British commandos and naval personnel who went on a daring raid to destroy the Normandie dock at St. Nazaire. Its real name was the Forme-Ecluse Louis-Joubert dock, named after the president of the St. Nazaire Chamber of Commerce. The decimation of this raiding party, although it was successful in its mission, reflects the strong defenses that had been developed in these ports and their importance.

OPERATION CHARIOT

On March 27, 1942, the German soldiers and sailors in the port of St. Nazaire were dressed in their best uniforms in anticipation of a visit to their base by Admiral Donitz, commander of the German submarine force. The admiral had visited St. Nazaire and Lorient immediately following the occupation of France and designated these ports as principal bases. Fourteen submarine pens were planned and Admiral Donitz would inspect the nine that were completed. The U-boat flotilla commanders were Kapitanlieutenant Herbert Sohler (7th Flotilla) and Kapitanlieutenant Wilhelm Schultz (6th Flotilla).

During the course of the inspection, Admiral Donitz asked, "Tell me Sohler, what would you do in the case of an English attack for the defense of your base?" The young officer, somewhat taken aback, paused for a moment and then answered that he thought an attack on the base would be hazardous and highly improbable. Donitz raised his eyebrows and said, "Are you sure, Sohler?" It would not be long before they would both reflect on this conversation, as events were already under way that would prove Sohler wrong. He was right that such an attack was improbable, but the British commandos were legendary for doing the improbable.

The geography surrounding this submarine and dry dock base was all but unapproachable by stealth. The Loire River empties into the sea by a large estuary that actually runs east and west. This estuary, very wide at the mouth, narrows as it becomes the Loire River. St. Nazaire was in a well-protected area, six miles from the open sea. A ship of any size had to stay in a narrow, twisting, deep channel or it would quickly run aground on the numerous shoals and mud flats. This channel was heavily defended with

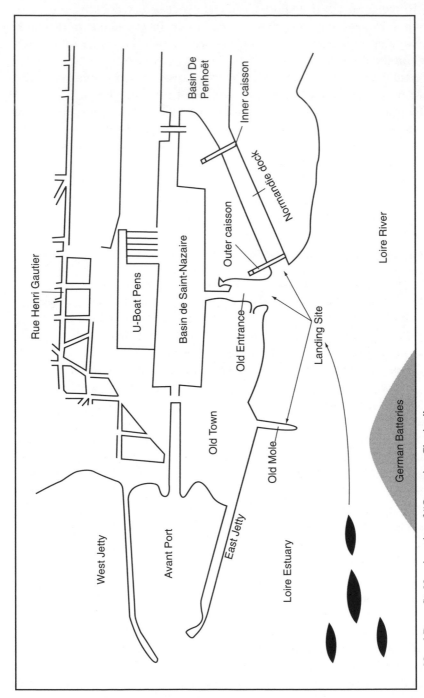

Naval Base, St. Nazaire, site of "Operation Chariot."

artillery and searchlight batteries along the north and south shore lines for the entire distance from the sea to the port. Any ship trying to come up this channel would almost certainly be destroyed. This eased the mind of Kapitan Zur See Zuckschwerdt, who was in charge of the gun emplacements.

The British admiralty began to develop a plan it hoped would destroy the dock. In August 1941, Admiral Sir Roger Keyes had tried and failed to draw up such a plan. In January 1942, Lord Louis Mountbatten, who had replaced Keyes as head of the Combined Operations Organization, was asked to look at the problem again. St. Nazaire was studied with the help of current aerial photographs, and Mountbatten came up with a daring plan. They would fill a ship with explosives and ram it into the front caisson of the dry dock. The plan was submitted to Prime Minister Churchill, who subsequently presented it to King George. Realizing the damage this raid could potentially accomplish, both approved it immediately. It would be designated "Operation Chariot."

One of the 50 destroyers that President Roosevelt had sent to Mr. Churchill was chosen to be filled with delayed explosives to give ample time for it to be cleared of personnel before exploding and fitted out to have the appearance of a German ship. It was now called the *Campbeltown,* previously named the U.S. *Buchanan.*

The assault force would be composed of 19 boats: the destroyer, a motor gunboat (MGB), a motor torpedo boat (MTB), and 16 motor launches (ML). Two additional destroyers would accompany the flotilla to and from the enemy coast but would remain at sea during the raid. The boats, of different capabilities, would each have a specific individual mission. The armament of the *Campbeltown* was enhanced and modified to weigh less so she could traverse the mud flats and shoals of the estuary without running aground. The participants included 63 naval officers and 293 ratings for a total of 356 naval personnel. There were 40 army officers and 225 soldiers of other ranks, giving a total of 265 army personnel. Two French liaison officers accompanied the raiding party, giving a total of 625 planned participants. Teams of commandos would attack targets such as gun emplacements, searchlight strongholds, and machinery.

Success of the mission depended on complete surprise. Two experts in ports and docks, Captain R. K. Montgomery and Captain W. H. Pritchard, were sent to study the dock at Southampton because it was almost a copy of the dock at St. Nazaire. This was where the men would train.

The Royal Air Force was to coordinate an attack just prior to the arrival of the assault group in the port. Sixty bombers were to attack St. Nazaire at 11:30 P.M. on March 27, 1942, to create a distraction and to engage the coastal artillery units. Churchill requested that only military targets be bombed and the town spared. The *Campbeltown* was to rendezvous with the two destroyer escorts at Falmouth on March 24. Owing to a serious shortage of ships, 16 "B" class motor launches were later substituted for the second destroyer. (Two destroyers were in the first plan, which was aborted.) Designed for inshore patrol and antisubmarine duties, these light ships were entirely unsuited to an assault role, yet they would now be required to carry a second contingent of commandos, approximately 15 to each ML. They were a mere 112 feet long and 18 feet across the beam; wooden and fueled by petrol, they presented a fire risk. Their armament would be enhanced and the naval complement increased in number on each boat. It was anticipated that a portion of this fleet would be lost. A specially equipped motor torpedo boat, *MTB 74,* would be added as well as a motor gunboat, *MGB 314.* Approximately one-half of the assault troops would ride in with the destroyer, and the other half would be split among the 16 MLs.

The plan was that the collective force would proceed together and approach St. Nazaire on a moonlit night. The destroyer would ram the gate then disembark the commando and demolition units. The remainder of the force would disembark at selected points for their special sabotage mission. So as not to endanger commando units operating nearby, the decision was made to fix the destroyer's charge in place prior to departure and fire it after the survivors of the force had left the estuary. To prevent the destroyer being towed away, it was to be scuttled in place, either against the caisson or across the sill if the caisson was found to be open. *MTB 74's* job was to use her torpedoes if *Campbeltown* grounded or was sunk. If the outer caisson was open, then the MTB would pass by the destroyer and torpedo the inner one. Otherwise, she would attack the lock gates in the Old Entrance. The attack was planned to last for two hours, and then the commandos and demolition troops would re-embark on the MLs for the trip home. Two destroyers, the *Tynedale* and the *Atherstone,* would accompany the flotilla there and back but would remain at sea during the assault. The submarine *Sturgeon* would be in place at a designated position before the force arrived and act as a beacon for navigational purposes.

Lieutenant Colonel Charles Newman's 2 Commando Group would make up most of the assault force and pave the way for the demolition teams. Newman would be overall commander of the ground attack with the title of military force commander. Major Bill Copland, somewhat older than Newman and a veteran of WWI, would be his second in command. Commander Robert Edward Dudley Ryder, RN, was chosen as the naval force commander. He and Newman would work closely training the men and ironing out all the details of this hazardous mission. Two better men would be hard to find. Newman was 37 and Ryder, 34. The operation was fortunate to have these two men as its leaders. Both were courageous, determined, and absolutely reliable. They had approximately one month to prepare for the attack.

Lt. Nigel Tibbits, RN, was appointed to head the navy's demolition party and, with the help of Pritchard, would transform the *Campbeltown* into a floating bomb. Lt. Tibbits proposed the ship be scuttled immediately after ramming and that the charge be exploded several hours later while she rested on the bottom, when the force had cleared the area. The charge would be sealed in place to avoid any interference. Tibbits was 28 years old, diligent, and gave tireless effort to this assignment, leaving nothing to chance.

Lieutenant Commander S. H. Beattie was chosen as commander of the *Campbeltown*. This pleased Ryder very much, as he and Beattie had joined the navy at the same time and been on a training ship together. The rest of the naval appointments included Lieutenant A. R. Green as navigator and Ryder's chief of staff. Sub-Lieutenant J. E. O'Rourke was to be signal officer. Lieutenant R. E. A. Verity was chosen as beachmaster. On March 10, a meeting was held in Plymouth for a final review. Beattie, Tibbits, and Pritchard were present. Lt. Commander Billie Stephens attended in the capacity of commanding officer (CO) of the 20th Flotilla; Lt. Dunstan Curtis, captain of the headquarters ship *MGB 314;* and Sub-Lt. Micky Wynn, commander of *MTB 74,* were all present. The "explosion plan" designed by Tibbits and the route to the objective were discussed and accepted.

During this time, the *Tirpitz* was reported to have sailed from Trondheimsford to intercept Convoy PQ12, which was headed to Murmansk with war materials for the Russians. A powerful British squadron chased her and the aircraft carrier *Victorious* got close enough to launch an air strike. A squadron of Albacore torpedo bombers flew from her deck but the attack was bungled, and the *Tirpitz* headed for home. This missed opportunity, unfortunately, cost the lives of many young soldiers and sailors.

Woods's 28th Flotilla

ML	Commander
298	Lt. Bob Nock
306	Lt. Ian Henderson
307	Lt. Norman Wallis

341	Lt. Douglas Briault
443	Lt. T. D. L. Platt
446	Lt. Dick Falconar
457	Lt. Tom Collier
447	Lt. Commander Woods

Stephens's 20th (four boats) and 7th (four boats) Flotillas

192	Lt. Stephens
262	Lt. Ted Burt
267	Lt. E. H. Beart
268	Lt. Bill Tillie
156	Lt. Leslie Fenton
160	Lt. Tom Boyd
177	Sub-Lt. Mark Rodier
269	Lt. C. S. B. Irwin

The last four MLs each carried two torpedoes.

Newman's force was reported as having 265 men in all, 173 of whom came from his own commando unit. Medical personnel and "office" staff joined at the last minute but were often not included in official figures. The military plan called for the assault troops to be broken down into groups according to their intended function. The "assault parties" were to overwhelm the defenses, and "protection" parties were to give close support to the "demolition" teams. Zero time was 0130, March 28, 1942. The bomber group was to start their bombardment two hours prior. All ground activity was to cease at 0330 followed by withdrawal, with exceptions for unfinished missions.

Training became intense. The commandos were boarded on the MLs for a 36-hour tour into deep water to get them used to traveling on the sea in small boats. Ryder and Newman made the trip on Billie Stephens *ML 192,* as the gunboat was not yet available. The weather deteriorated and many of the commandos got sick, but the trip did put the MLs through their paces in the worst kind of weather, and all held up exceptionally well.

MGB 314 finally arrived. She was slightly shorter and narrower than the other boats but had powerful engines and a maximum speed of 26.5 knots. Her armament was formidable. She was to be the headquarters ship for Ryder and Newman and was commanded by 31-year-old Dunstan Curtis. Because of a limited range, it was planned to tow her to the objective and back.

With personnel now assigned, the battle plan was as follows: The destroyer *Campbeltown* would charge at full speed into the outer caisson

The Mole. Prominent as a landing site for British commandos, March 28, 1942, during "Operation Chariot." Author's photo.

of the dock, and immediately thereafter Major Copland and several parties of commandos would scramble over the side, secure the immediate area, and wreck the dock's pump and winding machinery. At the same time, the MLs would discharge their parties at two other major points—the Mole and the Old Entrance. The Mole was a narrow stone structure jutting out into the Loire River high above the water and 50 meters south of the dry dock. It was heavily defended and the site of gun emplacements.

A third landing site was the Old Entrance, located between the Mole and the dry dock. Group 3, under Copland, would land with the ramming of the dry dock gate at one site. Group 2, under Captain Micky Burn, would land at the Old Entrance, and Group 1, under Captain Bertie Hodgson, would attack the Mole. All groups would be led by assault teams followed by demolition teams protected by squads of commandos. Bob Montgomery would oversee demolition in the dry dock and Bill Pritchard would oversee subsidiary demolitions. This would be a complicated attack with speed and split-second timing essential.

The order was given to leave and the 19 boats plus the escort destroyers *Tynedale* and *Atherstone* put to sea. The three destroyers were in line in the middle and the MLs were in columns on either side. The MGB and the MTB were towed by the *Atherstone* and *Campbeltown* respectively. Newman and Ryder were on the *Atherstone*. The small convoy traveled at 13 knots. The weather was calm.

As this second night began to fall, the convoy turned toward St. Nazaire and was at Point "E," a point of no return, 65 miles from St. Nazaire. *MGB 314,* commanded by Lt. Curtis, was at the head of the column with Newman and Ryder on board. Behind them was the *Campbeltown* surrounded by 16 MLs. The *Campbeltown* hit bottom at one point in the estuary but drove herself free. The flotilla was running the gauntlet of many fixed gun positions and searchlight units on both the north and south shores of the estuary. The submarine *Sturgeon* provided a navigational beacon by displaying a light seaward at 2200 hours.

The 62 Royal Air Force bombers were to attack from 2330 on the 27th to 0045 hours on the 28th. So many restrictions had been placed on this air raid that the effectiveness was questionable. The planes were required to stay above 6000 feet, bomb only military targets, and drop only one bomb at a time. (The weather deteriorated to the point that very few bombs were actually dropped.)

The German flag was raised on the *Campbeltown*. She was to strike the caisson at 0130, March 28th, at which time she would be flying the British flag. As leader of the formation, the gunboat carrying Ryder and Newman would support *Campbeltown* as she made the final dash. When she was in place, Newman and his group would disembark. The two non-troop-carrying torpedo MLs, *160* and *270,* were to be a small striking force on the way in.

The plan of the attack, published in detail in Dorrian's treatise, *Storming St. Nazaire,* is too detailed for inclusion here, but each boat, assault group, demolition group, and protection group had its own individual assignment of destruction. The ramming of the outer caisson of the Normandie dock was the purpose of the mission, but it involved many secondary assignments.

The first order of business was getting to the target with the flotilla intact. This involved the elements of surprise, confusion, and stealth for slipping by other ships and fortresses of cannons on the shores. The plan itself was very complex and, by most standards, one almost impossible to achieve. Fragile, vulnerable, wooden boats and small groups of men would be up against one of the most fortified of the German bases with 5,000 troops ready to respond. The commandos had no reserve forces. Failure of each small group would take its toll on the mission. Brave men against tremendous odds.

There was one encounter with a German U-boat, *U-593,* but it dived. After a pursuit and the dropping of depth charges, the destroyers returned to the convoy and by 0900, all was back in order with the group of boats continuing to their target on time. At 11:35, French trawlers were encountered. The crews were taken off and the boats sunk. Neither carried wireless. Valuable information about other boats in the area was obtained through interrogation of the crews.

At 2000 hours, with darkness falling, the small convoy reached the point to turn straight north to make the final run. The motor torpedo boat and the motor gunboat slipped their tows from the *Atherstone* and *Campbeltown* and were on their own. The gunboat with Newman and Ryder was now the headquarters ship.

The first casualty was *ML 341*. It developed an unserviceable engine and could not keep up. The personnel aboard were transferred to *ML 446*. At 2200 hours the submarine *Sturgeon* flashed its light to signal its position. Remarkably, timing and position were right on target. They were 40 miles from the objective.

At 2330 hours, the bombers began their run. The Germans responded, lighting up the night with their searchlights and the flash of many cannon. St. Nazaire, known for its antiaircraft guns, stood up to its reputation. Unfortunately, the weather had deteriorated into clouds and rain with a ceiling of only 3,000 feet, so most of the planes returned home without releasing their bombs. It was frightening to those in the approaching boats that the bombardment ended when strategically it should have been at its peak.

At 0122, March 28, the German searchlights on both shores came on, lighting up the convoy of little ships. Request for identification was flashed to the convoy by a German boat. The English sent back this message by a signaler who could send in perfect German, "Urgent—have two damaged ships following enemy engagement. Demand immediate entry." The shooting from the shore batteries, which had begun before the challenge was issued, now paused. The English then sent the enemy the signal for "a vessel considering herself to be fired on by friendly forces." A few more precious moments of cease-fire occurred. The firing resumed.

At 0128, they were one mile from the target. Captain Beattie issued the order to take down the German flag. Firing from the coast batteries became intense. The leading gunboat was closing fast on the harbor with the last boat in line approximately one mile in the rear. The German guardship, *Sperrbrecher*, was encountered but bypassed successfully. Following the gunboat, the *Campbeltown,* although being hit continuously, was making good progress at 19 knots. Members of assault and demolition groups began to take casualties.

The *Campbeltown* cleared the Mole, leaving only 500 meters to go. As the destroyer neared the dock, the commandos on board braced for the shock. With only seconds to go, the antitorpedo net was breached. Finally, IMPACT! occurred at 0134, only four minutes late. The ship became wedged more than 10 meters into the structure. Eighty commandos arranged in small groups slid to the dock on ropes and ladders and disappeared into the night. Many sailors had been wounded and lay on deck. On the way in, a team of experts had set the explosive charges on the interior of the ship. Another group prepared the back of the ship with explosives so its removal would be more difficult. Flak positions east and west of the dock were being attacked by the commandos as were gas and diesel reservoirs. Three demolition groups had the mission to destroy the pumping station and all of the machinery at the north and south caissons. Roderick's team of about 14 men successfully knocked out four gun emplacements with "tommy-guns" (fully automatic weapon similar to a submachine gun) and grenades but lost at least four of their team. Captain Roy's team was also successful in their goal but lost a good percentage of their team.

Copland was well satisfied with what his commandos had accomplished but was unaware that the boats destined for the two landing places had failed, as many of the MLs were destroyed by gunfire. Landing groups One and Two were almost complete failures. A mere 15 commandos were landed at the Mole by Lt. Collier's *ML 457,* and in the Old Entrance the only boat to make it straight in was Sub-Lt. Rodier's *ML 177.* Of the forward striking force, Boyd's *ML 160* was engaging targets upriver, and Irwin's *ML 270* was circling out of control.

With *Campbeltown* already sinking by the stern following the explosion of her scuttling charges, the crew prepared to evacuate. Having put his commandos ashore, Rodier, in *ML 177,* came alongside and took off some 30 men, including the wounded, a physician, and Beattie, who was the last to leave. It then headed out to sea. Copland, unaware of this disembarkment, went through the *Campbeltown,* evacuating more wounded men and with them headed for the Mole, anticipating re-embarkation. The caisson winding huts and pump house with its machinery were destroyed but with a significant loss of men.

The small boats, no match for the stationary gun emplacements on shore, were destroyed one by one and left burning on the water. The men had to take to the cold sea and many succumbed to the cold and their wounds. Those who made it to shore were captured. The last vessel had left, leaving the commandos to their fate, unaware that there were no boats to take them home. Copland tried to get back to Newman's headquarters but ran into heavy machine gun fire. He had been successful with most of his assigned missions.

There were approximately 100 ground troops remaining, many of them wounded. Newman knew nothing of the destruction of the fleet and fully expected the boats to be there waiting to take them home. "Tiger" Watson

Destroyer *Campbeltown* resting on outer caisson of Normandie dock, embedded there during "Operation Chariot." Courtesy: The Grand Blockhaus Museum, Batz-sur-Mer, France.

later wrote: "When we saw the river before us, we stopped, appalled. The surface of the water was lit up brightly by sheets of flaming petrol, while thick, oily, black smoke rose above the flickering glow. A few blackened hulls, some still smoldering along the waterline, were all that remained of the MLs to take us home. We stood speechless. For a moment all seemed suddenly silent to me, despite the guns which were still firing down by the river. Major Bill Newman was already organizing a defensive perimeter."

Newman established his headquarters near the Old Entrance and most of the groups eventually make their way back. Copland and Day were reunited with Newman and they decided to exit the town and eventually split up into small groups of 20 men, each group to try to fight their way out. Of Newman's group, about 30 were captured while hiding in a basement. Another group of 17 surrendered. Only five escaped, crossed France, and made it back to England. One soldier, Private Howard, was hidden by a schoolteacher and eventually made it back to England three months later.

One hundred and six sailors and 109 commandos were sent by truck to La Baule and eventually to Stalag 133 in Rennes. The wounded were

St. Nazaire, April 1942. German officers saluting brave British commandos for their courage in attacking the Normandie dock. Courtesy: The Grand Blockhaus Museum, Batz-sur-Mer, France.

treated at L'Hermitage de Baule. One hundred and four English sailors and 65 commandos were killed.

Campbeltown exploded at noon on March 28, 1942, and the dry dock was destroyed. A large group of German officers and civilians were touring the ship at the time and were killed. Metal fragments and human debris stuck to the walls of the basin. The next day was quiet; the cleaning process to begin the following day. On the 30th, *MTB 74*'s delayed-action torpedoes exploded, prompting the Todt workers to flee from the docks. Their khaki uniforms somewhat resembled the English uniform and nervous German soldiers fired on them, killing many. The homes of the townspeople were searched for possible hidden commandos, and the nervous soldiers killed numerous civilians who raised their suspicions. They even fired on the car of a German officer returning from Nantes.

Meanwhile, having lost six of his ships within the harbor, Ryder's remaining 11 boats had cleared the port by the time of Newman's final push from the Mole. Within an hour, three more were struck and destroyed, leaving 8 of the 17 that had sailed into the estuary. By 0400, these were making good progress for Point "Y," which was the first possible rendezvous site with *Tynedale* and *Atherstone*. *ML 306* reached "Y" first and went on to the secondary position "T." *MLs 307, 160,* and *443* reached "Y" together and pressed on. Falconar's *446* had come across the limping *156* and they proceeded together for awhile. The gunboat *314* was badly damaged and kept afloat by a bucket brigade. It stayed with Irwin's *270* for awhile.

ML 306 was making good progress when it sighted five German destroyers heading for it. It was still dark. Lt. Henderson, although totally outgunned, decided to make a fight of it when one destroyer, the *Jaguar,* left its position and came toward them. Henderson was killed in the violent fight that ensued, as were most of his men. Lt. R.O.C. Swayne, the only officer left, surrendered. The German commander picked up all living and dead in the water and made sure the wounded were given the best medical care available. He obviously had a lot of respect for the crew of this grossly outmanned vessel.

The *Atherstone* and *Tynedale* came within sight of the four remaining German destroyers and *Tynedale* was fired upon. After a brief exchange, *Tynedale* broke off. The Germans did not pursue but headed to port. The two English destroyers then set course to the back-up rendezvous, Point "T." They encountered the remaining MLs at 0700, March 28. Two other destroyers, the *Cleveland* and *Brocklesby,* were sent to assist getting the MLs home and met at Point "T." At 0900, *MGB 314* and *MLs 446* and *270* joined the group. Ryder, now outranked, was relieved of further responsibility.

Commander G.B. Sayer, the commanding officer of the destroyers and few returning MLs, grew more and more concerned about their progress, as the MLs were just not making headway fast enough and they were still 100 miles from the enemy coast. There were still three MLs they had not encountered yet that had wounded on board. Against the wishes of Ryder, Curtis, Irwin, and Falconar, Sayer ordered all three crews to board the destroyers and *MGB 314* and *MLs 270* and *446* to be sunk by gunfire. At the time of this decision, the bucket brigade was still working to keep the gunboat afloat. The destroyers, after sinking the MGB and MLs with cannon fire, sped off at 25 knots to find the remaining three *MLs—307, 341,* and *443*—which were traveling together.

Dr. David Paton, the physician traveling with the three remaining MLs, treated the wounded on each boat as best he could with a shortage of supplies and poor conditions. A lone German plane tried to bomb them. They were attacked again at dusk on Saturday. On Sunday morning, March 29, they could only guess their position. They were fearful of missing England altogether. With some of the wounded needing urgent treatment, they broke radio silence and found that they were headed directly for Falmouth. By noon they were approaching the harbor, led by *ML 443*. The wounded were quickly removed and taken to hospitals. The remaining sailors and commandos were given a warm welcome.

Fate of Small Boats

ML 192 — Hit by several heavy shells. Caught fire and burned, just off the Mole.

ML 262 — Made it to shore but forced to re-embark commandos in the face of heavy fire. Attempted to withdraw but was set on fire and abandoned. Later exploded.

ML 267 — Hit while attempting to land troops. Caught fire and sank.

ML 268 — Blew up during approach to Old Entrance. Most of crew and commandos were lost.

ML 156 — Hit numerous times and forced to withdraw. Later scuttled at sea.

ML 177 — Successfully landed troops. Evacuated many of *Campbeltown*'s crew Attempted to withdraw but set on fire. Abandoned with heavy loss of life.

ML 447 — Attempted to land troops but severely hit and set ablaze. Later abandoned.

ML 457 — Successfully landed troops but crippled by enemy fire and abandoned with heavy loss of life.

ML 307 — Did not land troops. Driven off by heavy enemy fire. Withdrew. One of only three boats to return to England.

ML 443 — Failed to land troops. Withdrew. Returned to England in company with MLs 307 and 160.

ML 306 — Failed to land troops. Withdrew. Engaged enemy destroyer and was sunk.

ML 446 — Heavily hit during approach. Failed to land troops. Withdrew and was later scuttled.

ML 298 — Succeeded in task of drawing enemy fire but was set ablaze and abandoned with heavy loss of life.

ML 270 — Hit and initially disabled. Limped out to sea and was later scuttled.

ML 160 — Attacked targets of opportunity. Embarked survivors from *ML 447*. Hit and damaged but succeeded in returning to England.

ML 341 — During approach to St. Nazaire, developed an unserviceable engine and returned to England after transferring commandos on board to *ML 446*.

MTB 74 — Fired torpedoes at Old Entrance lock gates. Attempted to withdraw. Stopped to pick up survivors in the water. Heavily hit. Set ablaze and abandoned.

MGB 314 — Landed commandos of Commanding Officer's party. Engaged shore positions and attempted to withdraw with many survivors on board. Hit many times and reached open sea in sinking condition. Later abandoned and scuttled.

Back in England, Bill Savage, who died in the battle of *ML 306* against the German destroyer *Jaguar* but was brought home by his comrades, was laid to rest with full honors. It was the end of this quiet, modest man's life, but the beginning of a legend in which this lone sailor's courage, just as was the case with Tommy Durant, also a hero of that battle, would come to stand as a symbol of the resolution and fortitude of ordinary men, qualities that are all that ever really shield us from tyranny.

EVACUATION, BOMBARDMENTS, AND U-BOATS

Shortly after the violent raid by the commandos on April 12, 1942, permission was requested and granted to evacuate 1,500 civilians of Old St. Nazaire who were being held at a race course. They departed with few possessions. Schoolchildren were evacuated to Chenaire for the boys and Metaire for the girls; both being in the region of Nantes.

Bombardments occurred on April 15 and 16 at St. Nazaire that killed 19 people and damaged 650 homes. On April 20, 1942, the headquarters for the Legion of French Volunteers Against the Bolsheviks (LVH), a collaborationist organization that recruited Russian soldiers from the Eastern front to fight for the Germans, was destroyed with explosives. The Germans attempted to take hostage 20 prominent Nazariens, but 9 of them escaped. The incarcerated 11 hostages were released two days later.

Multiple bombardments occurred in May 1942. London broadcast to the French to evacuate, because more intense bombing was planned. Fifty children were sent to Switzerland and others to Algeria and Tunisia. The worst bombardments that St. Nazaire was to experience occurred on November 9, 10, 14, and 17, 1942. At this time, school officials decided to close the schools still attended by 1,200 students.

On November 9, 1942, high-flying planes came over in daylight. It was the Americans bombing St. Nazaire for the first time. A second and third wave dropped bombs, and in final analysis, 186 people were killed, including 150 shipyard workers. The whole city, as well as some of the Germans, turned out for their funerals.

The next day the bombers returned and hit the shipyard and railways, leaving 8 people dead and 15 wounded. On November 17, two waves of bombers severely punished the town, killing 78 people and wounding 200. The surgeons of the hospital worked 48 hours without stopping. Some of the casualties had to be transferred elsewhere for treatment.

In spite of the commando attack on St. Nazaire and the subsequent bombardments that followed, business went on as usual and there was no evidence that these events had any inhibitory effect on submarine activity. In May 1942, the U-boats sunk 120 Allied ships and in June, another 119.

However, the Allies were beginning to gain a technological advantage with the development of new electronic devices. Radar (radio detection and ranging) sent out radio waves that bounced off solid objects and were reflected back to the sending sets. Direction, speed, and range could be determined. Surfaced U-boats at night could no longer hide. Asdic (Sonar—a variant of radar) and radar collaborated well. This began to play a role in defense against the U-boats and in the counterattacks.

The ship-borne high-frequency direction finder, which the British sailors nicknamed "Huff-Duff," was another electronic device that could tune in on high-frequency coded transmissions and locate a U-boat by radio. The "Huff-Duff" was installed on shore stations and ships and became a valuable adjunct to the Allies in locating the German submarines.

The very high-frequency radio-telephone was developed, which made it possible for ships in a convoy to communicate with each other. It could also be used between ships and aircraft, greatly enhancing the teamwork between the two.

During the spring and summer of 1942, the numbers of ships sunk off the United States's East Coast decreased. For better hunting, Donitz shifted many of his U-boats to Russia's Arctic coast to intercept convoys taking lend-lease supplies and armament to Russia. Roosevelt and Churchill knew that it was essential to support Russia, and large convoys left Iceland for Russia frequently. The convoy PQ-17 left Iceland June 27, 1942, with 35 merchant ships loaded with planes, tanks, guns, and other essential war materials. This convoy was guarded by 47 escort ships. Things went well at first.

An air attack sunk two ships and then a quiet period followed. While PQ-17 was making forward progress, the admiralty learned that the German battleship *Tirpitz* had escaped surveillance, and they thought that it and several other battleships were headed for the convoy. In somewhat of a panic, they ordered the convoy to disperse and each ship to proceed on its own without escort. This was gross misjudgment. On July 5, 1942, the Luftwaffe and U-boats attacked and on the first day sunk 14 ships. On the 6th, 7th, and 8th, two, two, and one ship were sunk respectively. Two more were sunk on the 10th. Of the 35 ships that set out for Archangel, only 11 reached the Russian port. One hundred and fifty-three men, 22 merchant ships, 430 tanks, 210 aircraft, and 99,316 tons of supplies were lost. A bitter lesson was learned regarding the convoy system.

Chapter 4

1943

BOMBARDMENT INTENSIFIES—
THE APOCALYPSE

This was a crucial year for the Allies. Preparations were already underway for the invasion of France, and England was filling up with United States troops. The United States Air Force had many large units there that were effectively bombing targets all over Europe. Multiple infantry and armored divisions with attached units were in advanced training, preparing for the big show that would take place the following year. Two hundred thousand soldiers with IQs over 115 were placed in colleges all around the country to become engineers, doctors, dentists, and language experts in case the war was extended. Little did they know that after their academic venture, they would become riflemen, filling the ranks of infantry and armored divisions that would be committed in 1944. The Resistance in France was expanding and would spawn the Free French of the Interior (FFI). These new and young recruits would provide 30,000 to 40,000 troops in Brittany and were destined to carry a large part of the combat following the Invasion.

Lucien Francois, now 14 years of age and still living in Lorient with his family under the worst hardships, recorded in his memoirs about this period:

> In 1943, the days went by and in spite of bombardments, censure, curfew,
> and the attitude of the German occupation forces increasing their dominat-

ing oppression, and the food supply in a shocking state, the people of Lorient kept on living the best that they could to survive. While the Todt organization was increasing their labor force to accelerate their works under the heavy pressure of the high Command, Lorient was to become a huge fortress to protect large packs of U-boats. Admiral Donitz, regarded by the German sailors as "The Great," became Chief of the Kriegsmarine on January 30, 1943, and advised the Fuhrer of the necessity to increase the production of submarines and to build new types with better performance. The Allies had to react to win the battle of the Atlantic. At the Conference of Casablanca during the beginning of January 1943, the fate of the city of Lorient was sealed. The decision taken at this conference resulted in some drastic actions.

This would be the worst year of the bombardment. On January 3, 1943, the city authorities decided that everyone except those with essential jobs would be evacuated. Pregnant women and women with small children would leave first, followed by the sick and elderly. The schoolchildren had already left. The town was destroyed, but the submarine pens remained intact and functional.

On January 14 and 15, the glow of fires seen by Nazairiens were those of Lorient, which was in ruins. The same fate would befall St. Nazaire. At the summit conference in Casablanca, the decision was made to step up the bombing raids on the submarine bases.

From January 15, 1943, on, all of those who could count on some relative or friend escaped from Lorient and the surrounding area. They took with them what belongings they could carry, depending on their mode of transportation. Life was scarcely possible in the town without water, electricity, gas, and food supplies. The authorities pushed for rapid evacuation but this was discouraged by the German command, who thought that the civilian presence there would discourage Allied attacks. This theory was wrong.

During this time, 33,000 persons left St. Nazaire and went to communities of the Departmente Maine-et-Loire. Six or seven thousand remained in this city of ruin. On Friday, January 16, the city was subjected to another bombardment by B-17 bombers. Two waves of bombers affected major damage and killed 27 people. The mayor's office was evacuated.

From the memoirs of Lucien Francois:

During the nights of the 14th and 15th of January 1943, the attack by Allied Air Forces was preceded by a radio message from BBC London addressed to some heads of the Resistance: "De Bosuet a Bourdaloue, les courgettes seront cuites deux fois… Je repete: de Bosuet a Bourdaloue…". The people in Lorient could not understand immediately the meaning of the warn-

Bombs hitting U-boat base and surrounding area. Courtesy: Hotel de Ville, Lorient, France.

ing message. Bosuet and Bourdaloue were Lorient and St. Nazaire located between Bordeaux and Brest. The "Squash" were the submarines. It will be Lorient from the ports who will be most martyred. On January 14, 1943, there were two raids, at 4:00 P.M. and 10:00 P.M., but probably reconnaissance flying. During the night of the 14th and 15th of January 1943, a loud roaring noise from a large formation of planes was approaching, and with egoistic thoughts, we were hoping it was going to be either Nantes or St. Nazaire, but it was for us. The 317th air raid on Lorient was going to end sadly in the history of the city.

From 1:00 A.M. in the morning until 2:30 A.M., then later during the day from 7:00 P.M to 9:40 P.M., over 20,000 incendiary bombs fell on the city. The German antiaircraft gunnery sent a deluge of tracers invading the sky toward the fleet of bombers from which the bombs were launched as well as some star shells or flares to light their targets. The fire in Lorient started to play havoc. Some people were able to save their homes themselves or with the help of neighbors when it was possible. Because incendiary bombs sometimes fall by clusters, the fire would spread very quickly and the people had to evacuate. In our street friends helped each other and that day they avoided the worst.

With the houses touching each other, the fire spread rapidly, roof to roof. The firemen could not be everywhere at once. Feeling powerless, the people could do nothing but look at the sad spectacle and to see their homes, souvenirs of a life-time, all going up in smoke, then leaving town for a shelter somewhere, to a parent or friend, or anywhere else far away from this inferno.

Firemen from neighboring towns came to help, even German army firemen, but water was cut off by a bomb destroying a main water line to the city and they were reduced to using sea water from the harbor. To add to the misery, a strong wind was blowing and accelerated the spread of the fire. You could find here and there unexploded incendiary bombs and by the heat they would flare up and start another fire. Grandfather found two or three in his garden. Some streets were impassable by the heat rising on both sides from the rubble blocking the pavement. People walked in the street without knowing where they were going, with a shocked, traumatic look on their faces.

On January 23, 1943, from 1:25 P.M to 2:13 P.M., planes with four motors dropped high-explosive bombs on all quarters of Lorient. The bombers returned from 7:45 P.M to 9:00 P.M. for a second attack with explosives and incendiaries, which demolished the town hall and 500 homes. The left side of the Arsenal was severely damaged. On that day, 14 civilians were killed and 25 were wounded. On January 26 and 29, more violent attacks with explosives and incendiaries occurred. Three-fourths of the town was in ruins. The surrounding communities were not spared.

Lucien Francois adds:

On January 23, 1943, when the inhabitants of Lorient were beginning to adapt themselves to the situation, two bombing raids occurred in the afternoon and evening during which 125 heavy bombers dumped explosives. This type of bombardment was scary by the continuous explosions, and was traumatic for the people. On the 26th of January from 8:15 P.M to 9:30 P.M. again explosives and incendiaries fell on the city. The city was 75 percent ruined and the prefect of Morbihan department was authorized by the German Command to evacuate the city. Some inhabitants had already left without waiting for the authorization because they had no house left to live in. This was January under rain and the winter cold. The problem was, where to go? It was too dangerous nearby the perimeter of the city. Some left to go far away from the region.

There was no longer any doubt about the destiny of Lorient. On February 3, 1943, the police commissioner obtained the authority for evacuation of the civilians. Forty thousand Lorientens began by any means possible to evacuate to less-exposed communities. Thirty thousand stayed nearby and six thousand left toward Mayenne and Indre-et-Loire. Others dispersed in every direction to find safe haven. Seine-et-Marne adopted the displaced townspeople. There were masses at the transportation stations carrying suitcases and bundles. Those who could not count on family or friends were forced to pay prohibitive transportation rates.

Despite the physical and emotional hardships of departure from their homes, time had run out for the civilians of Lorient. On February 4, 7, 13, and 16, 1943, waves of bombers dropped, without interruption, larger and more powerful explosives and incendiaries, putting the finishing touches on the destruction of the town. New buildings including St. Louis Church, the train station, and Bodelio Hospital were laid waste by projectiles weighing almost two tons each.

Only concrete German fortifications, causes of the disaster, remained in perfect working condition. By February 17, 1943, Lorient had been evacuated by most of its population. Its municipal services were devastated. Access to the city was restricted by barricades. Only those who were indispensable could go back. The personnel of the Arsenal and German dockyards were furnished special authorization allowing them to work there during the day. Consequently, the Allies had no hesitation on March 6 to carry out a very violent bombardment with explosives, which knocked down about 990 supplementary buildings.

Lucien Francois tells of the plight of the inhabitants:

The Allied bombing persisted on February 4, 7, 13, and 16, 1943, with bombs and incendiaries on what was left of the city. The next day, the last of the inhabitants left town leaving behind a pile of ruin. Souvenirs were destroyed and for a lot of them, their dear relatives were under piles of bricks and stones. There were also other raids of bombing on March 6th, April 16th, and May 17th, but Lorient was empty of people.

Our newspaper, *Laliberte of Morbihan,* reported the following:

104 people killed in one night on the 14th and 15th of January, 1943
60,000 incendiary bombs in one month
5,000 explosive bombs
3,000 buildings destroyed, without counting those they had to condemn for safety

Lorient is practically destroyed 90 percent, but the main German buildings were still untouched.

Lucien's family lost their home and became refugees. The hardships that this family endured are similar to those endured by hundreds of thousands in Europe. These refugees and displaced persons became a massive problem at the end of the war. How to feed them and get them back to their homes or to some stable location with shelter required a major effort by the Allies. Not only was nutrition a problem but acceptable preventive hygiene and health care were almost insurmountable problems.

Lucien's memory of this period of evacuation was as follows:

The population had abandoned the city not by choice but because of no more roofs over their heads. Those residing in the suburbs on the perimeter were less touched by the onslaught but had left also by fear, which was understandable. Some occupants would not leave, at any price, their home of many family generations. It was impossible for them to abandon a sacred spot of sentimental value.

For us, my family lived a little off the center of the city. Our street was not the worst hit during the first air raid. We were lucky we could extinguish some incendiary bombs ourselves. (Water won't do the job. From the beginning of the war people were advised to keep a supply of dry sand and a shovel in their attic, the only way to succeed over an incendiary bomb.) My grandfather spent many hours on watch in the attic, risking receiving some on his head, when the rest of the family was in the basement. He was a veteran of the First World War and gassed in the trenches and yet still had a will to fight.

We evacuated to 30 kilometers from Lorient to the village of Inguiniel where a friend of Grandpa had a convenience store. His name was Tourelin. A minimum of baggage was moved from our house and we made many trips back and forth to get clothing, furniture, dishes, and what we felt was of use to us. One morning when we arrived to pick up two or three loads to save practically all goods, we arrived to see our house in smoke, almost finished burning. The street was deserted. We were able to enter the backyard of the house by a neighbor's yard and save a blacksmith forge and bag of coal standing in a shop at the end of the garden. This piece of equipment was useful for some farmers to maintain their tools in exchange for food or other supplies necessary for us until the end of the war.

We were lucky to have Grandpa's old truck, which escaped the requisition because of its old age. The Germans used to take anything on wheels. It was running when we had gasoline and permitted us to save some of our family possessions. A good majority of people did not have this chance of transportation.

Dishonesty for profit was prevalent everywhere. Leaving the place was a must, but how? Some people could not afford to pay for moving their possessions but where would they go if they did not know any family or friend outside town? Some went by train, some went by foot pushing or pulling all sorts of carriages with just what they could take along and abandoning the rest except the favorite doll for that child or a stuffed bear for another. They had to run away from those smoking ruins. Then by order of the Germans after the evacuation on February 3, 1943, the city was closed to anyone who was not working at the Arsenal or on field work for the Todt organization, especially at the submarine base.

The German troops became very nervous and would shoot on site without warning for no reason. The inhabitants were dispersed in the countryside for miles around the city. The tide of refugees from the city was not always welcome among the country people, who in some small towns could not speak French, only their ancestral language of Breton. The city folk were invading the country folk. At the beginning some clashes resulted in rivalries, like churches in the village on Sunday. The service, sermon, and singing were in Breton or Latin and people exiled from Lorient complained to the mayor and priest that they wanted a service they could understand.

To survive, our family of eight people, including four children of 4, 6, 11, 12 years old stayed in an old abandoned building belonging to my grandfather's friend, all of us in one room with a fireplace and dirt floor, but a roof over our heads. No running water, no electricity, no toilet. Water was obtained from a well. To heat, we used dead wood we could find in the countryside. With spring coming, we picked dandelions, mushrooms, snails, and *ortie* (nettle) for soup. Wild weed was common but would give a rash on the skin when in contact but safe when cooked. We could buy some potatoes and chestnuts.

Summer coming, the city folks helped the farmers in the field. After the hardships of winter, relationships with the people in the country became smoother and they understood our predicament and began speaking French with us.

FEBRUARY 28, 1943—THE APOCALYPSE

On February 28, 1943, a virtual apocalypse occurred involving St. Nazaire and the surrounding territory. Three hundred B-17s dropped several hundred tons of bombs over a period of 26 minutes. Thousands of incendiary and phosphorous bombs consumed St. Nazaire. More than 600 fires illuminated the town. The firemen worked diligently trying to create fire breaks by knocking down some structures. Water to quell the fires was in short supply. Schools and hospitals were destroyed. The people sought shelter wherever they could find it; 300 huddled in the basement of a burning building. Thirty-nine died and thirty-six more were injured. Sixty percent of the houses were consumed. Commerce, water, electricity, and telephone service disappeared. The fire departments of Nantes and

Refugees with only the possessions they could carry awaiting a bus that would charge them greatly elevated fees. Courtesy: Hotel de Ville, Lorient, France.

Pouliguen sent help. The town archives were destroyed. La Clinic Gentin continued to administer to the wounded and sick.

On March 4, over 4,000 Nazairiens were evacuated. Secours National did its best to provide food for the evacuees. On March 16, total evacuation was decided upon. The bombers returned on March 21, and for 25 minutes rained destruction upon the city as well as the small towns on the periphery. Fifteen persons died and twenty were wounded. For the first time, the Americans used delayed bombs. Another bombardment on March 23 left four dead and one wounded.

Only one bombardment occurred in April. Seven members of the Angelo family were arrested and accused of hiding an American aviator who had been shot down. The father was shot and the rest of the family sent to prison. On April 16 and 17, 1943, bombing attacks on Lorient were severe but the inhabitants were warned beforehand by radio. The last bombardment occurred in May 1943, on the 29th. The town and docks sustained incendiary bombs, leaving 1 dead and 10 wounded. Three planes were brought down with antiaircraft fire. Although numerous alerts continued, there was no more air bombardment. The submarine pens remained undamaged.

During the years 1940 through 1943, 177 bombardments of St. Nazaire took place, killing 479 civilians and wounding an additional 576. More than 3,600 homes were completely destroyed and almost an equal number were damaged at least 50 percent.[1]

THE U-BOATS MEET RESISTANCE

At the end of 1942, the U-boats were still at their peak of destruction of Allied shipping. In November 1942, 509,000 tons of Allied shipping were sunk. Bad weather decreased these losses by 50 percent in December and January 1943. In February, the numbers had escalated. One hundred and twenty U-boats sunk 300,000 tons. In March 1943, the U-boats sunk 108 ships.

During this period, Donitz was shocked to learn that for the first time, U-boat losses had exceeded their production. United States production had replaced all of its ships lost to submarines since the beginning of the war. In just two months, a remarkable change for the better had occurred. In April 1943, the loss from U-boats was 227,000 tons, but 15 U-boats were sunk. In May, Allied loss was 212,000 tons and 41 U-boats were sunk. Hitler became unhappy with Admiral Straeder and replaced him with Admiral Donitz as commander in chief of the German navy. This gave Donitz the opportunity to upgrade the submarine service with boats, supplies, and personnel without having to go through other admirals.

The tide began to change in favor of the Allies. United States air power entered the battle with radar to find submarines. The mid-Atlantic gap was closed with long-range American Liberators. Centimetric radar was developed and, in the spring of 1943, was installed in aircraft and crews were trained in its use. Resonant cavity magnetron, a transmitter that would give out pulses of very high power with wavelengths of only a few centimeters, became functional. This was very small and placed in planes and ships. U-boat losses began to increase. The "wolf packs" were caught in a tightening technology vice. In May 1943, the Germans lost 43 U-boats, twice the number produced that month. Donitz lost a son who was on a German U-boat. The American planes had huge searchlights installed so that once they picked up a sub on radar, they were able to visualize it on the surface and attack after cutting off their motors and approaching the submarine quietly. During this period, 218 U-boats were attacked at night, with 27 sunk and 31 severely damaged. They were also able to launch a torpedo that honed in on the submarine's propeller.

Massive destruction of city buildings. Courtesy: Hotel de Ville, Lorient, France.

United States Admiral Ernest I. King developed a plan to divide the Atlantic into three sections and make each of the Allies responsible for a specific section. Long-range aircraft were to work anywhere they were needed, regardless of the country in need.

Admiral Sir Max Horton was King's counterpart in Britain. He had been a submariner in WWI and now had sufficient warships and support groups, such as escort carriers, to escort the convoys. With the battle of Convoy ON-5, in May 1943, against 50 to 60 U-boats, Horton's strategy was convincing. The convoy lost almost one-third of its ships, but six U-boats were sunk. Donitz broke off the attack, as he knew aircraft from Newfoundland would soon be approaching. In the early days, this many U-boats would have been devastating.

When the war was over, Admiral Donitz said, "The German submarine campaign was wrecked by the introduction of the convoy system." Several things accounted for this. Operational Research, a small backroom unit of the admiralty, studied convoy losses and made recommendations as to the size, formation, and escort service. Their studies and recommendations were instrumental in greatly reducing the number of ships lost. For instance, if five U-boats attacked a convoy, the same number of ships would be lost in a 30-vessel convoy as in a 60 vessel convoy, escort being the same. In other words, the larger the convoy, the fewer ships lost.

FRENCH FORCES OF THE INTERIOR—ORIGIN

The year 1943 was a formative one for the Free French of the Interior (FFI). Sensing that the invasion of Europe would take place the following year, there began an acceleration of enlistment into the FFI or various organizations that eventually become absorbed into the FFI. There was also growing intolerance with the Vichy regime, especially at local levels such as villages and towns governed by Vichy-appointed officials. The Resistance had stepped up its pace of information-gathering and sabotage.

Eventually, when the Allies did invade Europe, these organizations began to attack the Germans. A great number of the patriots migrated to St. Nazaire and Lorient. At first, they were mostly untrained, ill-equipped, and in need of guns and munitions, but by the end of the war, there were approximately 40,000 French soldiers on the St. Nazaire and Lorient pockets who were well trained, equipped, and absorbed into regular French army units. This large group of volunteer French soldiers proved to be an important ally to the American units assigned to these two heavily defended strongholds.

In an effort to research the origin of such a large French force, a search was made for key people who could give accurate firsthand accounts. Fortunately, such a source was found during a celebration in 2000 of the veterans of the 8th Cuirassiers, which was one of France's most celebrated regiments. General Pierre Dumas-Delage, from Lyon, the president of the 8th Cuirassiers Veterans Organization and former *chef de corps* of the 8th Cuirassiers, wrote a summary of the origins of some of the best French units who fought in the southern sector of the St. Nazaire pocket.

After the French were defeated by the Germans in June 1940, the Germans authorized the formation of a French army of 100,000 men in the unoccupied zone. In November 1942, when the Germans occupied this *Zone Libre*, all of the units were dissolved. This Army of the Armistice became a hotbed for Resistance recruits, many of whom became prominent in the pockets of St. Nazaire and Lorient.

The "Chef d'Etat Major" of the 9th Military Division in Chateauroux, Colonel Raymond Chomel (later to become General Chomel), was made responsible for the liquidation of the Army of the Armistice and all related activities. He was able to stay in touch with the military and secretly joined the Organization Resistance de L'Armee—Army Resistance Organization (O. R. A.). This Resistance organization gave Chomel the responsibility of contacting the many officers of this Army of the Armistice and, hopefully, reinstating the dissolved units and create a brigade or division. This was difficult, since many of the soldiers belonged to different Resistance groups, some of which were greatly at odds with each other.

In 1943, another group appeared on the scene, the First Regiment of France (1st RDF). The creation of this regiment took place in July 1943. Officers and noncommissioned officers were carefully chosen to establish high standards. The regiment quickly attracted many young people from 18 to 20 years of age, half of whom were military students. Thus, the 1st RDF had many future officers, some of whom reached top levels in the army.

The command of the 1st RDF was given to Colonel Berlon, who became a general in April 1944. The second in command was Colonel Segur, who had a reputation as a Gaulleist and had been Chef de Corps of the 8th Cuirassiers in November 1942 before its dissolution. Many officers and noncommissioned officers of the 1st RDF were secretly associated with the Resistance. The regiment was extremely anti-German in spite of some of the members' attachment to Pétain because of his past accomplishments in WWI. General Berlon was replaced by Colonel Segur to command the 1st RDF. Segur visited Chomel on August 12 and joined the O.R.A. He was clearly on the side of the Resistance.

Orders arrived from London stating that members of the 1st RDF could be accepted in the French army but were not to be given commanding positions. Although Segur wanted to regain command of the 8th Cuirassiers, he could not be considered under these new laws. Chef d'Escadrons de Beaumont, formerly in the 8th Cuirassiers in Chateauroux, was chosen instead. Colonel Chomel moved fast and, in August 1944, re-created the 8th Cuirassiers by unifying the two cavalry squadrons of the 1st RDF and the two squadrons made up of troops affiliated with the Resistance that claimed to belong to the 8th Cuirassiers from Chateauroux. In one of these was Lieutenant Jean Buneaux Pusy Du Mothier, Marquis de La Fayette, direct descendant of the General Marquis de La Fayette of Revolutionary War fame.

At this time, many soldiers who had fought for France against the Germans in 1940 began coming back into French units to fight again. Typical of this group was Francois Kauffmann Tardivel, who now resides in Cannes.

In 1938, Francois left his home and joined the 8th Cuirassiers. In December 1939, he assumed the duties of a liaison officer with British troops. He spent time on the second line, first line, outpost, and as a commando, then pulled back in reserve. While attached to an antitank regiment, he was wounded during the Aras counterattack. Because the wound damaged his sciatic nerve, he sustained permanent foot drop. He escaped from Dunkirk to England, where he spent three months in the hospital.

After returning to France, Francois became a member of the Resistance in 1942, then joined the FFI and fought in Paris in the area of Place de la Concorde and Tuilerie. Following the fighting there, he joined another unit and proceeded to a position south of the Loire River on the outskirts of St. Nazaire. When the FFI was absorbed by the regular French army, Francois was discharged because of his wound and the resulting disability. He, like many others who were evacuated from Dunkirk, returned to fight for the honor of his country. The thousands of French soldiers who fought at St. Nazaire and Lorient spared many soldiers for the fight on the eastern front at a time when Allied manpower was suffering.

Colonel Chomel was made general and commander in chief of the Forces Francaises de Loire Inferieure (FFLI) that became the French 25th Division. His brigade was ready for the operations in the pocket of St. Nazaire. One of the most revered French officers to fight at St. Nazaire, Chomel had served as liaison officer in the French 4th Armored Division under General de Gaulle at the battle of Montcornet in 1940.

When the armistice between Germany and France was signed, Chomel remained as a regular French officer with the "Baby Army," which was authorized by the Germans to aid Pétain in keeping order as a police force. Under the code name of "Commandant Charles," he secretly began recruiting regular army officers to help the Allies when France was invaded. His group became a brigade and included the 8th Cuirassiers, the only French cavalry regiment still in existence at that time. Chomel named his unit the "Charles Martel Brigade." Charles Martel is well known to all French boys and young men as the "Prince of the Francs," who stopped the Arabs arriving from Spain on October 25, A.D. 732, by defeating them at Poiters. The prestige of that name caused many youngsters to join in spite of the risk of being caught by the Germans.

Chomel was given a much larger command after the Normandy invasion and was put in charge of all French troops south of the Loire River. His leadership and contribution to the campaign in Brittany became legend. He was at General Hermann Kramer's side when the Germans at Lorient and St. Nazaire surrendered. Following WWII, he spent three years in Indochina as a commanding officer and returned to take command of the French Forces of Occupation in Stuttgart, Germany.

NOTE

1. One would wonder why the Allies persisted with this intense bombardment of Lorient and St. Nazaire when, in reality, very little damage was done to the military targets.

Chapter 5

1944

GERMANS ON THE DEFENSIVE

The year 1944 brought many changes and put the Germans on the defensive. Bombardments of St. Nazaire and Lorient ceased on May 29, 1943. The Allied air forces were concentrating on targets in Germany and those on the coast of France significant to the invasion. The buildup in England escalated. Multiple infantry and armored divisions in the United States were in advanced training.

The Allies were now able to remain on the offensive and accelerate their missions to destroy the U-boat armada. Admiral Karl Donitz was losing more U-boats than he could replace. In the year before the Normandy Invasion, only 92 Allied ships were lost out of thousands carrying supplies to England. The U-boat menace, however, continued until the end of the war, as evidenced by the tragic loss of so many fine, young soldiers of the 66th Infantry Division, who were on the troopship *Leopoldville,* when it was torpedoed Christmas Eve, 1944. The 66th Division subsequently played a major role in containing the Germans in the U-boat fortresses of St. Nazaire and Lorient, by greatly reducing their effectiveness by daily artillery bombardment and an aggressive ground war.

On May 5, 1945, the last U-boat, *Fuchs,* left St. Nazaire. Only two boats remained. When Germany surrendered, Admiral Donitz ordered all U-boat captains to surface and turn their boats over to the Allies. One hundred and fifty-nine did, but 203 were scuttled by their crews.

A section on the Army Specialized Training Program (ASTP) is included here because the 66th, 83rd, and 94th Infantry Divisions, major participants in the ground war at St. Nazaire and Lorient, were ASTP and air force cadet divisions. This meant that they were 3 of 35 divisions, mostly infantry, that received large numbers of ASTP soldiers and air force cadets when both programs were aborted in the spring of 1944. These soldiers, with IQs of 115 or better, had a very positive impact upon the combat performance of these divisions, as well as the many other divisions that received them prior to going to Europe.

Although it is difficult to determine who supplied the initial "monument of thoughtfulness" that spawned this program, there is no doubt that its godfather was Secretary of War Henry L. Stimson. In essence, this program "red-shirted" approximately 200,000 inductees in the spring and summer of 1943 for future positions of knowledge and leadership in the event that the war continued for more than several years. All participants had to go through basic ground force training prior to actually entering the program.

Louis E. Keefer has written an excellent book on this program, *Scholars in Foxholes.* Both from historical and human interest perspectives, Keefer's book is enlightening, very readable, and provides a forum for evaluating the many and varied opinions as to the value of this program to the armed services, which range from criticism to praise.

In the spring and summer of 1943, officer candidate schools and air force pilot training programs were glutted with far more candidates than needed. Graduating seniors from Reserve Officers Training Corps units were commissioned and juniors assured a place in officer candidate schools. During the preceding year or two, many commissions had been given outright based on certain qualifications. This left a large number of college students who had joined the Enlisted Reserve Corp and who had better-than-average IQs with little opportunity for advancement. Many inductees during this period were singled out for ASTP, having scored 115 or better on the Army General Classification Test (AGCT).

After the war, Stimson, secretary of war 1940–1945, wrote in his book, *Service in Peace and War,* "Each step of the ASTP story was tied in with ups and downs in the Army's estimates of its manpower requirements. In all such changes, the college training program, as a marginal undertaking, was very sharply affected. The choice was between specialized training and an adequate combat force."

Probably the single most important event leading up to the creation of the ASTP—and the navy's V-12 Program—was the American Council on

Education's National Committee on Education and Defense collaboration with the United States Office of Education to co-sponsor the largest conference of college and university leaders ever held on January 3–4, 1942. Many plans and ideas were presented to utilize the nation's educational institutions to train personnel for the army. Initially, the armed services were not ready to study the question.

Three weeks later, William O. Hotchkiss, president of Rensselaer Polytechnic Institute, recommended a "War Technical Training Corp." He enthusiastically sent his ideas to some of the highest officers in the government, including Stimson. This probably set the stage for the important steering committees that formulated plans for, and initiated, the ASTP and the navy's V-12 Program.

College leaders, experiencing drastic reductions in enrollment, continued an aggressive campaign to convince military leaders of the advantage of utilizing the campuses for training. President Roosevelt urged Secretary Stimson and other members of his cabinet to study the proposals carefully. As a result, Brigadier General Joe M. Dalton was ordered to develop a program. By the end of two months, he had developed a plan for the formation of ASTP.

In opposition was General Leslie J. McNair, commander of the army ground forces. He was against any program that took away young men needed for combat roles and felt the program should be put on hold until it was determined that the war would continue beyond 1944. After much study and planning, the "Joint Statement of the Secretary of War and the Secretary of the Navy on Utilizing of College Facilities in Specialized Training for the Army and Navy" was published December 17, 1942. A description of the Army Specialized Training Program was printed in the *New York Times.* Following this announcement, there was much pro and con opinion among military personnel and college educators.

General George C. Marshall, army chief of staff, described this new training: "The Army has been increasingly handicapped by a shortage of men possessing combinations of intelligence, aptitude, education and training in fields such as medicine, engineering, languages, science, mathematics and psychology who are qualified for service as officers of the Army. With the establishment of the minimum selective service age of eighteen, the Army was compelled to assure itself that there would be no interruption in the flow of professionally trained and technically trained men who had heretofore been provided in regular increments by American colleges and universities." Essentially a soldier who had a high school diploma and scored more than 115 on the Army General Classification

Test qualified. Trainees started coming into the program in April and May of 1943. There was a great influx of these soldier students during the summer, and the program peaked in the fall. When the program began, it was estimated that 1.3 million young soldiers would be potential candidates. At first the response was less than positive, so General Marshall demanded more support by telling those in command to make sure that their men knew about the program. The response was positive. Some soldiers even thought they were placed in it by their commanders involuntarily.

Initially, 151 colleges were selected, 35 of them having both Air Cadet Programs and ASTPs. More colleges were included later. In December of 1943, it was estimated that 127,000 ASTP members were on college campuses and that approximately 74,000 were studying engineering, 15,000 advanced engineering, 14,000 medicine, 13,000 languages, 5,000 dentistry, 4,000 advanced Reserve Officer Training Corps, and 2,000 veterinary science.

The objectives of the program and its ultimate goals were never clear. Many trainees were under the impression that they would eventually receive a commission, but the army never made that commitment and there had been no promises. At any rate, there were a lot of young soldiers in college but losing their chance for promotion. On the other had, they were enhancing their education and remaining out of harm's way. This became important later when the program was abruptly aborted.

Colonel Herman Beukema was named director of the Army Specialized Training Division in which the ASTP was placed. His approach was disciplined and professional, and he made certain that ASTP men would be "soldiers first and students second." He was assisted by a high-level Army Specialized Training Division (ASTD) Advisory Committee, which sent 200,000 soldiers to 227 colleges and universities. Criteria for candidacy for the program were established. Basic infantry training had to be completed first.

In November 1943, General Clayton Bissell proposed that the ASTP be reduced to 30,000 soldiers, most of whom would be studying medicine or related subjects. The remainder would be returned to ground force units. Lt. General Leslie McNair concurred, with Secretary Stimson's support, and the decision was made to reduce ASTP to 62,000 trainees by the end of 1944.

The cause of this major reduction was the manpower crisis and congressional debates about fathers being drafted. After considering using some existing units, such as coast artillery and antiaircraft units for replacements, Marshall wrote to Secretary Stimson on February 10, 1944, to request the ASTP reduction.

I am aware of your strong feeling for the Army Specialized Training Program. However, I wish you to know that in my opinion, we are no longer justified in hiding 140,000 men in this training when it represents the only source that we can obtain the required personnel, especially with a certain degree of intelligence and training, except by disbanding already organized combat units. I recognize that it would be desirable, if circumstances permitted, to withdraw personnel from the Army Specialized Training Program only as they completed scheduled terms of instruction; however, our need for these basically trained men is immediate and imperative. I, therefore, propose that a maximum limit of 30,000 students to be established, this number being required largely for the supply of doctors and dentists and such other highly trained technicians as the Army may be unable to provide from other sources.

The outstanding deficiency noted in our divisions is the number of non-commissioned officers who are below satisfactory standards of intelligence and qualities of leadership. The men from the Army Specialized Training Program made available by the foregoing proposal should materially raise the combat efficiency of the divisions now scheduled for shipment overseas.

President Roosevelt approved the proposal on February 18, 1944. The ASTP was reduced from 145,000 soldiers in training to 35,000, a greater reduction than had previously been planned. The only alternative was to disband three tank battalions and 27 antiaircraft battalions.

Thirty-five divisions, infantry and armored mostly, received an average of over 1,700 ASTP students each. Twenty-five of these divisions also received an average of 1,000 aviation cadets each. Some infantry divisions received more than 3,000 combined of the two groups.

An unusual situation was created. If measured strictly by IQ, there was great disparity between the noncommissioned officers (non-coms) and this college group of soldiers they were to train. Since the non-coms were much better trained militarily, there was bound to be a cultural clash. The attitude of most non-coms was, "we'll show them college boys who have been goofing off," and try they did.

The training program was grueling. The "college boys" adopted their own "do-or-die" attitude and demonstrated physical ability and stamina to more than match anything already existing in their companies. Also, at sessions on map reading, current events, or anything relating to "book smarts," they nailed the instructors to the wall with their probing questions designed to expose the non-coms' lack of knowledge on the subject.

There was a gradual social and military amalgamation, each group gaining respect for the other and many long-lasting friendships between low and high IQs developed. The advanced infantry training that summer was hard but created a "togetherness" in the company that went with it to the European Theater of Operations (ETO).

The 66th Infantry Division, destined to wrap up the ground war at St. Nazaire and Lorient, like many other ASTP divisions, was sent to the ETO in the latter part of 1944, arriving in England in November and in France in late December. In Europe, ASTP soldiers were selected to fill probably 90 percent of vacant non-com positions. This demonstrated that intelligence is strongly related to performance, initiative, equanimity, dependability, and leadership.

ASTP divisions fought in Brittany, the Huertgen Forrest, and in the Vosges Mountains. They were at the Battle of the Bulge and the Siegfried Line and in the battles to cross the Elbe and Rhine Rivers. The 106th Infantry Division, which was overrun during the Bulge and suffered many casualties, was an ASTP division.

George M. Illis, an ASTP soldier in the 102nd Division, gave this story: "When we went overseas, I could estimate that 65 percent of my company were former members of ASTP. By the end of the war, I would estimate that less than 5 percent of the company had been members of that program. The rest had been killed, wounded, or captured. I was the only survivor of that group in my platoon out of twenty ASTP soldiers. There is no question about it, if they lived long enough, the ASTP boys became superb soldiers."[1]

Another important opinion on the ASTP and its soldiers is given by Peter Mansoor in his book, *The G. I. Offensive in Europe, The Triumph of American Infantry Divisions, 1944–1945*. It is as follows: Thirty-five divisions benefited from an infusion of an average of 1,500 ASTP students each and 22 divisions each received 1,000 Aviation Cadets. The divisions assigned the bulk of these men to the infantry, and training and morale— by no coincidence—soon improved.

These actions came too late. The transfer of the men from the ASTP, the Aviation Cadet Program and the Zone of the Interior service establishments improved the quality of the personnel in the divisions in the United States but these men had only a limited time to train with new units before deployment overseas. If the War Department had assigned these men to combat divisions in the first place, many of them already would have filled positions of leadership in their units. By 1944, soldiers who had been quickly released from ASTP and other programs were just more "warm bodies" needed to fill gaps in the ranks. As matters stood, many qualified soldiers ended up serving in their new units under less qualified officers and non-coms. The 102nd Infantry Division received 2,760 soldiers from the ASTP before deployment: about 100 of them eventually earned battlefield commissions after rising to non-com leadership positions in battle.

The Siegfried Line, Lorraine and the Vosges campaigns demonstrated the ability of the American divisions to perform well during their initial entry into combat. The official historian of the Siegfried Line campaign observed: "In Normandy, it had become almost routine for a division in its first combat action to incur severe losses and display disturbing organizational, command and communication deficiencies for at least the first week of combat indoctrination. Yet in no case was this tendency present to a similar degree among these divisions receiving their baptism of fire during the Siegfried Line campaign."

It is probable that those who survived would have filled the junior officer ranks had the war lasted another six months. Many ASTP soldiers have distinguished themselves in civilian life. Former Senator Bob Dole, former Secretary of State Henry Kissenger, former mayor of New York Edward Koch, and author Gore Vidal were all in the ASTP. Mayor Koch went to the Timberwolf Division, Senator Dole to the 10th Mountain Division, Secretary Henry Kissenger to the ETO as an interpreter, and Mr. Vidal to the Transportation Corps.

One can only speculate on the value of the ASTP and air force cadet soldiers in the enlisted ranks, as there are no objective criteria with which to judge them. There have been many high-IQ non-coms in the ranks ever since the United States has had an army, but never in such numbers and in such concentration as were sent to Europe in the summer and fall of 1944. They were not of the "drill instructor" mode but managed their units (squads, sections, platoons) with leadership by example. Their judgment promoted security among their charges. There are numerous examples of their resourcefulness in completing projects against great odds and with intelligence and perseverance, terminating successfully, often beyond the call of duty. Three of these stories are included as examples of that "little bit beyond" that some of these soldiers possessed. In no way is this meant to take away from the many brave and dedicated soldiers who were not blessed with a better-than-average IQ or the opportunity to have an education; it is merely to recognize this special group of soldiers.

A few days after the 66th Division entered the campaign against the Germans in Brittany, the supply of signal flares (parachute flares) was almost exhausted. There was a dire need for these by the front line soldiers to light up the area in front of their positions when enemy infiltration was suspected.

Ray Roberts from Bridgeman, Michigan, was a T-5 (technical) corporal in the 766th Ordnance Company of the 66th Division and was stationed in the small village of Messac near Lorient and St. Nazaire. Ray's first sergeant told him to report to the Division Ordnance Headquarters in Rennes. Being only a T-5 corporal and sensing some important mission, he questioned the first sergeant as to why he was chosen. He was told that he was the only one left and available. (The others were out picking up the company's vehicles in Antwerp, Belgium.) When he reached Division Ordnance, he was given papers and instructions by Lieutenant Colonel Embree Reynolds. He was to go to an ammunition depot, which was either in eastern France or southern Belgium, and pick up a supply of signal flares. These flares were only stocked in one depot in Europe and the location was classified, so Ray was not given a definite location but only an area. He was told that it was imperative that he return within seven days and, if not, two more GIs would be sent on the same mission. To put things in proper perspective, Ray had not traveled much prior to entering the army. Now Ray was headed to his third foreign country in as many weeks with a driver he did not know, during the Battle of the Bulge, and in a snow storm with an open-cab truck that had a canvas roof.

Ray and his driver, Herman, took off in a Dodge weapons carrier with orders and a map and headed for Belgium. Herman was a Private First Class (Pfc.) from the 66th Quartermaster Company. He was 20 years old, grew up in the Green Point section of Brooklyn, and had worked as a delivery truck driver for Macy's department store. Ray told him that he was driving too slowly and Herman informed him that he had no experience driving in snow and ice. His family had not owned a car.

Just outside of Rennes, on the road to Le Mans, they were going down a hill. Herman hit the brakes hard, went into a spin, and ended up in a shallow ditch. Ray saw that Herman was obviously "shook," so he volunteered to drive. Most of Ray's driving experience was back and forth to work at the Ford Motor Company in Dearborn, Michigan, and back and forth to night school at the University of Detroit. The going was slow, and when they pulled into an Ordnance Depot to spend the night, they had only gone about 60 miles. (If you were a GI traveling with orders, you could get food, gas, and a place to sleep—usually on the floor in your sleeping bag.)

That evening, Ray asked every GI and officer if they knew the location of the ammunition dump (ammo dump) that he was assigned to find. No one knew anything about it. At the motor pool the next morning when he was filling the truck with gas, a sergeant told him some of the drivers had mentioned a large ammo dump somewhere near Liege, Belgium. The previous evening, Ray had seen an issue of *Stars and Stripes,* the GI newspaper, and it described the Battle of the Bulge surrounding Bastogne, which is about 45 miles south of Liege. They would have to pass near the front of "The Bulge" in order to find the dump. The sergeant in the motor pool had told Ray that the ammo dump was called A123 and that this identification would begin to appear on wooden arrows nailed to posts at major road intersections when he got to Belgium.

They left Le Mans in cold, snowy, foggy weather, headed for Paris. For the third time, in a moment of panic, Herman spun the vehicle into a ditch. After a long day of Herman's bad driving on icy roads in lousy weather, they made 80 miles and arrived in Paris late in the afternoon. The sergeant at the motor pool had told Ray that there was an ordnance office in Paris and if he showed them his orders, they could direct him to Ammo Dump A123. Here is what happened, in Ray's own words:

> We managed to find the building and the proper department on the fifth floor of this fancy headquarters building. Everyone was dressed in khakis and olive drab uniforms with ties, decorated Eisenhower jackets, and shined shoes. Into this area, I walked with muddy boots, fatigue pants, a combat jacket and wearing a knit cap, not having had a shower or change of clothes for three weeks. Eventually, I was ushered into the plush office of a Captain of Ordnance. I asked if he could tell me where Ammo Dump A123 was located.
>
> He replied: "What the hell do you want to know that for? Don't you know that is classified information?"
>
> "Sir, I have orders to pick up signal flares for the 66th Infantry Division in western France," I replied.
>
> He looked at my orders very carefully, then dismissed me and said that no one in Paris would reveal that information to me and that I was lucky not to be arrested.[2]

Discouraged but undaunted, Ray and Herman found a motor pool in the center of Paris, parked their weapons carrier, and were directed to a small GI hotel. They were assigned beds and served a good meal. Having had a very discouraging and difficult trip thus far, the only thing to do now was what any good GI worth is salt would do and that was to have a night on the town. Who knows when one might "be arrested" for trying to carry out his assigned mission. A fellow GI directed them to the best show in town and helped them get tickets, and they were soon on the Metro headed for Montmarte.

After a walk through this poor section of Paris, they came to a gorgeous theater and attended the "Follies Bergere." Fifty years later, Ray is still ecstatic about the show he saw. Not only was that the first time that he had seen a topless dancer, but the stage was full of them. He said that the show negated the unwarranted bawling out that he had received from the desk-bound ordnance captain.

The next morning he and his driver checked up on "The Bulge" and found that a direct line to Liege would take them too close, so he headed north-northeast and entered Belgium at Mons, then drove east on a road along the Meuse River. Road conditions had improved. Ray did most of the driving.

On this third day they began to pick up signs to A123 and made 175 miles. They stayed overnight at Namur, Belgium, and were fed and given some delicious red wine (captured) by a group of cooks from the 106th Infantry Division who had escaped in the mess truck when their division was overrun by German troops near Bastogne.

The next morning they continued in weather that had turned snowy, overcast, foggy, and very cold. At the city of Huy, 25 miles west of Liege, the A123 signs directed them onto a road headed north. Shortly thereafter, they experienced a weather condition called a "white out"—a combination of thick fog, blowing snow, and roads completely covered by snow, creating a condition similar to a white sheet being placed across the windshield. Ray rubbed his eyes to clear them, but nothing happened. Going at a snail's pace and sometimes walking in front of the truck to make sure they stayed on the road, they finally reached a stretch that had telephone poles that helped guide them.

After what seemed an eternity, a GI tent appeared and a sign that marked the entrance of this classified, secret, hard-to-find, ammunition dump A123. They entered and talked to a sergeant in charge who filled out a picking ticket and directed them to another area of the ammo dump where they would find the flares. While there, a German buzz bomb came in over the tent with a high-pitched whine and exploded 15 seconds later. The sergeant was unconcerned and said that even though they sent one every hour, they rarely hit anything. They were finally loaded and ready to head back. (If the attacking Germans had been able to reach Liege, they would have captured this massive ammo dump and a gasoline dump not far away, which would have helped them reach their goal—the port of Antwerp on the North Sea.)

Driving west through Brussels, they found better roads and were able to move faster. Herman was now driving at least 50 percent of the time. At the end of the fourth day, they were still 500 miles from Rennes. With some searching, they found a mess hall and were allowed to sleep on the floor in their sleeping bags.

On the way back, they bypassed Paris and arrived in Rennes the afternoon of the sixth day, just before two more GIs were to be sent as a backup mission to secure the flares. They delivered the flares and Herman went back to his outfit, and they never saw each other again.

Here was a 23-year-old GI in a foreign country experiencing its worst winter in 40 years, embarked on a lonesome, scary journey, trying to find the secret and classified ammunition dump A123 that no one wanted to talk about, and being threatened with arrest for trying to locate it. But he and Herman had avoided danger around Bastogne while driving in the worst possible winter weather and returned with the badly needed signal flares. No promotion, no medal, not even a pat on the back. Just a GI doing his job.[3]

When the 66th Infantry Division reached France, not yet having been in combat, it was already short approximately 3,000 men due to the deaths, wounds, and illness associated with the sinking of the *Leopoldville*. Replacements were hard to come by, as so many units were losing men on the eastern front especially due to "The Bulge."

The situation was so bad that a group of army prisoners were released for duty on the front lines. Sergeant Hank Andersen from Minneapolis needed a man in his mortar squad in E Company of the 262nd Infantry, and he was told to go back to Battalion Headquarters and pick out a replacement from this group. When Sgt. Andersen finally arrived, he found that there was only one soldier left—Johnny "O." (A fictitious name is used here to avoid any embarrassment to this soldier.) He was in such sorry condition that it was no wonder that nobody wanted him. He was dirty, had a beard and long hair, was foul-mouthed and arrogant, a real reprobate.

The history that Sgt. Andersen extracted from him, with some difficulty and patience, was that he entered the army at age 15 and after basic training ended up in the Aleutian Islands for three years. He suffered so much from prolonged isolation that he was sent back to the States and told that he would not have to serve overseas again. Typical of the army, he ended up in Europe. When he landed in France, he immediately went absent without leave (AWOL) and raised all sorts of hell. He was eventually imprisoned.

The guys in the squad and Sgt. Andersen were good to him, tried to gain his confidence and friendship, but it was a tough go. They deloused him, cut his hair, and tried to restore some sort of pride in him. Andersen made him his tent mate and did everything possible to overcome his alienation. It seemed hopeless.

Company E, 262nd Regiment, was pulled off the line for a few days of rest and rehabilitation (R&R). Passes were given to some to go to Rennes. These were three-day passes, but soldiers had to come back to the company each night. Johnny O. was still under guard and was not eligible for a pass. Sgt. Andersen decided to let him go and cover for him. It was his intention to show the man that he was trusted, and he hoped this might have some positive effect on his rehabilitation.

He didn't return the first two nights, and Sgt. Andersen began to get pretty nervous. When he did not show up the third night, Andersen became frantic and dashed into town. He began combing the "red light" district, determined to go through each house of ill-repute until he found his wayward squad member. He grew aggressive and started throwing doors open until he finally found his errant soldier very drunk and with a woman who was glad to get rid of him. Andersen, a big guy, 6 feet 5 inches, grabbed him, dragged him down the stairs, threw him into a jeep, and drove like mad to get back to camp. He sneaked around the back of the company HQ tent and threw his charge into the squad tent. Johnny O. was silent and somber the next day and remained so until the company went back on the line.

All of a sudden, a complete change took place. Johnny O. asked Andersen why he did this and they began to talk. Johnny O. began to open up and they had some profound discussions. His behavior became exemplary. He began to read and compose music. He seemed to be near genius and after the war he returned to his hometown, joined the Presbyterian Church, and became a well-respected member of his community.

This "save" was not accomplished by a board-certified psychiatrist in a plush office, nor by an ordained minister in the hallowed halls of a beautiful church. It was accomplished by a 20-year-old GI far from home but fortunate to have a thinking brain associated with a great deal of compassion for his fellow man, so much so that he was not afraid to take a risk if there was the possibility of rehabilitating this lonely, distraught soldier from the self-destructive road he was traveling.[4]

The last story, summarized only briefly here, is the subject of the book *First Class Privates* by William Watson Jr. It is an amazing chronicle of two young soldiers. "Bill" was raised in rural South Carolina near Florence. His area did not have electricity until 1937. Prior to going into the service, he attended The Citadel for two years.[5]

After basic training, Bill was placed in ASTP, scoring 146 on the qualifying exam, previously mentioned. When the program was aborted, he was placed in the 100th Infantry Division and endured the vicious Vosges Mountains Campaign and the battle at Wengen-Sur-Moder on the Elbe River. In December 1944, now 20, he was trapped in a basement, rendered unconscious by concussion grenades, and captured. With other prisoners of war, he spent five days on a boxcar without food or water under inhumane conditions that caused the deaths of some GIs. They were sent to Stalag IV-B outside of Muhlburg on the Elbe River. He and a platoon buddy "Sam" Samorajski, became fast friends and helped each other survive the freezing winter and malnutrition.

When the Russians were nearing Dresden in May of 1945, the commandant of the camp freed all the prisoners and attempted to lead them (approximately 2,000) toward the Allied forces to escape the Russians. A Russian plane strafed the column and Bill and Sam took off through the country and began getting much-needed food from farms. Eventually, they were told of an American consulate in Geising, Germany. They found the house and were taken in and treated royally by a small group of people who spoke perfect English. There was plenty of food, good warm beds, and even a tailor brought in to make new American uniforms complete with an American flag patch on each shoulder. Weapons were also supplied.

The people in this small town heard of their arrival and were convinced that they were the advanced guard of the American forces for which they were grateful, thinking they would shield them from the Russians. When a group told them that the burgomaster was hoarding food in his cellar while the children in the orphanage were starving, Bill and Sam paid the man a visit, pistols drawn. They escorted him to the cellar and made him open up. Sure enough, there was a large quantity of food, which they "liberated" and sent to the orphanage. The people then made them co-burgomasters and the town mechanic rehabilitated an old motorcycle with a sidecar so they would have some mobility while doing their duties in the town.

Two more very ill GIs arrived, and even though Bill and Sam were anxious to leave, they stayed another week to get these men strong enough to travel. Finally, it was discovered, as they had suspected, that their hosts were high-ranking Nazis posing as American consulates to evade Russian interference. The group of GIs finally got away in an old car and made it to the American zone 50 miles away. More than 30 days had passed since their liberation from the stalag. Quite an incredible tale for two young men who had traveled very little prior to army service.[6]

THE RESISTANCE MOBILIZES FOR WAR

The multiple infantry and armored divisions in the United States were not the only groups training diligently in 1944, in anticipation of deployment to the ETO. The Resistance movement became more militarized, and bands of 50 or more, sometimes reaching 1,000, were forming regionally. In 1944, these units joined forces as the Forces Francaise de l'Interior (FFI), by which time there were approximately 30,000. Unfortunately, increasing strength gave way to increasing temptation to use it, which resulted in tragic losses at Glieres, Montmouchet, and Vercors. In each case, the FFI, thinking the Allies would join them, started fights with the Germans and were overwhelmed, losing many Frenchmen.

Elsewhere, the Resistance and FFI played a successful part in defeating the German army and the Vichy government. They denied the French rail system to the Germans, disrupted road communications, destroyed mine fields, and obstructed the movement of German troops to Normandy. They defeated the Germans in a one-day battle at St. Marcel on June 18, 1944.

According to General Dwight D. Eisenhower, these groups were worth 15 divisions and shortened the war in Europe by two months. In no other area was their presence more effective than in the pockets of St. Nazaire and Lorient where they, in large numbers and with multiple infantry, reconnaissance, and artillery units helped to contain the Germans and, ulti- mately, to defeat them.

THE RESISTANCE MOVEMENT IN MORBIHAN
AND IN THE LOIRE ATLANTIC

The Department of Morbihan is a large section in Brittany that is similar to a county in a state in the United States. Lorient is located in Morbihan and St. Nazaire is located in the adjacent Department Loire Atlantique. The battle for these ports, which began after the Normandy Invasion, was pre- ceded by the activity of the "maquis," the Resistance movement in Brittany. This movement was the forerunner of the FFI in this area and served as the nucleus from which the FFI was organized.

At the time of the Normandy Invasion, there were approximately 150,000 German troops in Brittany. The heaviest concentration was in the west of Brittany, which was divided into security zones supervised by spe- cially trained units. German General Dolman, whose headquarters was in Le Mans, defended Normandy and Brittany with his 7th Army. Three divi- sions guarded the coastal area: the 84th commanded by General Marx, the 74th under General Koltz, and the 25th commanded by General Wilhelm Fahrmbacher (who eventually retreated into the pocket of Lorient and served as overall commandant there). The German forces were divided into northern and southern zones. The German 266th Infantry Division moved against the 6th Armored Division when it was headed to Brest.

These forces were supported by a number of reinforcement units that included parachute divisions and "Eastern Units" made up of Ukrainian cavalry and Georgians. There was also the 25th Fortress Regiment, which consisted of 29 companies.

The FFI in the Department of Morbihan began to organize in earnest just before the invasion. Unfortunately, on March 31, 1944, the Resistance movement in Morbihan was greatly damaged by more than 50 arrests, including many leaders.

Saint-Marcel, a village at the eastern end of the Department of Morbihan, was selected for the drop zone. Saint-Marcel had 500 people and two streets. The nearest town was Ploërmel with Vannes and Redon not too far distant. Between Saint-Marcel and Sérent, there was an area with open fields surrounded by a wooded area. It was far removed, near thickets, and easy to find from the air because of the Questembert-Ploërmel railway line and the Oust Canal. Its use was limited prior to the invasion for security reasons. WHALE was the code name for the drop site.

La Nouette was chosen as a base to store arms and food and, possibly, for parachute reinforcements.

Commandant Barthelemy (alias Hill or Barnat) arrived to inspect the performance of the FFI in Morbihan on May 15, 1944. He was satisfied with conditions at La Nouette. There followed a meeting of the Resistance leaders at La Nouette on May 22; a similar meeting took place to subdivide the FFI into five sectors. Several leaders were arrested while traveling to Paris but plans were carried out as scheduled. On June 3, 1944, Edouard Paysant, the new head of the Aerial Operations Bureau, arrived and gave orders to issue arms to their units. Orders were given to implement the GREEN PLAN and PURPLE PLAN, which concerned cutting aerial and underground telephone wires.

On June 4, a broadcast from London included the message "The dice are cast," and on June 5 came the message "It is hot in Suez." The first message was an order to launch GREEN and PURPLE PLANS and the second to launch RED PLAN (guerilla warfare). Railway lines were cut and maintained over several days but the RED PLAN required more weaponry. There were almost no rifles or submachine guns. The Aerial Operations Bureau had sent only 400 sten guns (a portable automatic gun), 150 pistols, 4,000 grenades, and a quantity of explosives. These were for sabotage but not sufficient for any major attack.

A general mobilization order was issued for the FFI battalions in Ploërmel, Josselin, Vannes, Auray, and Guémené. These combined would be a force of 3,500 men. The first of these was to rally at La Nouette (the Nouette Farm), the mobilization center that was to act as a permanent garrison. The other three would remain in place and stay on the alert. Urgent requests were sent to the Inter-Allied Command for more weapons to be dropped on Aerial Operations Bureau site WHALE. The Allies, although fully aware of the activities of the FFI in Morbihan in May, were not inclined to depend on it for a specific mission. There was always the risk that its function would be delayed or prevented by a series of arrests. They also lacked information on the size of the Resistance groups in occupied France. When planning OVERLORD, the Allies were not inclined to let the forces in France play a major role, as they could not share their plan with forces not under their control. Also, the role of the guerilla army in such a complex situation was difficult to define without precise knowledge of its capabilities. In June 1944, there were no plans to call upon the Resistance for help unless it was needed as support. (Note: The troops that parachuted into France on D-Day were ordered to contact local groups and gain their support with leadership and supplies.)

A plan was developed to drop French paratroopers into Brittany to carry out sabotage and infiltrate Brittany in order to establish bases and drop zones for future larger units. Commandant Pierre Bourgoin's battalion of 500 parachutists was selected for this first phase. Two bases were selected, one at Cotes-du-Nord and the other in Morbihan. Two forward units of nine men each were dropped into the two bases on June 5 and June 6. In Morbihan, Lieutenant Pierre Marienne's group landed at 4:45 A.M. on the night of June 6–7 at a spot that turned out to be 800 meters from a German observation post in Plumelec. They were surrounded by 150 enemy troops, most of them Russians, and fired on by automatic weapons. One corporal was killed and the wireless operator captured. The leader was left with several men.

Meanwhile, the other small group of parachutists, led by Lieutenant Henri Deplante, was dropped in Lilleran seven miles off target. Marienne and Deplante met at a designated rallying point and proceeded to La Nouette Farm. There they found Captain André (real name André Hunter-Hue) and Sergeant Löic Raufast, who had arrived the day before. La Nouette became the rallying point for the parachute troops. (The other base at Cotes-Du-Nord was dispensed with, so those who landed there were directed to La Nouette in Morbihan.) The parachutists were not aware that the Resistance movement was still alive and they would have to work with the FFI.

Anna Pondard was the young daughter of a farmer at La Nouette Farm and remembered when all of this activity first began. It was in August 1943 when a car from Ploërmel stopped by, and one of the men in the car was the leader of the Resistance in that area. He wanted to contact a member of the Resistance who was hiding there. Anna had seen the man who was hiding and her father make frequent short trips to check on weapons and supplies hidden in various places. This indicated that the Resistance began very early to prepare for the final encounter with the Germans.

Anna also noticed that on April 16, 1944, activity at La Nouette Farm began to increase and various members of the Resistance began to visit. Some only wanted food and moved on after a day or two. Others came to help train the maquis. A gradual buildup occurred and Anna remembered that sometimes there were at least 40 people sleeping in the house and that the house often resembled an arsenal. When the groups would leave, either on foot or by vehicle, Anna and other young people would follow behind them and erase their tracks with old clothes.

On May 20, 1944, orders were sent for the Resistance group there to blow up the train tracks nearby. Anna and the others heard the detonations in several places. They returned in different small groups during the night, so there was no sleep for those in the house.

On June 6, 1944, news of the invasion reached them and La Nouette became a virtual camp for training and collection of ammunition and supplies. Anna sewed arm bands for two days with little rest. This arm band was the only uniform that some of the maquis had.

The next morning, the leaders arrived with their radios and in the afternoon, the FFI began to arrive. Anna and others made the rounds taking coffee to the men. That evening, they heard a plane and went out of the house to see three paratroopers drop from it. The next night Lt. Marienne arrived with more paratroopers. They had been dropped off course and had a hard time finding the camp in the dark.

Now there were German patrols everywhere. In spite of this, paratroopers and Resistance fighters continued to arrive. Sometimes Anna and others were cooking for 2,000 men. Seven or eight bakers kept four ovens going continuously. There was always a shortage of food. The shoe shop was also busy mending boots and shoes. A nice consolation: the women enjoyed sleeping on the silk parachutes that had been dropped.

LA NOUETTE, 6 TO 18 JUNE, 1944

On the morning of June 6, all the local and departmental leaders of the Resistance were brought to La Nouette with their wireless operators. By afternoon, Resistance fighters from the Malestroit area had arrived and crowded into La Nouette. As volunteers continued to arrive, the leaders began to give them instruction and training. Food was brought in from other farms. A cobbler's workshop, a clothing workshop, and a vehicle repair shop were set up.

Marienne arrived on June 7 and was impressed with what he found. He sent an urgent radio message to Commandant Pierre Bourgoin advising him of the situation and requesting immediate deployment of men, arms, and supplies to La Nouette. He was told that 3,500 men waited his arrival. The departmental FFI command had a transport company at its disposal. Dr. Edouard Mahéo organized the medical corps to care for the wounded. Two infirmaries were set up.

Commandant Bourgoin parachuted in on the night of June 9 with some of his men. He was surprised by the atmosphere at La Nouette. Lights and people were everywhere. All of the civilians in the neighborhood watched the parachutes drop. The FFI men were filled with exaltation at the site of the parachutists dropping out of the sky to bring them arms and leadership. The 150 parachute troops enjoyed the prestige. They came from Britain and had fought in Libya.

Commandant Bourgoin invited the FFI battalions to rally at La Nouette (known as the St. Marcel Camp) to pick up the weapons the British were dropping each night. On June 13, 25 planes dropped approximately 700 containers and parcels, the largest parachute drop in occupied France. (Between 3,000 and 4,000 men were armed at St. Marcel.) The British furnished pistols, submachine guns, mines, grenades and antitank weapons, clothes, and tinned food.

Each day another group of FFI soldiers arrived to receive weapons and ammunition. After a few days of training by the parachutists, they returned to their own sector. Maintaining food and water for this many men, sometimes numbering 2,000, was a tremendous task. Local farmers continued to bring in livestock, vegetables, and cider. On the night of June 13 to June 14, an FFI battalion of 900 men arrived. Bad weather delayed their departure.

The Germans were aware of operations by the Resistance but thought it was of limited nature and had not suspected a rallying point like La Nouette. They were more concerned with moving troops up to Normandy, but their movement to the front was hampered by the sabotage groups of the parachutists who operated in small groups.

There was so much activity at La Nouette, and so many people coming and going, that the Germans could hardly not take notice. On the night of June 17–18, five planes mistakenly dropped 120 containers on the railway station at Roc-Saint André. After examining the contents of the containers, the Germans thought it best to patrol the area.

Commandant Bourgoin and the general staff were well aware that the base would be discovered sooner or later. They were anxious to receive orders to proceed toward the Allied forces in order to act as guides. At this time, they received orders from General MacLeod to avoid a pitched battle at all cost and to continue all-out guerilla warfare and arming the FFI. It was decided to disperse the units but, unfortunately, it was too late.

On June 18 at 4:30 A.M., two cars with German soldiers came by on the road from St. Marcel to L'Abbaye. They were probably seeking information regarding the increased activity in the area. The first FFI post opened fire. The first car ran the barricade but the second was destroyed by mortar fire. Three of the eight Germans were killed, one was wounded, and three were captured. One escaped and raised the alarm. An attack was now imminent. The camp was defended by 2,400 men, which included 140 parachute troops under the command of Captain Larraide.

THE BATTLE

The Germans reached St. Marcel at 8:15 A.M. approximately 500 strong. Their attack directed toward the north west was spearheaded with a company of 200 men. Using hedgerows for cover, they approached the first group of FFI and killed them at close range. This first firing sounded the alarm. The first German patrols, thinking they were only dealing with a small group of Resistance fighters, proceeded single file and were decimated. They then began to cross open fields with smoke cover. The French counterattacked and drove them from the farm, killing many of them.

Loic Bouvard was a 15-year-old farm boy whose mother, Madame Bouvard, still occupied the Chateau of Sainte-Genevieve with her six children. Loic and his younger brother, Guy Michel, were awakened at 5:30 A.M. on June 18, 1944, by the gunfire that came from the checkpoint that had fired on the two cars of Germans. They quickly put on their clothes and ran over to the farmhouse command post. A mass was being held and the chaplain told them that the Germans won the first round but they would win the second with the help of God. He also told them, "Let us prepare to fight." Loic then went to a shed to get a rifle and was questioned about his age. He told the captain distributing arms and ammunition that his mother had given her permission. His younger brother tried to get one but was turned down and began crying. Loic placed him with a family that was leaving the camp.

Shortly thereafter, several German companies arrived and attacked immediately. Loic and other maquisards were hidden in the bushes and killed many of the advancing Germans. He then went with Captain Puech-

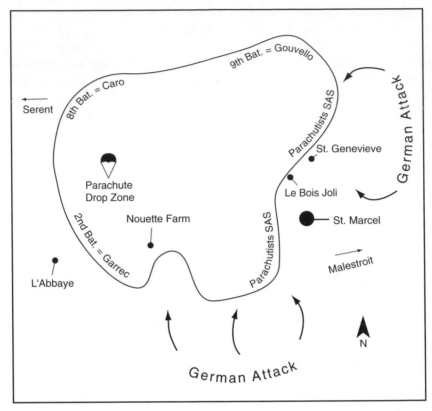

The Battle of St. Marcel.

Samson, who wanted to make some adjustments in the defense. They got into an area that was the middle of the fight and guns were shooting everywhere. Commandant Bourgoin was there and giving orders. Lt. Marienne was also there encouraging the men to hold the line. Captain Puech-Samson was wounded and Loic took him to an ambulance, which transported him to a medical treatment area. Loic then went to the command post and assisted a captain there.

Anna Pondard remembers that from 8:30 until 9:30 A.M., machine guns could be heard from an attacking German force. Marienne left with a group of his soldiers and Anna was sure that they would all be killed. At noon the officers warned the women and children to leave. They gathered a few things together as they were leaving. Marienne came up in a jeep. He had been wounded in the face and had blood all over his shirt. After he had something to drink, he returned to the fight and fought like a lion. He said later that he had probably killed 40 Germans.

At 10:00 A.M., the Germans launched a second attack with twice as many men and used mortars to attack the edges of the woods. The French, with the use of a light machine gun, halted them again and killed many in the cornfields and meadows. Large numbers of wounded were evacuated. The French wounded were taken to the Chateau of Sainte-Genevieve, given first aid, and then moved to the camp's field-dressing station. The attack was over at midday.

At 2:00 P.M., the Germans launched their third attack on a front covering 2,500 meters using reinforcements including German parachutists, Georgians, and a tactical deployment group from the 275th Infantry Division. The Georgians gained the chateau through the breach. Automatic weapons then stopped them. In the center, the Germans launched a fierce attack and captured the farm, driving the French forces back 300 meters.

Jacques Jacir, a parachutist, described the fighting:

The Fritz (Germans) came in great numbers this time but believing that they were facing a small group of maquis soldiers, their first patrols were isolated, one behind the other. They were systematically destroyed. Two companies occupy the village of St. Marcel, and from there they approach toward Marienne's position. He stands his guard well.

The Germans seem confused and are being killed at an incredible rate. They come forward, standing in the middle of fields, without understanding what is going on. After a while, they react and form a front, a line of battle that gives them a chance to have a good understanding of the opposing forces. They install machine guns and organize firing zones. The farm Bois-Joli is taken by the Germans. They try also to take Chateau of Sainte-Genevieve, as they believe it to be the maquis headquarters, which it isn't. It is still occupied by Madame Bouvard and her children. Her son, Loic, age 15, is fighting with the maquis and has an American rifle.[7]

Allied aviation intervened at about 3:30 P.M., after Commandant Bourgoin had requested assistance of the general of the Special Air Service (S.A.S.). Planes were airborne 70 minutes after the request was transmitted. For almost one hour, fighter bombers struck and bombed enemy positions and columns of reinforcements. Once the planes had left, the battle raged again.

At 7:00 P.M., the French launched a violent counterattack on the enemy's flank. The area around the Chateau of Sainte Genevieve was retaken. By 8:00 P.M., the Germans were gaining ground. New German troops arrived from Coetquidan. These troops were fresh and their attack brutal. They continued to advance in spite of heavy losses, and with their incendiary bullets set the woods on fire behind the defense. The FFI contained the enemy, but the pressure continued to mount.

At about 8:00 P.M., the central command post in La Nouette learned that trucks filled with German reinforcements were arriving. It was suspected that the northern sector would be attacked soon as the advanced posts could see groups of enemy forces assembling south of Saint-Abraham.

It was obvious to the command group that the Germans were moving in with overwhelming numbers and to fight them would deplete all of their ammunition. They expected an attack at daybreak with artillery and possibly tanks. Commandant Bourgoin and Colonel Paul Chenailler decided to disperse the base before it was encircled. This would be in compliance with the orders received from London before the battle. The Resistance and parachutists were to carry out sabotage and avoid rallying in large numbers in one place.

Anna and her family left and found refuge a few kilometers from the farm with another family. At midnight they were awakened by very loud detonations. They thought it was the end and that they were all going to die. It turned out that these were the French exploding all of their ammunition and guns that they could not carry with them as they withdrew from La Nouette. They did not know until the next day that the soldiers had retreated from La Nouette during the night.

The retreat began at 10:00 P.M. One company of parachutists remained as rear guard gave covering fire, while more than 2,000 men, 20 trucks, and four ambulances slipped off into the night. The parachutists retreated at midnight, having suffered no more losses. The FFI returned to their original sectors, leaving much of their equipment behind.

Parachutist Jacques Jacir describes the end:

> Gradually, the Germans became stronger. British planes appeared and sprayed the area with machine guns but when they leave, the battle rages again. In spite of heroic fighting, especially by our seasoned parachutists, the Germans receive reinforcements and gain ground. Darkness falls.
>
> Finally, the time comes for fold back toward Callac in the dark, rainy night. One by one, the different groups disappear. As a bloc of gelatin, the camp seems to liquefy, to lose little by little, its structure and it is pretty soon only a devastated site. Everything that could be transported by car is gone. Captain Puech-Samson ignites the remaining ammunition, which destroys the remaining vehicles.[8]

The results of the battle were that 30 Frenchmen were killed and approximately 60 wounded. The wounded were treated in secret at farms.

The German losses were estimated to be much higher, around 300 or more killed. The Germans made serious efforts to track down Chenailler and Bourgoin.

The Germans, not knowing that the base was evacuated, fired artillery on La Nouette the following morning. Enraged, they murdered all wounded found in the vicinity. Commandant Bourgoin sent a message to General Marie Koenig asking that French troops fighting in Italy be informed. The FFI commandant informed the German command that any German soldiers falling into his hands would suffer the same fate, officers included. The Germans searched meticulously for the "terrorists." The population was terrorized and arrests and murders carried out on isolated people. A notice was published in Vannes that anyone leaving the road as the Germans approached would be shot on sight. The castles in Sainte-Genevieve and Les Handys-Béheléc were burned, as were the farms and village of St. Marcel.

The Germans were surprised that the French could muster such a force to oppose them. These forces inflicted heavy losses and the Germans were unable to subdue them. By the Allied planes participating in the battle, the Germans knew that the French forces were in immediate contact with the Allied command. It made the Germans uneasy not to know the strength of their opposition. The major accomplishment of this battle was that it inspired more citizens to join the FFI.[9]

NOTES

1. Louis E. Keefer, *Scholars in Foxholes: The Story of the Army Specialized Training Program in World War II* (Jefferson: McFarland, 1998).

2. Ray Roberts and Embree Reynolds, *A Tale of Two Panthers* (Bridgman: Ray Roberts, 2001).

3. Ray Roberts has, within recent years, published three books on the sinking of the *Leopoldville,* the last entitled *The* Leopoldville *Trilogy.* He also collaborated with Colonel Embree Reynolds and published *A Tale of Two Panthers,* which is a collection of stories associated with soldiers of the 66th Infantry (Black Panther) Division.

4. Hank Andersen continued his education soon after discharge, finished college, and completed graduate studies at McCormick Theological Seminary (Presbyterian) in Chicago, Illinois. His last church was Fairmont Presbyterian Church in Cleveland Heights, Ohio, where he served for 16 years. Now retired, he is active in local, national, and global church affairs.

5. Bill Watson was a classmate of mine at The Citadel before the war and the University of South Carolina after the war, but we were not acquainted at either time. It has been a pleasure to know him through correspondence about his story.

6. Bill Watson finished his education at the University of South Carolina and did graduate work at Harvard University. He became deputy director of the Centers of Disease Control (CDC) in Atlanta, Georgia. After retirement from the CDC, he was director of operations for the Carter Presidential Center for five years. He is now involved with global philanthropic activities regarding child survival.

7. Patrick Maheo, *Saint-Marcel. Haut lieu de la Resistance Bretonne* (Ploermel: Rue Des Scribes Editions, 1997).

8. *Ibid.*

9. There is an excellent museum at St. Marcel devoted to the French Resistance. The exhibits are very authentic with life-size wax figures, much of the equipment used by the Resistance, and excellent movies pertaining to their activities.

First names of Resistance leaders were not often recorded in records and journals, as they were known by many aliases. For the sake of accuracy and to avoid confusion, these were not used in the foregoing section unless first name was known beyond doubt to be accurate.

Chapter 6

1944—JULY, AUGUST, SEPTEMBER

BREAKOUT AND ENGAGEMENT

When the breakout from the Normandy beaches occurred, there was a period of about one month when the war assumed an intense volatility in Brittany, especially around the pockets of St. Nazaire and Lorient. Large numbers of FFI seemed to materialize overnight and engage the Germans at Rennes, Vannes, Nantes, St. Nazaire, and Lorient. They were the initial force that began to drive the Germans into the pockets.

Large German forces were trying to escape the oncoming Allies and went through small villages and towns, foraging, destroying, and killing. Their presence precipitated artillery battles with the FFI. Destruction intensified, as did atrocities against the populace. The Germans were in a panic. The FFI and the Resistance were intent on destroying them.

The United States Third Army's 4th and 6th Armored Divisions entered the battle in Brittany in early August 1944. The United States's 83rd Infantry Division came in on August 20, but would stay only one month. The 94th Infantry Division took over September 9 for the 6th Armored Division and was relieved by the 66th Division on New Year's Eve 1944. The 66th would remain until the end of the war.

The breakout from the Normandy beaches occurred on July 31, 1944. It was significant to this campaign that many retreating forces were left to the relative security of the ports on the western coast of France, ports that could have been useful to the Allies and, in the opinions of Generals Eisenhower and Omar Bradley, essential to supply the Allied advance eastward.

During the German retreat to the east, large garrisons were left to hold Le Havre, Brest, Dieppe, St. Malo, Lorient, and St. Nazaire. The German high command wished to deny these ports to the Allies, as the ports were critical to the supply of the advancing Allied armies. Special efforts were made to strengthen St. Nazaire and Lorient because of the submarine pens. Eisenhower's and Bradley's pre-invasion plan was to commit General George Patton and the Third Army once the breakout occurred. Patton was instructed to turn right into Brittany and advance to Rennes and the Loire River. They were strongly in favor of this plan to secure these ports, especially St. Malo and Brest. Patton was opposed and thought it should be scrapped, but they insisted. They did, however, allow Patton some modifications. The original plan was for the whole Third Army to turn into Brittany, but when Patton so strongly objected, Eisenhower and Bradley relented and allowed him to attack Brittany with one corps and advance to the east with two corps.

General Bernard Montgomery was in agreement with Patton and wanted to abandon the plan to overrun Brittany, for, in his view, all possible forces should pursue the Germans eastward with haste so as to give them no time or chance to set up a defensive line. If this were successful, St. Malo and Brest would be less important.

On August 3, 1944, the 6th Armored Division had traveled 150 kilometers from Avranches toward Brest when a communication from corps headquarters got through to General Robert Grow, commander of the 6th Armored Division. General Troy Middleton, corps commander, told him not to bypass the stronghold of Dinan and to concentrate on St. Malo. Grow protested the order and disobeyed it. He left part of his force well out toward Brest rather than calling it back. Other parts of the division would capture St. Malo. It was the first of the ports to fall after a bitter battle on August 4, 1944.

General Grow and his staff were in a wheat field the next morning when General Patton drove up. He said to Grow, "What in the hell are you doing here? I thought I told you to go to Brest." Grow replied that his advance had been halted by corps headquarters. Patton read the order, put it in his pocket, and said, "I'll see Middleton. You go where I told you to go." Grow received another message from General Middleton to return the 6th Armored to its original mission against Brest. A day had been lost, and the 6th Armored reached Brest on Sunday, August 6, 1944.

Grow submitted a call for a surrender to the Germans, which they refused, on August 8, 1944. Grow then prepared to attack on August 9, but learned that parts of the German 266th Division were approaching from behind. By the time the 266th Division had been disposed, valuable time had been lost and reconnaissance determined that the fortifications in Brest were too strong for a single, armored division. The delay caused by Middleton's orders of August 3, 1944, became a controversial subject. The premise was that Middleton allowed the Germans to withdraw their coastal garrisons from all over western Brittany into Brest, thus making it a more formidable fortress, which Grow could have taken had he arrived a day earlier. Brest finally fell September 19, 1944. Damage was so great that it was not restored by the Allies to a serviceable port.

Major General John S. Wood, commander of the 4th Armored Division, was bitter about the diversion into Brittany to secure the ports and was very vocal about it. He, like Patton, was a cavalry officer and wanted to pursue the Germans before they had a chance to stop and set up lines of resistance. When interviewed by historian Sir Basil Liddell-Hart post-war, he said: "I protested long, loud, and violently and pushed my tank columns into Chateaubriand and my armored cavalry units to the outskirts of Angers and along the Loire, ready to advance to Chartres. I could have been in the enemy vitals in two days. But No! We were forced to adhere to the original plan." General Troy Middleton, Wood's corps commander said, "Looking at it in hindsight, Wood was right of course. But the high command at the time was absolutely right in wanting the ports."

Nevertheless, the 4th Armored, like the 6th Armored, was on the move, the two units making one of the most rapid advances during the war. Both Grow and Wood were "hell-for-leather" commanders and wanted to be cut loose to chase the Germans eastward.

At this time, the 4th Armored Division was out of gasoline. When the combat commands began a sweep around Rennes, the transportation had been sent to Avranches to bring the 13th Infantry forward to occupy Rennes. Finally, on August 4, a direct route was opened through which gasoline could be delivered. On August 5, 1944, General Wood sent Combat Command A (CCA) to Vannes, a distance of 70 miles. The FFI had already captured the airfield and guided the tank column to the best approaches. The attack was accomplished rapidly and Vannes was captured before the Germans could prepare demolitions.

Near Vannes, the 4th Armored ran into the remainder of a French paratrooper unit that had been dropped into France on D-Day. They were led by a one-armed major and had been fighting in small bands for two months. The Forces Francaises de l'Interior also enthusiastically lent its support. The French patriots gave information about the enemy, guided tankers, harassed the German communications, and mopped up residual enemy pockets. In *Patton's Best: An Informal History of the 4th Armored Division,* authors Frankel and Smith refer specifically to this group of FFI. "They were everything the French Resistance was supposed to be. These soldiers were masters of infiltration. They blew bridges, they sniped officers, they wouldn't let a jeep or truck go by without blowing it. I met one once—a big, bald 'mother' with a broad smile who communicated mostly through affectionately obscene gestures. His English was negligible and even his French was atrocious. He spoke Breton and fought for Brittany. Hitler could keep Normandy for all he cared."

During the rapid advance through Normandy, the XIX Tactical Air Command (TAC) of the Ninth Air Force coordinated with the Third Army for one of the most successful air-ground offensives during the war. The XIX TAC support parties swung their vehicles into the 4th Armored's leading columns and called in P-47s for bombing and strafing ahead of the tanks. "Yellow Leader" was the air group code name and "Egg Cup" was the ground control unit. When "Egg Cup" called "Yellow Leader," the response was immediate, with a bombing run followed by a strafing run, clearing many German units out of the way of the advancing armor.

On the 6th of August, the enemy counterattacked from Auray and drove back the outposts of CCA. Colonel Clarke sent a strong task force that cleared Auray and went beyond to seize a bridge across the Blavet River at Hennebont. When they arrived, they found the bridge demolished. During this time, General Dager's Combat Command B (CCB) had driven directly toward Lorient. They reached the city on the 7th of August and, finding strong defenses, turned north through the village of Pont Scorf. As the advanced guard entered the town, German artillery became overwhelming and they could go no farther. This is described in *The Fourth Armored Division: From the Beach to Bavaria* by Captain Kenneth Koyen:

> The CCB Headquarters vehicles had just pulled into the two fields when the first shells whistled in. For two hours, the headquarters and infantry from the 51st were held down and blasted by murderous shell fire. At least one battery of German artillery rained high explosive rounds into an area less than 500 yards square.. The artillery was carefully observed and corrected. Shells sought out single halftracks and blew them up with direct hits that exploded mines, shells and gasoline. Men were killed crouching beside and under vehicles. Hedges were no protection. Shells hit on both sides and on top of them. Splinters slashed tires, halftrack plates and flesh. Finally the German artillery observers, a lieutenant and a sergeant were hunted out on a nearby hill and killed. Twenty 4th Armored men were killed and 85

wounded. Five halftracks, six jeeps, two trucks and armored cars were destroyed completely and a score more vehicles badly damaged. The dead were buried one day later where they fell south of Pont Scorf. The French still tend the graves.[1]

There is a large monument near Pont Scorf where the 4th Armored was stopped. This monument honors the 4th and 6th Armored Divisions and the 94th and 66th Infantry Divisions as well as several French units. It might be said that this violent attack was a forerunner of what would have happened if the Allies had tried to take Lorient and St. Nazaire. It would have been costly in loss of men and materials because of the concentration of seasoned soldiers and artillery in these two heavily defended ports. The arrival of CCA in the Lorient sector made it possible to establish a thin line from Hennebont to Pont Scorf. The division probed the defenses to try to discover approach routes, but by August 9, it became clear that more than one armored division would be necessary to take Lorient.

German army and naval forces in Lorient outnumbered the 4th Armored more than five to one. An estimated 500 field pieces were placed throughout the base and sources concurred that they had plenty of ammunition. Antitank ditches, mine fields, and interlocking fields of fire were strong and well organized. Coastal defenses and naval guns were well supplied with large stockpiles of ammunition. The flak was so heavy that the Allied observation planes could not operate. The FFI reported that the Germans had large stores of provisions, including herds of cattle, so they could hold out for a long period of time.

During the approach to Rennes from Vannes, the 4th Armored ran into a unit of cavalry on horseback, which turned out to be Russian mercenaries, and both men and horses were killed with a barrage of cannon fire. The American soldiers were more upset at killing the horses than the Russians, as they considered the horses innocent victims that should not have been forced to die in a war that was not of their making.

It became obvious that an attack against Lorient would require support from the sea to neutralize guns on Quiberon Peninsula and Belle Isle. General Wood was gratified to receive orders from General Middleton to hold the armor at arm's length from the fortress. "Do not become involved in a fight for Lorient unless the enemy attacks," Middleton ordered. "Take a secure position and merely watch developments."

General Wilhelm Fahrmbacher, German commander of the Lorient Pocket, later claimed that if Wood had developed a strong attack between 6 and 9 August, the fortress probably would have fallen. As time went on and the sector became more organized, Fahrmbacher felt that he had an adequate defensive position. Previously, preparations were made for 12,000 men, but 25,000 Germans ended up there after the breakout with retreating Germans entering the pocket. There were also 10,000 French civilians remaining who were a further drain on supplies. Many of the German naval and service personnel were retrained for artillery and infantry units.

GENERAL FAHRMBACHER'S REPORT POST-WAR ON PREPARATION OF THE DEFENSE OF LORIENT

General Wilhelm Fahrmbacher, German commander of the Lorient pocket, was required by the French army to write a summary of his report, a condensed version of which follows:

Conversion and Measures Taken Until 8/1944

As part of the Atlantic Wall, Lorient was ranked only secondary, however, it was the most efficient among the U-boat bases. Therefore, it was converted into a fort and it was supposed to prevent anybody from coming ashore along the Central Breton Coastline. Defensive units were set up in close proximity to the fort, at the Anse Pouldhu, at the Bay of Quiberon, on the peninsula itself and on the islands of Belle Isle and Ile De Groix. (Batteries were listed.)

The fort commander had a staff but no troops at his disposal. This was provided by the respective division. (The last one was the 265th Infantry.) His activities were limited to preparing the defense on paper. To compound matters, there was no sea commander in Lorient to command the marine artillery. The division was in charge of all areas outside the fort. While the units of troops were relatively strong at the coastal flanks and on the islands, the actual fort was a lot weaker in its defense capabilities.

During the years '42 through '44, Lorient was hit several times during its expansion from heavy air raids. The city, the French shipyard and the French Arsenal suffered badly. The combat units and the U-boat structures were hardly damaged at all. Business was as usual within a few days.

There was one important loss for the fort, when in June, 1944, parts of the trained troops had to leave for Normandy, and especially when the 265th Division, which was familiar with the situation and surroundings, had to take over the section of St. Nazaire and concentrated their efforts there. The front, as it was established, was more a coincidental one that had to be supported by a number of improvisations and had to be staffed by troops, that with only very few exceptions, had no idea of what they were supposed to do.

On the evening of August 3, 1944, the fort commander, coming from Pontivy, arrived in Lorient and established the operational post in U-boat bunker Keroman III. With the move of trained command posts and the troops away from the fort to other assignments, a tremendous amount of uncertainty prevailed.

Colonel Kaumann, the fort commander, was put in charge of all army units and the few ground units of the air force. Vice Admiral Mathias was put in charge as sea commander. The marine units and the shipyard personnel were combined. All others were kept at the commanding general's disposal. The troops inside the fort represented a motley crowd. Only a few were trained for combat on land. The majority of the trained troops were gone.

Of decisive importance were the immediate measures that concerned supplies. The fort had enough food for a lock-in period of 56 days for 12,000 troops. It was easy to see that about 25,000 men had to be fed and that staying power of more than 56 days would be required. Store rooms and ammunition stock had to be moved quickly inside the fort. A population of 10,000 would be included.

Finally, the tasks of the troops on the islands of Belle Isle and Ile de Groix, the Quiberon Peninsula and Concarneau had to be clarified and regulated through appropriate measures. One thousand men from each of the island troops were called up and transferred to Lorient in order to be utilized as infantry along the main line of resistance.

If the enemy should attack Lorient within the next few days, the fort will face a very difficult situation. It is not yet ready for defense. Every day without an attack can be considered a win.

Preparing the Fort for Defense

Once the enemy's pressure decreased after August 10, 1944, the commanding general did not anticipate an attack on Lorient. Everybody now concentrated on getting the fort ready for defense. The following were considered important:

1. Leadership. The fort commander, Colonel Kaumann, was wounded by a mine and disabled. The commanding general took over control of the fort.
2. Establishing defensive sectors.
3. Combining the entire artillery under an artillery commander.
4. Retraining marine and air force troops for infantry land battle.
5. Establishing reserves.

6. Clarifying the responsibilities of the islands and the Quiberon Peninsula.
7. Organizing a news service.
8. Securing supplies.

On August 16, 1944, the commanding general took over the total control of Lorient. The following command was issued to the troops during a meeting with the commanders:

> Fort Lorient will be defended. With keen observation and an active reconnaissance party, a clear vision of the enemy should be guaranteed in order to prevent any surprises. The fighting activities should be limited to smaller but well prepared operations and to the firing on visible and worthwhile targets. Large undertakings are not planned for the time being. The number of mines positioned should be increased.
>
> The battle front was separated into four sections: East, North, West and South and each staffed with one regiment consisting of two to four battalions.
>
> The artillery was divided into four groups with a total of 52 batteries and several individual guns that could increase its firing capacity to its maximum. In order to deceive and to decrease the enemy's firing power, a number of batteries were supplied with only two or three guns. (Several diagrams were furnished showing the position of German batteries in Lorient.)[2]

From August 6th to the 16th, while trying to talk Lorient into surrendering, the 4th Armored Division did little more than contain the garrison and await another force to free the division to resume cavalry warfare. During the first 12 days of August, the division took 5,000 prisoners and captured or destroyed approximately 250 German vehicles. In the process, of the division members, there were only 98 killed, 362 wounded, and 11 reported missing. Only 15 tanks and 20 vehicles were lost. Despite the success, it did not take Lorient, the assigned mission. In hindsight, it has been theorized that if Middleton and Wood had been more aggressive toward the Quiberon Peninsula and Lorient, the division might have arrived before Lorient had had a chance to strengthen the defenses with additional forces that took refuge there in the retreat from Normandy.

General Wood remained bitter about the 10-day delay in carrying the battle eastward with cavalry warfare. General Patton also remained critical of Eisenhower's and Bardley's decision to detain the cavalry for these Brittany ports and for not having turned the cavalry loose to chase the Germans eastward, thus denying them of a chance to stop and set up an effective defense line.

In accordance with orders received August 12, 1944, the 6th Armored started redeploying troops to carry out the new mission of containing Brest and relieving the 4th Armored Division in Lorient. When arriving at Vannes, they found Vannes taken and in the hands of the FFI. The CCA column of the 6th Armored Division went to Plouay. CCB of the 4th Armored was relieved that day. The 6th Armored found that the line naturally divided itself into three sections. One was the Quiberon Peninsula, the second was the sector between Belze and the Blavet River just below Hennebont that included a section west that lay between the Scorf and Blavet Rivers. This latter sector was strong and included many gun positions. The third and most important sector, which included the main approaches to Lorient and the bulk of the defenses, extended west from the Scorf River to a point approximately three miles south to the coast. By 0600 on August 15, the 6th Armored had completed the relief of the 4th Armored on the Brittany Peninsula.

General Robert Grow, commander of the 6th Armored Division, recalled the relief of General John Wood and the 4th Armored Division: "I drove up to General Wood's command post as it was moving out to go east. Our relief was the most informal and brief I have ever heard of in military history. Neither of us got out of our vehicles. He said words to the effect: 'We're off, its all yours! And we're gone.' "[3]

To increase the battle training of the division and to destroy all enemy personnel and material possible, General Grow directed the following tactics in the performance of this containing mission:

1. (a) Every stratagem be used to "mouse trap" enemy patrols. This meant that enemy patrols were allowed to advance well forward and then artillery fire would be brought down on them.

   (b) Enemy troops were permitted to penetrate the line as deep as a mile before being cut off and attacked by local reserves.

2. A system of patrolling deep into enemy territory was carried out in the sector from the coast west of Lorient east to the Scorff River. Each patrol consisted of 25–30 men, which included an infantry and artillery officer.

3. All fronts were to be extensively mined and booby-trapped. This resulted in a comprehensive system of booby-trapping the entire front from the west coast of Lorient to the Blavet River. They made it difficult for any patrol to get through without activating a mine.

By August 17, United States troops were engaged in combat at St. Nazaire, Lorient, Dieppe, Brest, and LeHavre. Aided by 20,000 FFI soldiers, General Middleton challenged all ports. Resistance was fierce.

Dieppe fell on August 31, 1944; Le Havre on September 7, 1944; and Brest on September 19, 1944.

On August 22, 1944, CCA of the 6th Armored Division was relieved at Brest by six battalions of the 2nd Infantry Division. The command headquarters moved to Lorient. Between August 23 to August 27, the 6th Armored was involved in minor engagements and captured some Germans, guns, and other material. Each day the division carried out vigorous patrolling and exchanged artillery fire frequently with the Germans. By the end of August, the FFI, estimated at 40,000 men in the Brest-Lorient area, became a formidable force, effectively reducing the numbers needed from the United States to contain the two ports.

On August 22, 1944, General Grow drove 312 miles to General Patton's headquarters northeast of Orleans to try to convince Patton to relieve the 6th Armored at Lorient so they could proceed east and be restored to the pursuit of the Germans. Patton explained the situation to Grow and gave the reasons why he must keep the 6th Armored in the battle. Grow continued to be unhappy with a containment role and persisted with a visit to General William H. Simpson, commander of the Ninth Army, as Grow expected his division would be released from the Third to the Ninth Army. He was encouraged in being told that he would soon be relieved but later disappointed to learn that there would be a further detainment of his division there.

Evaluation of the defenses of St. Nazaire and Lorient caused the Allies to decide against trying to capture them, as it would require too many men and supplies, thus hindering the main force in their progress eastward. The decision was made to contain them until troops and supplies were available. In view of the violent encounter that the 4th Armored Division had when first on the scene near Pont Scorf, the decision probably prevented the loss of lives of many American soldiers and the loss of many vehicles and much equipment.

Finally, it was decided that the 94th Division, newly arrived in the European Theater, would relieve the 6th Armored Division. The relief process for General Grow was frustratingly slow. The 94th Division commander arrived on September 5, but the leading troops did not arrive until September 10, 1944. The complete relief was effected by September 16.

At one time, the 6th Armored was stretched out for 460 miles, from Brest to Auxere. The central section of approximately 220 miles from Redon to Orleans was covered by patrols of the 83rd Division, which spent about a month on this line. The 6th Armored finally received confirmation of its relief from the Lorient sector on September 16 and closed its command post and left to link up with Patton's Third Army. The Brittany Campaign was finished for the 6th Armored. The unit had driven a distance of 230 miles, cutting a swath 20 miles wide through the center of the Brittany Peninsula, disrupting and destroying communications. This precipitated the complete disorganization of the enemy's garrisons, about 60,000 troops. Approximately 4,000 enemy troops had been killed and 6,700 troops with 1,100 guns had been captured. Numerous vehicles were knocked out or abandoned.

The 301st Infantry Regiment of the 94th Division commanded by Colonel Hagerty began relieving the 6th Armored Division on September 9, 1944, and completed the transition in two days. The sector to be controlled was bounded on the east by the Blavet River and on the west by the Laita River. The front line ran parallel to and south of Quimperlé, Rédené, Pont Scorf, Hennebont, and Nostang.

Colonel Johnson, commanding officer of the 302nd Infantry, opened his post near Plouay on September 15, 1944, with his tank company and 1st Battalion. The next day the 2nd Battalion arrived and all three battalions were committed to the line. Their line stretched from the Scorf River to Nostang. Shortly after organizing their positions on the line, the mission was extended to include the German forces in the pocket of St. Nazaire. Plans were formulated to shift the bulk of the infantry to the St. Nazaire sector. The artillery was split between the two sectors with the greater strength remaining at Lorient. The armor had departed. In was now an artillery and infantry campaign and would remain so for the duration.

The war in Brittany, surrounding the two U-boat fortresses, extended well outside their bounds and brought about the destruction of many small villages and towns, most of which had no military targets. They were just in the path of wayward bombs, artillery duels, and firefights between the Allies and the Germans. The Germans, when retreating into Lorient, came down the Blavet River and through Hennebont. There was a fight for possession of the village. It joined the list of others such as Pont Scorf, Rédené, Quimperlé, Nostang, and Etel that were equally devastated.

HENNEBONT

Hennebont was a small, beautiful village on the outskirts of Lorient. And like so many other villages, wayward bombs and ground war reduced it to rubble and killed many people. Today Hennebont is again a beautiful, picturesque village. From one vantage point, one can see the magnificent L'Eglise Notre-Dame du Paradis, the Porte-Prison, and the gardens of the

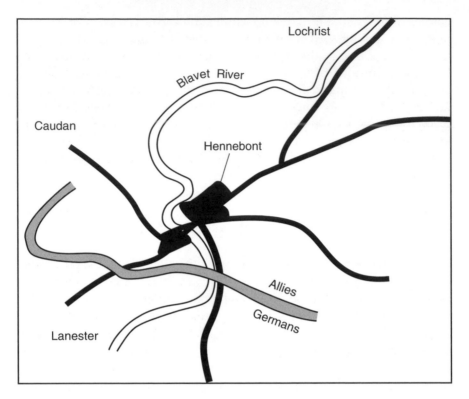

Hennebont.

Ramparts. The Blavet River skirts the town and hosts sailing and fishing boats. The streets are neat and clean and flowers bloom in the town square. The people stroll the streets content and happy, with no thought of any danger. The usual daily activities of walking to the bakery for fresh bread and to the butcher shop for meat go on as usual. Time passes quickly. It seems like only yesterday that GI patrols were stumbling through the rubble of this destroyed village to search for German observation posts.

The occupation of Hennebont began June 20, 1940. The Resistance became well organized with acts of sabotage. Living under the scrutiny of the Germans with limited food, fuel, energy, and water, plus the periodic bombardments focused on Lorient by the Allied air forces, was difficult enough. Add to this the reprisals by the Germans against the civilian population each time a convoy was fired upon or a segment of railway or communication lines destroyed.

As in other occupied villages, the people in Hennebont exhibited mixed behavior regarding the Germans. Some were heroic and actively carried

Hennebont: Town square, The Prison Gate, destroyed during the war and subsequently rebuilt. Photo 2001. Author's photo.

out resistance. Others collaborated, and the remainder tried to remain indifferent and carry on as best they could. There were arrests and deportations.

The period of liberation for Hennebont was August 6–12, 1944. Rallying points for the FFI were set up usually at farms away from the mainstream, and recruits from nearby towns, villages, and farms began to arrive. Most were young men 17 to 20 years of age who had no prior military training or experience. They were given a rifle, part of a uniform (sometimes no more than an FFI armband), and were put through a short training period, mostly weapons instruction. Some regular French soldiers stationed in England were parachuted in as training cadre and to fill the positions of leadership in the newly formed companies and battalions.

Food was brought into these camps by local farmers. Weapons, ammunition, and explosives were dropped in by the British. Radio contact was maintained with Great Britain. The Germans, sometimes noticing the disappearance of young men from a town or village, would search for these newly formed camps. They realized that the Resistance movement was growing.

On August 3, 1944, French General Marie Koenig, "Guerilla of all of Bretagne," communicated with the FFI, which had formed in the Hennebont sector in April 1943. General Koenig encouraged them to intensify their attacks on German convoys and soldiers particularly around Languidic and Branderion. They captured a number of German soldiers. Other elements of the group operated around Hennebont.

The Normandy landing forced the Germans to retreat, but it took the Allies longer than expected to break out of the beachhead area. By August 4, thousands of Germans and White Russians equipped with heavy material, including artillery pieces, fled from the advancing American tanks of the 4th and 6th Armored Divisions and headed toward Lorient and St. Nazaire. Many of the retreating Germans passed by Hennebont, causing destruction. Some came into Hennebont with the pretext of searching for terrorists with the real purpose of pillaging.

During this time, the Americans advanced to Rennes and then to Vannes. There was a delay for a day or two because of a shortage of fuel for the 4th Armored Division. On Sunday, August 6, the citizens of Hennebont heard a grinding sound interpreted as the American tanks coming. They were exalted as the Germans took flight over the Blavet River before the bridge was blown. On this same day, the Germans counterattacked from Auray. The Americans responded offensively and occupied Hennebont after detouring by Lochrist to cross the Blavet River. The Germans had blown the bridge at Hennebont.

On Monday, August 7, the Germans placed a badly wounded American soldier on a road near the village. The Americans stopped to give him aid, and, knowing this might be some sort of a trap, scouted the surrounding countryside. The diversion allowed the Germans a little more time to escape.

That morning the inhabitants came out onto the village square to celebrate and to welcome the Americans. Both the FFI and American soldiers pleaded with them to take refuge as the battle was far from over. In reality, it was just beginning. The Germans, in any sector that they regained, inflicted executions and sadistic cruelty while looting and burning crops.

At approximately 9:00 A.M., August 7, the large viaduct across the Blavet River was dynamited and cannon fire from both sides lasted the entire day. The Americans were on the left bank of the Blavet and the Germans were on the right. The German artillery of St. Nudec and Lorient joined in and turned the center of town into an inferno. Dead and wounded were on both sides of the river. Trees were defoliated. Most of the remaining inhabitants took flight.

Toward evening, the cannon fire subsided but those in shelters stayed put, as any activity caused more firing from the Germans. The population of the

Hennebont: The church of Notre-Dame du Paradis, rebuilt and functional since its destruction during WWII. Author's photo.

village remained very frightened. There was much confusion, and families became separated from one another. They took refuge in destroyed buildings or in any place where there was some protection from shelling. People were bruised and battered and their clothes were torn. One witness gave this account, "From the beginning of the bombardment, an explosion occurred at my house and my wife and I gathered a few things and we left to try and cross the Blavet River. A mass of people began to move around. The damage to the town was terrible."[4] There were 100 dead and 350 wounded. The time of liberation, which had been a pleasant expectation, turned into a horror and the town was 75 percent destroyed.

Devastation from aerial bombardment in Hennebont. Structure in center is the ancient Prison Gates surrounded by the Gardens of the Ramparts. Courtesy: City Archives and Le Mairie d'Hennebont (City Hall).

The Germans became barbaric and inflicted merciless atrocities against an unarmed population. The massacres of Kerroch on August 7, 8, and 9 accounted for 26 victims. Two days later, nine more persons were savagely killed. Three of these were a father and two sons who were made to pull a cannon to a new position. They were then shot and nailed to crosses. The Germans continued a brutal path of destruction, destroying homes and killing the elderly.

On Friday, August 11, more farms were burned. At Villenue, nine males were killed and their bodies thrown into flames. Francis Magnannon, in describing these tragic hours stated: "It would require the pen of Dante to describe the horrors perpetuated on the civilian population at Hennebont during the period of liberation, on the right bank of the Blavet in particular."[5]

The Germans fell back to Lorient after attacking Lanester, south of Hennebont, and a line between the Allies and Germans stabilized running by or through Quimperlé, Rédené, Pont Scorf, Caudan, Hennebont, and Nostang. After positioning themselves on the Etel River, the Germans continued heavy artillery fire, killing and wounding many civilians in small

Devastation of ancient prison wall with L'Eglise Notre-Dame du Paradis in the background. Courtesy: City Archives and Le Mairie d'Hennebont.

66th Infantry soldiers guarding Germans just after their capture by a combat patrol on outskirts of Hennebont. Courtesy: City Archives and Le Marie d'Hennebont.

villages on the right of the river. On August 12, Hennebont was finally liberated after having paid dearly for its freedom. The Germans held St. Nudec and Lanester as well as Lorient until May 1945.

There has to be great satisfaction in knowing that the Allies defeated Hitler and his cruel henchmen and thus allowed so many victims of the war to return to their homes in hundreds of villages and towns similar to Hennebont and to live there in peace and freedom. For those who were lost during the war, though the loss of each one was a tragedy, there is some small compensation in knowing that their sacrifice was not in vain, as they restored life to a great mass of people who were on the verge of losing it.

FRENCH FORCES MOBILIZE FOR WAR

On June 17, 1944, at a conference of the Supreme Headquarters of Allied Expedition Forces (S.H.A.E.F.) French General Marie Koenig was placed in command of all of the French Forces of the Interior under General Eisenhower and instructed to form a staff of 20–25 officers for its administration to coordinate a liaison with the Allied forces. With time growing near for the European invasion, the FFI units were standing by ready to help.

After the breakout from Avranches, the 4th and 6th Armored Divisions of General Patton's Third Army moved swiftly and liberated Vannes on August 16. CCB of the 4th Armored Division was in the suburbs of Lorient on August 7, 1944. The Germans evacuated Nantes on August 14. Between August 4 and September 7, 1944, groups of the maquis were formed south of the Loire River in the St. Nazaire sector. Most of the maquis units were eventually absorbed into FFI units, but a few remained independent for the remainder of the war. They were aided by the Tony and Simon Jedburg (code name) teams who administered the distribution of arms and ammunition, usually by parachute. A Jedburg team was usually composed of one French officer, a British or United States officer, and a radioman. The United States Office of Strategic Services (OSS) was very active with the Jedburg teams. These small teams were parachuted into France to aid the FFI. The first unit constituted south of the Loire was the First Ground Mobile Reconnaissance Squadron commanded by Lt. Guy Besnier and was based in Arthon. (Lt. Besnier later became a captain.)

The maquis were much like the militia in the United States during the Revolutionary and Civil Wars. Most were groups of young men from the same location who joined the local or regional military unit, usually led by someone with former military experience. Some of these leaders were in the French army when it was defeated by the Germans in 1940. They were re-entering the war to fight again. Typical of the young men who joined the Maquis was J. Bertrand, who recorded his story at The Grand Blockhaus Museum at Batz-sur-Mer.

I was in Maquis D3 under Captain Renard. I was appointed corporal as section head of a machine gun. On Sunday, August 13, 1944, at Champagne St. Hilaire at Rothschild stud farm, our Maquis group attacked a German position where 20 Senegalais prisoners were kept. They were successfully freed after Lt. Etienne courageously made contact with the men disguised as an electrician. The FFI captain wanted "his" victory so the fighting continued until the Germans brought in reinforcements. Nine Germans were killed.

At that time the whole of France was in insurrection. New units of Maquis were being formed rapidly, mostly from young men who wanted to get the Germans out of their villages. In principle, the FFI was unified under the command of General Koenig, a comrade of General de Gaulle.

At this time, the Germans were retreating, many of them southward to strong points like St. Nazaire and Lorient. Units of Maquis and FFI were trying to catch them on the roads by ambushes. (There were some independent Maquis units who had not yet joined the FFI.) Our own group waited for them on Pont de L'Isle on the river Clarente. We had six machine guns and converged on the bridge, which was already damaged by our troops. On the 27th of August, in a fog at dawn, a caravan of trucks came slowly through the fog and stopped on the bridge. The soldiers got out and we could hear them talking. We opened fire but being seasoned troops, they quickly responded with machine guns and mortar fire. Our Captain, Rogez, who was a seasoned veteran ordered our retreat. Having participated in much guerilla warfare, he knew to strike and get out. I was charged with protecting the withdrawal for several minutes. My escape route included having to climb a ladder and go over a wall. Machine gun bullets spattered all around me but fortunately, I was not hit. Incidentally, the bridge was called Pont des Chansons! (A bridge of songs.)

The terrain was ideal for ambushes—hedgerows and small fields. The Maquis would hunker down behind the hedgerows along a route. The group continued to harass this column of Germans who were on foot, slowing them up to 10 kilometers a day. They [the Germans] never reached their destination as all were killed, wounded or captured.

The Francs Tireurs Partisans (FTP), which was really a communist organization, became very active at this time and fought well. They all had German weapons including a heavy machine gun. Among them were Spaniards who were seasoned fighters. To them the liberation of France was only a step toward the liberation of Franco's Spain. The French communist members thought that they would eventually take over the power in Paris.

Our unit was then sent to Bernerie, six kilometers from Pornic and we were involved some small fire fights there with the Germans. Next we went to Bouaye. There we worked the lines and formed ambushes and patrols. On one occasion we killed ten Germans and only had one comrade wounded. That was Videau who was one of my machine gunners. He had to have an arm amputated.

On December 22, we were resting at Bouaye, 15 kilometers behind the lines. We were alerted and left quickly. Our truck broke down and we had to go on foot. We supported the troops that were falling back from a German advance. We waited on the Germans behind a hedgerow with a concentration of machine guns and stopped them cold. Our artillery entered into the dance. I didn't even know we had artillery. What a pleasure. This offensive coincided with that of Von Rundstedt in the Ardennes. Hitler wanted to break through towards Paris and the Germans in the Atlantic pockets wanted to meet up with them or form a diversionary tactic.

In January, progressive reorganization was done. General Edgard de Larminat was placed in total command of the front of the Atlantic. That of St. Nazaire-Pornic became the command of the 25th French Division under General Raymond Chomel. Our regiment became the 21st R.I. Captain Rogez took command of the battalion and he was replaced in our company by Lt. Du Paty de Clam. I became chief of the section.

Bertrand goes on to describe small firefights, patrols, and other fighting that his unit continued to do on a small scale. They finally got some English uniforms in March and continued to harass the Germans until the end of the war. Like many other soldiers in this campaign, he had a great respect for the German 88 millimeter cannon and in detail described its accuracy.

By August 18, the line between the Allies and Germans began to stabilize. Hitler gave orders that St. Nazaire and Lorient were to be held to the last man, no matter what the cost. There was to be no surrender. Vast mine fields were placed along "no-man's land" by the Germans, which marked off the pocket of St. Nazaire. Leaving Pénestin, the line passed Vilaine, Saint Dolay, Fégréac, the canal from Nantes to Brest then south to the mouth of the Loire River. It reached the sea in the area of Frossay. Approximately 27,000 Germans regrouped there, including 7,000 naval personnel.

Members of the Resistance either joined the FFI or remained in the background as "shadow soldiers." Both the Resistance and the FFI remained well organized and active, the FFI openly in combat with the Germans and the Resistance seeking and passing on information about German troop strengths, locations, armament, and gun locations. It was their plan, if the Allies attacked St. Nazaire, to work at the Germans' rear with acts of sabotage.

Opposing the Germans were units of the FFI and FTP, making sure the Germans could not escape. The French were joined by the United States 94th Infantry Division commanded by General Harry Maloney in early September. Later, the United States 66th Infantry Division would replace the 94th. The French FFI and FTP units were under the command of Colonel Chomel (later promoted to general) and the 66th under the command of General Herman Kramer.

Chateaubriand had fallen on August 4, 1944, to Patton's Third Army. The Resistance there reorganized and formed a reconnaissance group led by Lieutenant Guy Besnier. The first mission of this newly formed First Ground Mobile Reconnaissance Unit (1st GMR) was to guard the abandoned German depots. On August 12, arms and ammunition were parachuted to them. On August 26 and 28, Besnier's 1st GMR was ordered to cross the Loire River at Nantes and reconnoiter the territory south of the Loire. The party reached Saint Philbert-de-Grand Lieu. Numerous light arms as well as two 81 mm mortars were recovered. Two automatic rifles were also found and repaired.

The pocketed Germans began to experience some hardships, especially where food was concerned. During August 1944, they sent out foraging parties for livestock, grain, eggs, and any other farm products available. During these expeditions, under the pretext of looking for terrorists, they carried out acts of repression. On August 10, Emanuel Caut, a young resistant, was killed by a patrol. He was the son of a former mayor of St. Nazaire. Two people were killed at Notre-Dame de Grace on August 10 and three more the next day at Lance. A woman was killed at Fégréac on August 21.

The Resistance was everywhere in the St. Nazaire pocket and quite active. A collective cooperation existed between the various Resistance groups. The network included Georges France, 31; the Group Litoux; the Network Kimily; the Group Dubois; and the Francs-Tireurs Partisans—all organized under Colonel Doudevil. The principal activity of these Resistance groups, besides collecting information, was maintaining the line of demarcation separating the pocket from Free France. German deserters and civilians wishing to leave the pocket were allowed to pass. Numerous fishing boats were allowed to pass and go to Vannes. Many reconnaissance missions were carried out by the 1st GMR, commanded by Lt. Besnier. The 1st GMR worked closely with the 8th Cuirassiers, the French cavalry unit.

It was important to identify German locations between Pornic and Paimboeuf that passed by Saint-Pere-en Retz. Lt. Besnier ordered one of his patrols to destroy the bridge at Prighy, which was used by the Germans between Bourgneur and Pornic. On September 4, Lt. Besnier, accompanied in a sidecar by Lt. Juton, made a reconnaissance around Pornic. They were turned back by a violent artillery barrage. Their conclusion was that it would be impossible to liberate Pornic, as it was so heavily defended.

Lt. Besnier set up his headquarters at Arthon-et-Retz and his was the first unit on line to face the enemy. A week later they were joined by the first mobile group of the FFI, a force of 2,400 men. In the beginning of September 1944, the Germans launched attacks against the 5th Battalion at Loire-Inferieure and elements of the United States 4th Armored Division around Saint-Etienne-de-Montluc and Blain and also in the Foret De Gavre (Forest of Gavre—a large forest near Blain).

The Americans were quick to respond with a violent artillery attack on the zone around Bouvron, Guenrovet, and Camphon. Nearly 25,000 shells hit the villages. On September 16, the Germans launched another attack against the Foret de Gavre. The Americans pushed them back out of the forest by October 2. The Germans established a line of resistance from Clions-Sunmer to La Taminais, which passed by Saint-Pere-en-Retz and Groix. They were well dug in. The Germans sent out parties into the countryside near Retz and along the Nantes-Brest Canal. The Germans and the French Resistance groups exchanged raids and ambushes.

Besnier, later to become a captain, was one of the outstanding French soldiers fighting in the area of St. Nazaire, south of the Loire River. He and his unit distinguished themselves many times with their aggressive patrols and attacks. Also, Lt. Besnier took a group of mechanics to Normandy and rehabilitated 15 vehicles of various sorts that had been disabled there and brought them back to their unit near Chauvé, just outside of St. Nazaire.

Besnier was a reserve officer in the French cavalry and, prior to going to the cavalry school in Laumur, received a degree in engineering at the Ecole Centrale, which is the premier engineering school in France. During 1939–1940, he was an officer in the tank corps and fought the Germans in Belgium and France. He took the initiative of forming a special Resistance group to capture German tanks and other armored vehicles, including some Panhard armed cars.

The Panhard armed cars, seen in many pictures of the 1st GMR, were used at the outbreak of the war by the French. Many of these were captured by the Germans and used in their own units. After the invasion, the French were able to reciprocate in capturing them back and using them in their reconnaissance units.

Under the order of Colonel Chombart de Laure, alias Colonel Felix, who was department chief of the FFI, the residents organized 20 battalions that were composed of a force of 12,000 men. One-third were assigned surveillance of the southern zone. The FFI received much support from the United States 94th Infantry Division. Dr. Varliac (alias Commander Paulus) put together the members of the movement "Liberte" with other resistance fighters for a company of 503 men. Meanwhile, the Germans retook Frossay on October 15. Henceforth, the line remained fairly stable.

There was a high point of land, Moulin Neuf, on the road from Paimboeuf to Nantes where the Germans established an observation post. On September 12 at 2:00 P.M., two French civilians approached it wearing FFI arm bands. Their names were Alfred Martin and Jean Rondineau, and the latter had a revolver. They encouraged the Germans to desert. The Germans wounded them but they escaped only to be captured and led to the Moulin Neuf. Oberleutnant Werner Kretzchmar, chief of the post, arrived and sent his men to find four people on the road to come and bear witness to what was to take place. The two men were executed. He then informed the four witnesses that the same fate would befall all who would bear arms against German soldiers. The two men were buried on the banks of the Loire River, later to be exhumed and given a proper funeral with honors. After the war, Oberleutnant Werner Kretzchmar was condemned to hard labor for life by a French military tribunal at Angers.

83RD INFANTRY DIVISION CAPTURES 20,000 GERMANS

The 83rd Infantry Division, having completed its combat assignment at St. Malo, was sent to the St. Nazaire area to help to contain the Germans in that pocket and to patrol the Loire River on the right flank of the advancing Allied armies, more specifically for the United States Third Army. The area covered by the 83rd Division extended from St. Nazaire east along the Loire River to Orleans. This assignment was begun on August 20, 1944. The 331st Infantry Regiment of the 83rd Division moved to the vicinity of Heric and Nantes. They cleaned out residual pockets of Germans that had been passed by United States cavalry units. The Germans were contained although they tried on several occasions to breach the line in an effort to rejoin the German army. The 83rd patrolled the wide area between Angers along the Loire River to Nantes, a distance of 93 miles, then northward to Redon.

At regular intervals the intelligence and reconnaissance patrols crossed the Loire at Nantes to assess enemy strength and positions. During these patrols, they probed deep into the enemy territory. Additionally, they had to defend their positions against enemy attacks, as happened on August 27, when a battalion of German infantry and three tanks of self-propelled guns attacked a unit of the 331st near Blain. The enemy was repulsed with heavy losses.

Again, on September 2, a patrol of highly armed nazis attempted to enter Fay-de-Bretagne but was overcome after a short fight. From then on the major activity of the 83rd Division was active patrolling. Parts of the extended front of the 83rd were occupied by FFI units, who were valuable for the information and warnings extended to the 83rd.

An advanced command post was established in Nantes to aid the administration of the third-largest city in France. There were 150,000 civilians remaining there, and food, water, and fuel had to be provided while an active defense was to be maintained against the Germans.

On September 9, 1944, the day after the renewal of the attack on Brest, the Ninth Army received word from the 83rd Division that a German force of some 20,000 soldiers, located south of the Loire River, was desirous of surrendering. It came about as follows:

Soon after the United States 7th Army began its march north to join the Third Army following its landing in southern France, the Germans began to realize the precarious position of their troops in southwestern France. They decided to evacuate the area in an orderly fashion and move toward Germany.

They organized this retreat to appear as an offensive campaign with the objective of clearing all resistance in their path. This was done in order to keep the morale of the troops high. This massive body of soldiers was divided into Group South, Group Middle, and Group North. It was during this time that the 83rd Division accomplished the major coup of capturing 20,000 Germans without firing a shot.

Each of the three large German groups was assigned an assembly area, a route of march, and a mode of travel. Because of the advancing Allied armies and their opportunities for escape decreasing, plans were changed on August 27, now calling for a subdivision of the groups into fast-moving vehicles, slow-moving vehicles, and foot-troops. One foot column, designated "Foot March Group South," was under the command of Brigadier General Botho Henning Elster.

General Elster's command was moving as rapidly as possible to reach the Loire River before it was cut off. They arrived at Poitiers on September 3, 1944. When strung out two days later between Poitiers and Chateauroux, they suffered two air attacks and sustained numerous casualties and losses of supplies and equipment. The FFI and French civilians were harassing them. At this point General Elster wisely decided that it was futile to continue.

Patrols of the 83rd Division had started crossing the Loire to reconnoiter German positions. Lieutenant Samuel W. Magill, of the Intelligence and Reconnaissance platoon of the 329th Infantry Regiment, slipped south of the Loire and contacted the FFI who had been harassing the German force. They reported that Foot March Group South was near Issoudun and would probably consider surrender if approached by the Americans. Lt. Magill contacted General Elster at Chateauroux. The general wanted to surrender but wanted a mock battle to save face. He wanted the Americans to prove that there were at least two Allied battalions south of the Loire. At that time there were only 18 regular Allied soldiers within 70 miles of the Germans, but Elster was told if he did not surrender, his force would be bombed out of existence. To enforce this threat, the Tactical Air Command flew over the Germans in force and General Elster quickly accepted the surrender terms. The formal surrender took place September 16, 1944, at Beaugency Bridge. Twenty thousand Germans, including 754 officers, became prisoners of war.

The 83rd Division did not stay long on this front and were relieved by the 94th Infantry Division on September 22, 1944. The 83rd Division assembled at Montargis and began its move east on September 23, 1944. The 83rd and 4th Armored Divisions had outstanding records during the multiple battles during the remainder of the war.

NOTES

1. Kenneth Koyen, *The Fourth Armored Division: From the Beach to Bavaria: The Story of the Fourth Armored Division in Combat* (Germany, 1946).

2. General Fahrmbacher's report was old and had gone through at least one translation but evidently is pretty accurate as to the conditions in Lorient and his initial concern about being able to ward off a significant attack.

3. *Combat History of the 6th Armored Division in the European Theatre of Operations 18 July 1944–8 May 1945* (Yadkinville: Ripple Publishing, 1945).

4. Morbihan Hennebont, *Les Heures Tragiques De La Liberation* [Booklet in city archives] (Hennebont, France: Imprimerie Artisanale, Pont Scorf, France, 1985).

5. Ibid.

Chapter 7

1944—OCTOBER, NOVEMBER, DECEMBER

GROUND WAR—94TH INFANTRY DIVISION TAKES OVER

At the beginning of October 1944, the lines between the Allies and the Germans were pretty well established. Boundaries would be altered but not appreciably. Both sides had affected strong defensive positions facing "no-man's land."

The 94th Division was on board as the controlling unit. The French were there in considerable numbers defending the eastern section of Lorient and the area south of the Loire River in the St. Nazaire sector. Meanwhile, the 66th Infantry Division, which would later become the major player in this campaign, had received orders for deployment to Europe and was preparing to move to a port of embarkation.

RECORD OF 94TH INFANTRY DIVISION

After the 6th Armored Division departed, the battle surrounding St. Nazaire and Lorient became an infantry and artillery campaign. The defensive line between the opposing forces remained fairly stationary. The geography of the two pockets varied significantly. The enemy occupied approximately 100 square miles in the Lorient pocket and approximately 680 square miles in the St. Nazaire pocket. The Lorient pocket was punctuated with hills and valleys whereas St. Nazaire was flat and contained large areas of swampland. At Lorient, three rivers—the Laita, Scorf and

Blavet, flowed southward into the Bay of Biscay from the American through the German territories. At St. Nazaire, the perimeter was partially outlined by the Vilaine River and the Brest-Nantes Canal. The German and American forces opposed each other across these two rivers. There was no water barrier separating them in the east. The Loire estuary and river coursed through German territory.

The terrain of both sectors was crisscrossed with hedgerows. In St. Nazaire, especially, there was often a small sunken road between the hedgerows. The terrain was conducive to very effective camouflage, observation positions, and mines. A hedgerow could conceal a machine gun position perfectly, as the embrasure was cut through the hedgerow. Observation was so well done by both sides that one could not cross an open field but had to stick to the hedgerows. This laid the foundation for ambushes and close-encounter firefights.

When the 94th Division relieved the 6th Armored Division, it faced an estimated 25,000 troops at Lorient and 35,000 at St. Nazaire. One-half of the German troops were infantry and there was also a large contingent of artillery units. The remainder were naval, Luftwaffe, service personnel, paratroopers, and even some Russian troops taken on as mercenaries. Many of the latter were converted to infantry by an intensive training program. Lt. General Wilhelm Fahrmbacher assumed command of the Lorient pocket. Brigadier General Werner Junck, a former infantry commander, took command of the German forces in St. Nazaire when it was formed in August 1944.

There were approximately 500 functional artillery pieces in Lorient, of which 300 were stationary; the other 200 were capable of high mobility. They ranged from 20 mm antiaircraft guns to the 340 mm coastal defense guns, which had been turned to fire on the land troops. In St. Nazaire there were an estimated 525 artillery pieces ranging up to 340 mm and well supplied with ammunition. In addition to St. Nazaire and Lorient, the Germans occupied the islands Re, Groix, Belle, and the Quiberon Peninsula—all well fortified. The Quiberon Peninsula, extending out into the Bay of Biscay and located between the two pockets, was one long line of antiaircraft guns.

Because of the proximity of the opposing forces, the 94th Division used strict security measures concerning communications and laid abnormal amounts of wire to minimize the use of radios. The Signal Company had over 2,000 miles of wire connecting positions. Each artillery battalion laid approximately 80 miles of wire mainly from forward outpost to fire direction centers.

Because of the vastly extended front, the supply situation was difficult. During the four months that the 94th Division was there, 1,847,888 rations and 1,357,108 gallons of gasoline were drawn by the division and its attachments. Two separate railheads at Baud and Messac were utilized where prisoner of war labor was available. During the period from September 10, 1944, to December 31, 1944, 6,287 tons of ammunition were placed and, of this, 3,487 tons were expended on the enemy.

When General Harry Malony and the 94th Division took over the pockets, they discovered the presence of thousands of Frenchmen fighting in units of the FFI. The 94th Division, realizing the potential value of these groups, helped them organize; obtain supplies, weapons, and uniforms; then participated actively to upgrade their training. The Americans eventually supplied them with 2,344 rifles, 1,817 carbines, 283 machine pistols, 24 mortars, 19 105 mm howitzers, 5 155 mm howitzers, and 19 other artillery pieces and ammunition. The artillery units attached to the 94th were instrumental in training the French to effectively use these weapons. The French, although remaining under the overall command of the American forces, opened up headquarters in Vannes and Nantes and railheads at Redon and Nantes.

Coordination with the French was very poor at first due to internal politics and the language barrier. General Maloney continued to request more supplies for the French but because of the needs of the American First and Third Armies, the FFI was given low priority. Finally, on October 2, 1944, a conference was held in Chateaubriand to which the ranking French leaders were invited. This meeting, the first of many, did much to build better relations with the French and resulted in a much more cohesive effort between the Americans and French with rations, gasoline, arms, and ammunition. Shortly thereafter, the French Navy began operations in the Bay of Biscay with small armed vessels, which were effective in gathering information and passing it on to the American G-2 (Intelligence unit). Also, in early October, the French air squadron, Groupe Patrie, came under the control of the 94th Division. They had 11 A-24 dive bombers that were used primarily for reconnaissance. In addition, during the first month with the 94th, 84 sorties were flown and 30,900 pounds of bombs were dropped.

The last major shift in French command was on October 26, 1944. General Edgard de Larminat, overall commander in this sector, placed Colonel Raymond Chomel in charge at St. Nazaire and gave command of the Lorient area to General Borgnis des Bordes. By the time the 94th was relieved at the end of December, there were 21 battalions of French infantry at St.

Nazaire and 13 at Lorient. The 94th Division continued an intensive training program for those units.

The 301st Infantry Regiment of the 94th Division was first on the scene and relieved the 6th Armored September 9 through 11. Their regimental responsibility was bound on the east by the Blavet River and on the west by the Laita River. The line in their sector ran from south of Quimperlé to Rédené, Pont Scorf, Hennebont, and Nostang. The first contact with the enemy was an attack on an outpost commanded by Company K. This was repulsed and on that same day, Company E reported that two of their soldiers had been killed and that the enemy tried to burn the bodies on a hay stack. Members of Company E recovered the bodies before they were burned. On September 11, the first artillery rounds were fired by the division artillery. The 302nd Infantry Regiment arrived September 15 and took positions between the Scorf River to Hennebont to Nostang. The relief was completed on September 16.

Members of Company A, 302nd Infantry, were brought under fire the first day they were on the line. One soldier was killed and three were wounded. On September 19th, Lieutenant Herman Sidebottom led a patrol from Company F into the Caudan-Blavet River area and ran into Germans in prepared positions. The ensuing fight resulted in 4 enemy killed and 10 taken prisoner, including one officer.

The first Distinguished Service Cross earned by a member of the 94th Division was awarded to Private First Class Dale Proctor, Company K, 301st Infantry Regiment. He was a telephone operator and artillery observer who was severely wounded when the Germans concentrated artillery fire on his position. Despite his wounds, he remained at his post, continuing to direct fire while being treated by the medics. He pleaded to remain at his post and it became necessary to pry the phone from his hands in order to evacuate him. The following day this brave soldier died from his wounds.

Shortly after the 94th Division deployed to Lorient, their mission was extended to contain St. Nazaire. General Maloney flew to Le Mans and met with the commander of the 83rd Division, which they were to relieve. He then shifted the bulk of his infantry to St. Nazaire and split the artillery between the two pockets, with the greater strength remaining at Lorient.

On September 17, 1944, the 376th Infantry Regiment, not yet committed, relieved the 331st Infantry Regiment of the 83rd Division. On that same night, this new regiment suffered its first casualties when the Germans loaded a boxcar with explosives and sent it down the tracks into Blain. The car jumped the tracks just outside of town, rolled into K Company area and exploded. One soldier was killed and several were wounded.

The lines taken over by the 376th Infantry extended 22 miles, stretching from the Loire River through Le Temple, Fay-de-Bretagne, and Blain, then northwest to a road junction in the Foret de Gavre. The 331st had organized these towns' centers of resistance with intervening strong points. South of the regimental sector were several FFI units. The regimental Command Post (CP) was at Heric. Colonel McClure, regimental commander of the 356th requested a limited advance to straighten out the line. This was done, putting the towns of Le Temple, Fay-de-Bretagne, and Blain behind the front. Reconnaissance troops were valuable in helping maintain contact with elements of this extended front. On October 3, 1944, Companies B and C of the 302nd Regiment cleared the southern position of the Foret de Gavre, moving the front forward 3,000 to 5,000 yards and shortening the line.

Ninth Army next informed the 94th Division that their line was to be extended east to Auxere. General Maloney requested the light reconnaissance troops for extensive patrolling. Elements of the 15th Cavalry Reconnaissance Group answered the call.

An additional order on September 21, 1944, extended the 94th Division's mission still farther to include protecting the right flank of the Ninth and Third Armies from Quimper to Auxere (southeast of Paris, in central France). This resulted in a front of 450 miles from Quimper to Nantes, then along the Loire River to Auxere. Extensive cavalry patrolling was eased somewhat by all bridges across the Loire River having been destroyed.

Not only had the area of responsibility for the 94th expanded, but its complement of troops was now up to 35,000 American and French troops. It was the only division in the ETO that could boast its own navy and air force, Groupe Patrie.

During the period from November 25 to 26, two French battalions replaced elements of the 301st Infantry between the Scorf and Laita Rivers, enabling the 3rd Battalion of the 302nd to pass into reserve. These French units, having been trained and equipped by the 94th Division, became valuable to replace a unit of the 94th, so that it could withdraw into reserve. With a unit in reserve in each sector, the division commander had a force that could be deployed quickly.

General Maloney, restrained by orders against offensive action, decided to commit the division to a period of intense battle indoctrination by stepping up the emphasis on patrolling and the cooperation of armor, infantry, and artillery. Combat and reconnaissance patrols were constantly sent out from all levels—company, battalion, regimental—and coordinated to avoid firefights between friendly forces.

On the 2nd of October, Company K, of the 301st, sent out a strong combat patrol of 50 American soldiers and three FFI soldiers. It was a daytime patrol, and they ran into an ambush with withering crossfire. Artillery was called for and directed. A relief patrol was organized from Company I but never could reach the isolated Company K group. Private Harry Glickman, a member of the Company K patrol described the event:

Everything ran well until we got about 5,000 yards from our lines. Then it happened. Two scouts dropped dead and two more were wounded as the crack of rifles was heard from all sides. Ambush! The patrol leader acted quickly and deployment started. "Call for artillery time fire to cover us," he yelled. If I ever loved the artillery it was then. It was probably the artillery that saved us from annihilation. Concentration after concentration poured in on the Heinies [Germans] as we withdrew to better positions.

Then it started. Those five hours of fighting against terrific odds. They threw everything at us. I saw acts of bravery that day which it seemed could happen only in motion pictures; men charging machine guns and wounded men firing their weapons with one hand. The Germans paid a heavy toll, but in the end we also suffered heavy casualties. Twenty-six wounded and five dead out of fifty men.

Toward the end, the enemy began to organize and charge. There was only one thing to do. "Concentration Seventeen...forty yards left...Time Fire.... For Effect."

Behind a hedgerow we waited. Forty yards wasn't too far for safety even with a hedgerow for protection. Twenty seconds later the "On the way!" was sent over the radio and we heard the far-away rumble of the artillery. Wait until you hear a 105 mm shell coming down on you. Wait until you hear twelve of them scream—scream like sirens as they start their descent. The sound was enough for the Germans. They dove for any sort of cover.... The top of the hedgerow snapped in pieces and came down on us.

But it was to no avail. The enemy had many more reinforcements and our relief was still far off and had been halted. A little while later, we realized the inevitable—the radio was on the blink, ammunition was low and men were dying of wounds. We were ordered to give in.

They didn't treat us badly. They let us keep our watches and other valuables (except cigarettes). What happened in prison camp and how we each lost about twenty pounds is another story, but I shall always remember the day the German captain called me aside.

"Please," he said, "tell me how soon do I get to America after I am captured. I have a cousin in Milwaukee."[1]

Only two members of this patrol escaped the trap. French sources gave information to the effect that 100 Germans had been killed, later confirmed by men of the patrol returning in a prisoner-of-war exchange.[2]

On October 6, 1944, elements of the 3rd Battalion, 376th Infantry, advanced to Bouvron to shorten and strengthen the line between them and the 302nd Infantry. The principal activity was along the Brest-Nantes Canal near La Pessouis. Company I jumped off south of the canal and immediately came under heavy artillery and small-arms fire. By late afternoon, they had taken the small village of La Pessouis. The artillery supporting the 302nd on the other side of the canal mistook them for enemy troops and began to fire on them. The Germans were doing likewise from the opposite direction. They had to withdraw and the Germans reoccupied the village. For the next two days, the Americans pounded the village, and on October 8, the town was again taken by the 3rd Battalion of the 356th and thereafter remained in American hands.

During the period from October 23 to 28, a series of truces were arranged to evacuate civilians in conjunction with the Red Cross. Approximately 9,000 civilians safely crossed the line.

On October 8, the 94th Division was placed under the control of the 12th Army Group commanded by General Omar Bradley. This allowed the Ninth Army to move on to the western front.

Early on the morning of October 20, a group of approximately 100 members of the 986th Kriegsmarine attacked positions of the 1st Battalion of the 301st. From prisoners it was learned that their objective was Grand Champ and it was their practice to repeat an unsuccessful attack in two or three days. The same day a force of 100–200 Germans penetrated the French line but were beaten back by the FFI. The French withdrew after sustaining an artillery bombardment. They were ordered back by division headquarters and reoccupied it before the Germans came in.

On October 28, the Germans repeated the attack on the FFI and at the same time pounded the 1st Battalion of the 301st in the Hennebont Sector. They were beaten back. Later in the same day another German force, estimated at battalion strength, attacked the FFI at St. Hélène south of Nostang. They drove the French back from the Etel River and occupied the high ground.

During the last few days of October, 12th Army Headquarters, on the basis of information supplied by G-2 (Intelligence unit) of Brittany Base section, issued orders for the division to hold a battalion in reserve for a counterattack against a possible German offensive of 25,000 to 31,000 troops occupying the islands of Guernsey and Jersey. The Normandy and Brittany coasts were constantly patrolled, but no landing force ever came.

A series of boundary changes were made November 21, 1944, which increased the zone of the St. Nazaire Sector. Furthermore, the St. Nazaire Sector was divided into North and South subsectors with Colonel Johnson, commander of the 302nd Infantry, commanding the former while Colonel McClure commanded the latter. All FFI and FTP troops within these subsectors came under their control.

Thought had been given many times to separate Lorient from the Quiberon Peninsula in order to weaken the German position. General Fortier decided to reduce the pillboxes and strong points at the base of the peninsula and organize a considerable force of infantry and artillery from units of the 301st and 356th Infantry Regiments and their attached artillery, engineer, and medical units. On a cloudy night, the engineers cleared an antipersonnel mine field and at 0833 hours, after an intense artillery bombardment, assault groups organized from several infantry companies jumped off and, with perfect coordination, took all objectives in 50 minutes, despite heavy mortar and artillery fire from west of the Etel River and Ile de Groix. Fifty-nine prisoners were taken, nine bunkers reduced, and the desired positions obtained. American losses were extremely low.

On December 15, an outpost between Belle Isle and St. Nazaire, placed there for the purpose of observing enemy shipping between St. Nazaire and Lorient, was attacked by a force of 80 Germans landed there by motorboat. At the same time a French naval motor launch carrying Staff Sergeant Love, supply sergeant to the four men on the outpost, was engaged by enemy craft. The captain of the French vessel was killed and Sergeant Love wounded and taken prisoner. The four men on the outpost were captured.

When Field Marshal Karl Von Rundstedt's winter offensive began, the 94th Division greatly intensified its security measures for fear of saboteurs and parachute troops being dropped to create confusion and disrupt communications. Also, the 94th was alerted to the possibility of the pocketed Germans trying to break out in order to divert American reserves. During the remainder of December, the German offensive had been checked.

A series of prisoner exchanges occurred during November and December and the credit goes to Andrew G. Hodges of the American Red Cross, who, on his own initiative, negotiated the exchange with the Germans and became somewhat legend among our troops. Hodges was from Alabama and was a former football and basketball star at Howard University. He had been kept out of the service because of a bad right arm attributed to a football injury. He joined the Red Cross and was shipped overseas with the 302nd Infantry and became Division Red Cross Field Director.

Hodges heard rumors that the Allied prisoners were not being treated well, so "Andy," on his own, negotiated with the Germans under a Red Cross flag and carried food, cigarettes, toiletries, and books to the prisoners of war at Lorient and St. Nazaire.

After several of such visits, he dropped the remark to the Germans that if a prisoner exchange were carried out, he wouldn't have to make these trips. Much to his surprise, on his next visit he was informed that the German command was willing to make such an exchange. The exchange was to be rank for rank, branch for branch, with equal physical conditions. There was difficulty finding Germans who wanted to be exchanged, but under the sanction of our high command, an armistice was arranged for November 17, 1944, for an exchange at Etel on the Lorient Sector. The Germans rejected 13 and 2 more decided not to volunteer. Hodges was informed that since there were not enough Germans to exchange for the 71 Allied prisoners, only 56 could be exchanged. Hodges informed the German officer that "a good soldier is never caught without reserves" and produced the necessary replacements.

The second exchange took place at St. Nazaire on November 29, 1944. Hodges noted that three Allied prisoners were not on the list: two Americans and one English officer. The Germans explained that the two Americans had escaped and that they would not trade the English officer, as he had escaped four times and been recaptured four times, and he knew too much. Hodges informed the Germans that it was an all-or-nothing proposition and unless he got the Englishman, the deal was off. The Germans wanted six Germans for one English officer and Hodges continued to refuse until the deal was sealed on his terms.

A third exchange occurred that included the four men captured at the observation post, a bomber group shot down on returning from a mission, and Sgt. Love, wounded and captured when the outpost had been overrun.

All in all, and to the credit of Andrew Hodges, 140 Allied prisoners were returned, including 105 Americans, 32 FFI soldiers, and 3 British. With one exception, the division recovered all prisoners that had been captured.

General Maloney had been trying for some time to get the 94th Division relieved of its containment mission so that it could go to the eastern front. Numerous trips were made by him and his staff to headquarters to plead his case. Several times he was promised relief only to be disappointed later by cancellations. The last disappointment occurred with the promise that the 11th Armored Division would relieve the 94th on or about December 19, 1944. An advance party actually came to Chateaubriand to make plans for the relief, but Von Rundstedt's winter offensive began and while the 11th Armored was unloading on the beaches of Normandy on December 18, higher headquarters cancelled the proposed relief and the 11th Armored was sent to support the eastern front.

Finally, according to *History of the 94th Infantry Division in World War II*, relief was on the way when the troopship *Leopoldville,* carrying 66th

Infantry Division soldiers across the English Channel to Cherbourg on Christmas Eve 1944, was torpedoed and sunk with the loss of 802 lives. In addition, numerous soldiers were lost with wounds, frostbite, and pneumonia. Much of the equipment was lost, further crippling the division.

The report goes on to say: "Whether or not the division would have relieved the 94th if it had not been for this tragedy, will never be known. It was known, however, that General Bradley had long been anxious to get the 94th to the eastern front. Official word of the impending relief was received on the 21st of December. Three days later, according to the records of the 94th, General Herman F. Kramer, Commanding General of the 66th Division, arrived at Chateaubriand with his advance party to plan the relief and to be oriented on the situation.

"On the 26th, the shaken-up 66th began occupying positions in the line but all troops did not arrive in the area until after the departure of the 94th."

The above report is very confusing. If General Kramer was in Chateaubriand three days after December 21, he was there before the *Leopoldville* was torpedoed. If this is accurate, the 66th was destined to relieve the 94th and it was not because the 66th had been crippled in the Channel. It has always been thought by most soldiers of the 66th that their division was headed to "The Bulge" and was diverted to these pockets because of the Channel losses. This never seemed logical. One would think it poor strategy by those in command to send a green, inexperienced division on an emergency mission to "The Bulge," when a battle-tested, experienced division like the 94th was immediately available, provided there was a suitable replacement. If the story above is correct, it would support the concept that it was planned for the 66th to relieve the 94th prior to the *Leopoldville* disaster.

On the other hand, Ray Roberts, who was in the 766th Ordnance Company, related that during the first week of January 1945, all of the truck drivers and sergeants left Messac, where the company was stationed, and drove to Antwerp, Belgium, to pick up the company's trucks and wreckers and drove them back to Messac. He raises the question of why the vehicles would have been sent to Antwerp had it not been originally intended for the 66th Division to be sent to "The Bulge."[3]

FRENCH BATTLE GERMANS SOUTH OF THE LOIRE RIVER

During this same period, in the fourth quarter of 1944, the French units in the two pockets were very aggressive against the Germans. With the help of the 94th Division, they became better organized, trained, and equipped. At that time also, the 66th Infantry Division, soon to enter this battle, was training in England and was well aware that their call to duty would come soon.

The operation of the French forces of the west was created October 14, 1944, by General Charles de Gaulle, president of the provisional government of the French Republic. Through this organization was formed "French Forces in Operations on the Western Front" (FFO), which he entrusted to General of the Army Edgard de Larminat. The soldiers humorously interpreted the FFO to mean the "Forgotten French Forces."

Five geographic battle sectors were organized, only two of them relating to St. Nazaire. On October 27, General Larminat set up his headquarters at Cognac and a secondary one at Angers where he put Colonel Marius Marchand in charge. Colonel Marchand was instructed to maintain a liaison with the Americans north of the Loire. General Larminat established a liaison with the Allied organization in Paris. Thus, the American and French commands were divided. The two divisions were the following:

Zone North—Under the command of an American, General Maloney, who was commanding the 94th Division, and later by the 66th Division, commanded by General Kramer. Zone North included Lorient.

Zone South—Under the command of the French commandant of the FFO and under the authority of the 6th Army Group.

On October 15, 1944, the Germans began an offensive to gain 35 square kilometers of land to establish their line on a route from Saint-Pere-en-Retz to Frossay. Evidently, this was done to gain some tactical advantage for the defense of this section of the line, which was located south of the Loire River and controlled by the French. Serious clashes took place a few kilometers in front of Chauvé with the First Ground Mobile Reconnaissance (1st GMR) unit on the route to Saint-Michel-Chef-Chef. Andre Lemesle was killed and Pierre Jarno was wounded. The entrance into battle with these armed vehicles allowed the men to escape and the wounded to be treated at the Church Serot. Lt. Guy Besnier was promoted to captain.

On November 2, 1944, the Charles Martel Brigade reinforced the pocket and was commanded by Colonel Ghislain. The sector south of the Loire, where the French troops were deployed, was divided into two sections:

1. Secteur de port-Saint Pere, commanded by Colonel Claude
2. Secteur de Bourgneuf, commanded by Colonel Rochaud

On December 2, 1944, Besnier's squadron fell into an ambush near La Sicaudais close to Chauvé. Sergeant Pierre Jarno's group escaped and hid in a cabbage field. The remainder finally withdrew through a small wooded area. Sergeant Robert Bourreau was killed.

The French 8th Cavalry Regiment (8th Cuirassiers) was assigned to secure the front line. The 1st GMR played an important role when the Germans tried to take 85 square kilometers of the front but were denied by the French soldiers. On December 21, 1944, as in support of Von Rundstedt's offensive in the Ardennes, the Germans attacked La Bernerie, La Sicaudais, and the region of La Rogère. They succeeded in taking Sicaudais, which is near the coast, with the support of three gunboats of the Kriegsmarine from St. Nazaire. Two French battalions commanded by Colonels Thomas and Legrand opposed the Germans with the 1st GMR in the center. The French had been taken by surprise when the German artillery barrage began, and they did not have sufficient artillery.

General Chomel immediately met with all of his commanders, then put himself in the center of the battle to direct the French response. Initially, the two battalions commanded by Colonels Thomas and Legrand were driven back to Sicaudais and Chauvé. Lieutenant Maurice Pollono attacked with a mechanized patrol but came under heavy fire, which demolished the vehicles and killed Lt. Pollono and several other French soldiers.[4] The 1st GMR fired its cannons and mortars on the Germans at La Bumiere and Landes Fleuries. The 8th Cuirassiers attacked near the center of the battle and lost 2 men with 10 more wounded. Lieutenant Mazarquil's squadron was one of the leading elements of the counterattack.

On the following day, the French regained Chauvé never to lose it to the Germans again. The 8th Cuirassiers and the 1st GMR continued their combat patrols. On December 22 and 23, reinforcements arrived and the front stabilized. The French losses were 10 men dead and 38 wounded.

Two soldiers who fought in this battle have recently recorded their personal experiences with Luc and Marc Braeuer, curators of The Grand Blockhaus Museum located at Batz-Sur-Mer just west of St. Nazaire.

Sergeant Yves Bichan is a veteran of the First Ground Mobile Unit and relates the following:

> A few days before Christmas the Germans tried to take Vue. We were alerted for an operation on Clion for December 21, 1944. We prepared our armored car. The machine gun cartridge belts were inspected. We had 4,500 rounds. It was very cold. German artillery began from Bernerie and Sicaudais. We were at Arthon. We rode out of the center of Arthon and waited outside on the road to Sicaudais. Captain Besnier, Commander of the 1st GMR, had left and he directed us to proceed on reconnaissance to Poirier.

This photo of the *Leopoldville* was taken in 1939 by René Sottieaus, the chief steward. He survived the sinking of the *Leopoldville* but died a few weeks later on February 11, 1945, when the ship, *Persier,* which was returning him to Belgium was torpedoed by a German U-boat. Courtesy of granddaughter, Renee Wittebroodt-Sottieaus, and Ray Roberts, author.

The weather was extremely cold. We began having trouble with the vehicle motor. Shortly thereafter, we encountered a soldier retreating, who appeared very afraid. He told us the Germans were with 4,000 men and were advancing on Arthon. We were skeptical and proceeded, although uneasy.

We arrived at Poirier and encountered Commandant Joel who was wounded. He asked us to check the train station at Feuillardis to see if it was still held by our troops. We proceeded and then encountered Lt. Pollono who was guarding this important passage. He informed us that the enemy was on the offensive and making progress.

We began to advance slowly with Pollono towards Sicaudais. We knocked out a machine gun and its crew near La Roulais. We found we were near a greater concentration of Germans so turned around. The Germans were just about ready to set up an artillery piece near us so we withdrew. We received some reinforcements so proceeded forward again.

Lt. Pollono arrived and wanted to head back to Sicaudais so as to get into the countryside. We objected. Pollono left with four of his boys and wanted us to follow to help protect them. We followed slowly behind them to the crossroads of Lande Fleuris. The Germans were set up 100 meters away.

Panhard AMD 178 with 50 mm cannon and crew of 1st GMR. Courtesy: The Grand Block-haus Museum, Batz-sur-Mer, France.

Before I had time to spot their position, we sustained devastating automatic fire, which badly damaged our vehicle, showering sparks.

We destroyed their position with 25 mm fire and sent them to God the Father. A big shell knocked us off our feet but did not hurt us. I continued to spray the hedges and surrounding fields with my machine gun, thus permitting the Pollono group to fall back behind our vehicle. That group realized their maneuver was pretty useless. Our role of protection was done and we withdrew to where Hardy made his report to Mazarquil.

Shortly thereafter, the only survivor of Pollono's tracked vehicle arrived out of breath and quickly told us the sad tale that Pollono and several of his men were killed. Stragglers started coming back without leadership. Mazarquil was not too happy. He asked us to reconnoiter the area and we quickly took off.

We found a corpse, and near this a frightened soldier climbed out of a foxhole and told us the Germans were in the valley in front of us. We told him that reinforcements were coming and we proceeded on our mission. A squadron of the Cuirassiers arrived and took position near the train station at Feuillardais. The breach in the line was filled and the line now intact.

Lt. Mazarquil asked us to wait for him as he wanted to establish contact with Captain Besnier. The weather remained beastly cold. The Germans kept up a constant fire of small arms. Besnier asked us to make a rapid reconnaissance between La Feuillardais and the train station. We raked the hedgerow with the machine gun.

On the way back to Poirier, we set up the vehicle at a farm and had something to eat. The Germans began to shoot their 88s [88mm cannon] at us. Night fell quietly and the whole sector settled down.

22 December 1944

At 5:30 in the morning, Chauvé had been evacuated because of artillery fire. Captain Besnier asked us to go there and see what was going on. We passed two squads of the 8th Cuirassiers headed for Chauvé.

In the main square, we found the Curé, the local priest who was the Abbe Serot, the only person remaining in town. He told us about a German patrol that had just come through Chauvé. We stayed there to wait for the 8th Cuirassiers' squads to help them set up in Chauvé. We then returned to Arthon and toured the lines with Besnier. On returning to Arthon, we ran into General Chomel, who had come to evaluate the situation. Reinforcements soon arrived.[5]

In October of 1944, when Colonel Chomel received the mission to command and organize the front of the pocket at St. Nazaire, he had put Colonel René Blanquefort in charge of the artillery in the sector, which at that time was practically nonexistent. A French front was created around Nantes encircling 35,000 Germans who had fallen back on the powerful stronghold of St. Nazaire. This front extended from Vilaine to Pornic, and by Fégréac, Plessé, Saint-Etienne de Montluc, La Feuillardais, Arthon, and La Bernerie au Sud. The troops included the Charles Martel Brigade and the Maquis FFI de Vendee of Brittany, all converging on the retreating Germans.

Colonel René Blanquefort had managed to get a few cannon from the Allies, and with an aggressive effort the French forces in that area had captured some German guns and ammunition. On December 20, 1944, when the Germans became very aggressive and attacked the French positions through the Forest of Prince, Colonel Blanquefort was ready to put his newly acquired cannon to good use—killing Germans. The Germans launched an offensive toward Sicaudais and La Feuillardais. General de Larminat arrived and Colonel Blanquefort had a discussion with him. Blanquefort began deploying the batteries available to him strategically. Four captured German PAK/40s were taken to Melinet to improvise a battery that was placed under the command of Lieutenant Charpentier. Colonel Blanquefort describes the activity in his own words:

I took this battery over the Loire River and placed it on the German flank. Then I reconnoitered the line at Le Poirier and La Barre de Vue. Our line was in danger of capitulating under the pressure of the two German battalions

December, 1944. Section of Infantry FFI on St. Nazaire. Courtesy: The Grand Blockhaus
Museum, Batz-sur-Mer, France.

supported by three artillery batteries. One section of our line had fallen into
the hands of the Germans. We began shelling the Germans and gradually the
situation stabilized. The Germans fell back and our line reformed itself.

The southern sector required a lot of attention. There was some progres-
sion toward Nantes. On December 22, we had to put our cannon right on the
line. The four batteries under the orders of Lt. Charpentier were established
defensively south of Arthon with the 8th Cuirassiers.

Our problems continued to be a paucity of munitions, transportation for
the guns, compounded by severe cold and icy roads. Soon after this battle
we were able to capture a new battery of German 105s.[6]

Colonel Blanquefort and his artillery did such a superb job of accurately
bombarding the Germans that in reprisal the Germans knocked the steeple
off the church at Chauvé, which had served as an observation post to
locate German targets.

One of the most outstanding units among the French forces in the pocket
of St. Nazaire was the 8th Cuirassiers Regiment, as is obvious from this
three-day battle with the Germans. The 8th Cuirassiers Regiment was
formed in 1635 at the king's request and ordered by Cardinal de Richelieu to

wear the cuirass (armor). Campaigns included the Dutch Invasion, the Spanish and Austrian Wars, the French Revolution, and the First World War.

In 1940, they were the first French army unit to cross the Belgium border, May 10, 1940. Again, they distinguished themselves before France and Belgium capitulated. Many of them were evacuated at Dunkirk. Temporarily disbanded according to the armistice, they reformed as a Resistance unit at Chateauroux and fought the Germans with guerilla tactics.

The unit was officially reformed in October 1944, and on November 29, 1944, they replaced the Battalion Legrand around Chauvé. When the 8th Cuirassiers first arrived, they had six squadrons but only one was mechanized with light tanks—the 5th squadron under Lt. Mazarquil. This squadron, along with Besnier's, was the main intervention and counterattack force against German attacks in their sector. The unit represented the French at the surrender of St. Nazaire, May 11, 1945.[7]

SINKING OF THE *LEOPOLDVILLE*

The 66th Infantry Division was training in Dorchester, England, when the Battle of the Bulge began. The division was destined to play a major role in the campaign in Brittany surrounding the ports of St. Nazaire and Lorient, although most of the soldiers thought they were heading to the Battle of the Bulge. At noon on December 23, 1944, orders were received to be ready to move out by 6:00 P.M. Trains took the troops to Southampton for boarding on the HMS *Leopoldville* and the SS *Cheshire*. There was a lot of confusion in loading, and men were separated from their squads and companies.

Events that were seemingly unimportant could make the difference between death and survival in many wartime situations. An example is reported by Ebner Nicholson Jr. of Tucson, Arizona: "Our Captain saved our lives from getting on the *Leopoldville*. They were going to load us on but the captain said we were not to be loaded until his men had coffee and donuts. [Red Cross] They boarded F Company instead and F Company lost most of its men. They loaded us on the *Cheshire*. That is fate."[8]

The HMS *Leopoldville* was built in 1929 to carry 360 passengers, but it was loaded with 2,223 troops of the 66th and a crew of 237. It was a tired old boat, run-down and dirty. The crew consisted of 120 Belgians, 93 Congolese, and 24 British, who manned the guns. The ship had 14 lifeboats to accommodate 799 passengers and floats, which were designed to carry an additional 2,635, lashed by cables to the open deck. The SS *Cheshire* was

General Chomel, Commander of 25th Division (Fr.) on pocket
of St. Nazaire. Courtesy: The Grand Blockhaus Museum,
Batz-sur-Mer, France.

a similar vessel loaded with approximately the same number of troops and
had a more or less matching crew.

E. P. "Bill" Everhard of Phoenix, Arizona, was a 21-year-old second
lieutenant of Company B, 264th Regiment, 66th Infantry Division
assigned to a cabin that he shared with three fellow officers.[9] It was below
the waterline, crowded, hot, and stuffy. As bad as it was, Everhard said that
it was a palace compared with the troops' compartments. These were converted cargo hatches with wooden floors and steep wooden steps. Ceilings
were low and hammocks were strung four high. Aisles were narrow and

ventilation next to nil. The floors were covered with packs, rifles, duffel bags, and steel helmets. As the convoy got underway, the plumbing in the latrines failed at about the time that the seasickness of the troops began creating a very foul environment. The stormy weather kept the troops mostly confined to these crowded quarters. The atmosphere in these compartments became almost unbearable. Each unit was assigned to an assembly area on deck but there were no drills. Nor were there assignment to lifeboats or rafts.

The HMS *Leopoldville* and SS *Cheshire* left Southampton at 9:00 A.M., December 24, 1944, and joined several other ships, including HMS *Brilliant,* under the command of Captain John Pringle, who was also convoy commander. The water was rough and many were seasick. The severe cold forced most below deck. There was very little room in the aisles, so most soldiers retired to their hammocks and tried to read or sleep. Very few had any interest in meals, and the food wasn't very appealing.

A German U-boat was reported in the vicinity at 2:00 P.M. and the ships began to zigzag. At 5:45 P.M., a navy guard in the crow's nest shouted that he had seen the bubbles of a torpedo passing a few feet from the stern. A second later, he called, "Torpedo to the starboard!" This one would not miss. A torpedo fired from German *U-486* had struck the *Leopoldville* amidship!

Bill Everhard was in his cabin stripped down trying to get some sleep when the terrific explosion threw him out of his bunk (officers' quarters had bunks). An alarm bell began to ring and he and his three cabin mates were scurrying to put on their clothes. Two left and headed topside. As Bill was leaving there was a rumbling roar coming from within the ship. The floor pitched and he was thrown to the deck of the passageway. The cabin door slammed shut behind him with the remaining occupant inside. Water began covering the floor and rose rapidly. The cabin mate was hollering and both were trying to pull the door open. It was jammed and all of the pushing, pounding, and kicking were to no avail. The water rose to Bill's armpits and the lights went out. He could do no more and pulled himself along the ceiling toward the staircase. When he finally reached the stairs he was so numb that he could hardly climb them. He continued to climb until he reached the deck. He never saw his friend again.

Down in the compartments below the waterline on the starboard side, most of the soldiers were in their hammocks sleeping, resting, or trying to allay the seasickness with which so many of them suffered. Suddenly, the torpedo smashed through the steel hull of the ship and exploded. The compartments were obliterated and men smashed against the walls. Steel beams snapped and water poured in, drowning those who remained alive. Staircases were demolished. Cries of the wounded were quickly quieted by the onrushing water. Numerous men risked their lives by going down into these compartments by ropes to try to rescue survivors. Colonel Ira Rumberg, commander of the First Battalion, 264th Regiment, rescued many men, and, although wounded, had himself lowered one last time through a jagged hole to find others. His exhaustion overcame him and he was not able to save himself when the ship began to sink.

Walter Blunt of Company L, 262nd Regiment, was awakened by the explosion and was immediately engulfed in water as the compartment filled and there was total darkness. He gave this account:

> As the water buoyed me up, I felt equipment and objects bumping against me. I heard screams and muffled cries as my head surfaced above the water. I could taste the oil in the water and smell the stench of gunpowder smoke. I was dazed, but aware enough to wonder if I was now doomed to die. My next awareness found me wedged in a hole, which must have been the deck of "E" compartment. My head and part of my shoulders were above the floor but I could not move. I could see right out to the ocean. There were waves washing over me and then there would be a pause. I held my breath when the waves washed over me, but each time the water stayed longer. I thought it was a hell of a way to die. The next thing I knew, there was a light shining down on me and the voice I recognized was Captain H.C. Orr, my company commander. He said, "Give me your hand son, you'll be all right." After a few minutes of pulling and struggling, I was lifted from the hole.

Only one lifeboat left the ship carrying GIs. Blunt was in the boat along with others who had been wounded in the explosion. Seventy-four of the 181 men in Blunt's company were lost and 61 injured.

Away from the explosion area, things were comparatively calm and there was little confusion. Soldiers methodically tried to find their designated area on deck. It was a time of loneliness and despair and most were looking for someone they knew just for the comfort that that might bring. The death and destruction in the area of the explosion was not generally known at this time. Before the torpedo hit, the lights of Cherbourg had already been seen at an estimated distance of six miles. The soldiers were not aware that no one in Cherbourg knew of this disaster. Captain John Pringle, the convoy commander, had sent a message from the *Brilliant* to Portsmouth, England, but it was 45 minutes before his message was sent on to Cherbourg.

One report claimed that Belgian Captain Charles Limbor announced an "abandon ship" order, but it was in French and not understood by the soldiers. The deck lights and public address system were still operational, but little information was issued. The GIs continued to try to find their designated areas, but few reached them. The crew was running about and the order to "clear the deck" and "make way for the crew" was repeated many times. The GIs dutifully did so. Just before the lights and public address system failed, it was announced that they would be towed to port. The ship had drifted to within three miles of Cherbourg and the lights were more prominent, so the GIs took comfort and few realized that the ship was in real trouble. During the next hour, little information was circulated and the crew members began putting their personal gear in the lifeboats and lowering them into the water. The GIs thought that this was some sort of plan to begin evacuation by filling lifeboats and launching them, but they were sadly mistaken. The plan was to desert the ship and this they did. They used all of the available lifeboats and saved themselves. The GIs then tried unsuccessfully to loosen and remove the life raft tie-down cables but could not. No crew was there to help them.

Pete Wood of Bethesda, Maryland, related later that the soldiers actually cheered when the crew began to remove the lifeboats and put them into the water, as they thought it was for their benefit, but the cheering stopped when they realized the boats were launched for the crew only. Wood added that a very special event happened after that. A soldier began singing "The Star Spangled Banner" and others joined in until hundreds of soldiers on the deck followed, some not knowing the words and some not knowing how to sing, but all were trying. This occurred at a time when the lifeboats and rafts were snarled and the crew was abandoning the ship. Pete Wood still chokes up when he remembers.

The ship began to list badly. Everhard was convinced that it was going to sink. The British destroyer *Brilliant* came alongside and its captain called, "You are sinking fast, save yourselves." Everhard related, "This was the only 'abandon ship' ever heard. Some men never found life jackets. Others had discarded them during the long wait on deck. Now they wanted one. It was then that I finally saw a man from my platoon, a very young boy, sobbing and scared to death. I can see his face still. I tried to reassure him. He cried, 'I don't know how to swim.' I gave him my life jacket. I never saw him again. He was among the missing."[10]

Usually, in any kind of emergency situation or some situation caused by the unexpected, soldiers of the same company or platoon try to join some of their group at a designated area. The decks were so crowded and the confusion so great that very few units, even small as a squad, got together. When personal accounts were requested of survivors in 1999 and 2000, it was amazing how fresh this story was in their minds and the detail with which each survivor told his story. Most all of them are 77 years or older. One of the few accounts from soldiers who survived the sinking of the *Leopoldville* where a group known to each other stayed intact during the darkness and confusion came from Bill Moomey of Kearney, Nebraska. It was a very detailed letter from Bill Loughborough to his wife, both now deceased, that Loughborough sent to Moomey during an exchange of information. Until the censorship was lifted, the families of those who died were only informed that their family member was "missing in action." They were told nothing of this tragic event. A condensation of the letter is as follows: There was a group of soldiers from the weapons platoon, Company E, 262nd Regiment, who decided to go on deck and get away from the foul conditions in the ship. They were Bill Loughborough, Ole Jensen (deceased), Al Salata, George Miller, Hank Andersen, and Jack Yarbrough, all from the mortar section, and Bill Moomey from the machine gun section. They split up at one point with Andersen, Yarbrough, and Miller going to another deck. The remaining four stayed on "C" deck. Jensen went to the rail and threw up and just as he returned to the group, a terrific explosion occurred and a large piece of metal flew across the deck and rail, just where Jensen had been standing moments before.

Immediately after the explosion, in a calm manner, they got to their feet, began adjusting each other's life jackets and Loughborough remarked, "It looks like we've been hit." They then went back to the rear of "C" deck and met up again with the other three of the original group. They were all worried about the conditions in Compartment F-4, where their platoon had been assigned. Moomey was especially concerned, as he had not seen any other members of his machine gun section on deck. They knew the explosion had come very near their compartment.

According to Loughborough's letter, the group never considered that they were in danger and that the ship would sink. When a tug with British seamen passed by, there were the usual greetings hollered back and forth. There were some remarks and cheers of levity from the soldiers on deck leveled at the ineptness of the crew trying to man the lifeboats.[11]

At about 7:30 P.M., the destroyer *Brilliant* nosed up to their side and they found themselves on a deck not too high above the deck of the destroyer. Someone ordered all of them on that section of the deck to line up and begin jumping to the deck of the *Brilliant*. Still thinking they were safe, no one hurried. All was orderly. One by one they jumped, each calling back and encouraging those on the deck of the *Leopoldville* to jump. They were sent down to the galley and given soup and blankets. They were not aware when the two ships parted. When the news came into Cherbourg later that night that the ship had sunk, they were all appalled, as they fully expected the ship to stay afloat and get completely evacuated. The group of seven had no major injuries but were the sole survivors of the weapons platoon, except for the platoon leader, Lieutenant Donald MacWilliams (deceased—retired from the army as a general).

In his letter, Loughborough mentioned another survivor from E Company who was a runner for the company. He was actually washed out of the compartment, probably by the backwash, and pulled back onto the deck by soldiers who spotted him in the water. His name was McFall and he was a nonswimmer. The ship at this time was listing badly, according to Everhard's account. When the destroyer pulled up alongside, the heavy sea made it very difficult for the two ships to remain together. They would separate and then come crashing back together. Men started to jump, but many mistimed their jump and fell screaming into the sea between the ships. Then the ships would crash back together and crush the men in the water. Some lived but not many. Some men thought about jumping but after seeing bodies in the water, they backed away. The destroyer's crew members were yelling at the soldiers to "Jump, mates!" Lt. Everhard and several other officers assessed the situation and decided when the jump should be made. They then began to line the men up in rows, after advising them to take off their coats and helmets and leave their life jackets on. Lt. Everhard told a few men to stand on the rail and wait for the order to jump. They did so and as each group made a successful jump, more men took their places at the rail.

Some men held back too long before jumping and were lost, but none were lost when they jumped at the time the order to jump was given. Understandably, it was a hard order to obey as the ships were at the greatest distance apart and were just beginning to close when the order was given. Help in organizing the jumpers was plentiful and 10 to 15 men would jump at a time. The crew of the destroyer was lined up at the rail ready to reach for the men as they landed. Some were caught as they fell a little short and grabbed for the destroyer's rail. A couple of men, carrying a man strapped onto a stretcher, came to the rail and an effort was made to throw the stretcher with the soldier on it but the valiant effort failed. After just about clearing this area of the deck, Lt. Everhard and some of his helpers made the jump themselves, which was about 25–30 feet. Many arms and legs were broken during the course of these desperate escapes. Fortunately, some of the stretcher cases that were thrown from the *Leopoldville* to the destroyer were successful. One of the most unusual cases was that of Kenneth Kline of Hatfield, Pennsylvania, as told in his own words:

> When we were hit by the torpedo, I was lying in my hammock on the bottom deck of the hole. I was covered with water instantly. My foot was trapped and something struck me on my head and shoulder. Fortunately, I was able to get free from whatever was containing me and swam to the surface after being submerged a very long period of time. I saw a metal ladder on the side of the hole. I proceeded to the upper deck. Several men on deck gave me a dry blanket. Then I was taken to the crewmen's cabin. Two medics came into my cabin and decided to give me a shot of morphine. I was extremely cold. Sometime later I remember four men carrying me on a blanket down a stairway. On the deck I had my second close call. These four men swung me, unconscious at the time, with very good timing onto the deck of the destroyer, the *Brilliant*. At Cherbourg they found my shoulder was fractured and some bones in my foot were fractured. I had a very short stay in Europe, back to the States in two months. In hospital five-and-a-half months, then back to duty.

Another officer who was very instrumental in directing soldiers to make the jump to the destroyer was Lt. Ben Thrailkill Jr. of Greenville, South Carolina. He was a 2nd Lt. in K Company, 264th Regiment, of the 66th Division. He related the following:

> The torpedo struck close to the engine room about five feet below the waterline where there was a great cluster of troops. Hammocks were stacked four high. The conversion of this ship to a troop ship made mass rescue operation almost impossible since the flimsy walls were weak and a solid blast would seal off any recovery. Heroic efforts were made by many individuals to get the wounded to the ship's hospital. Colonel Ira Rumberg made 8 or 10 trips down a 40-foot ladder and each time brought up two soldiers, one hanging to his neck and the other hanging to his waist. Unfortunately, he did not survive his last trip; just as the ship began to sink. A friend of mine, Lieutenant Washko, and I helped organize troops for a jump to the *Brilliant* on a strictly voluntary basis. Some refused after seeing soldiers miss and fall between the ships. We were able to help quite a few make a successful jump, however. Finally, when the ship started sinking and the water was washing over the deck, we took off our overcoats and helmets, jumped into the water, and swam as fast as we could to clear the suction of the sinking ship. We were separated but both picked up by small boats and survived.[12]

So many of the survivors witnessed events that day that would haunt them the rest of their lives, and many have stated that in all these years not a day goes by without a terrible memory of this "night before Christmas" surfacing again. One comes from a soldier who prefers to remain anonymous:

> On the afternoon of December 24, 1944, I was lying in my hammock placed in a crew hole of a small ship carrying us across the English Channel. Soldiers were getting sick and I had to get some fresh air. To get on the deck, we climbed a wooden stairway that had been installed, converting the cargo hole for troops. A companion was with me and he suggested we go back and get our overcoats. I declined, not expecting to stay too long. I walked over to the railing and waited for him. It was gray cold day. There were some boats escorting us. In just a few minutes, a tremendous explosion shook the boat. A black volcanic eruption was being forced up from the compartment I had just left.
>
> Immediately after the explosion, there was complete silence; no talking, shouting, or yelling. Then all the troops started streaming onto the deck. After sunset we were in complete darkness. The ship began to list. At one time the boat shuddered and there was a muffled sound, which I assumed was a ruptured bulkhead.
>
> A British escort vessel came alongside and illuminated the area. The sea was rough and the boats could not be lashed together. Rope landing nets were unfolded to allow us to climb down and jump to the other boat. The two boats moved together and separated. As I was climbing down, a cruel wave sequence occurred. The small boat started up and suddenly reversed. Two soldiers jumped at this instance and landed in the water. I can still "see" this. Shortly after I got on, the boat headed in, quickly discharged us, and went back for more.
>
> Later I was asked to join a detail to go to a cemetery and try to identify bodies. The bodies were placed in a straight line. I was unable to make any identification. This is another part of the event that I still "see."

Bob Story of Madras, Oregon, carries the memories of seeing his buddies fall between the two ships. "When the torpedo hit, we were thrown out of our hammocks and against the bulwark of the ship. I was dazed and for a time did not know where I was. Soon thereafter, I made my way up to the deck. The *Brilliant* came alongside and we were told to wait until the destroyer was close and on her upward thrust before jumping to her. We would hold onto a rope, swing out over the *Brilliant,* and let go. I prayed, Lord. It seemed like I fell 20 feet before hitting the deck and my feet hurt badly. I remember watching some of my buddies who did not make it to the *Brilliant.* I remember seeing three ropes break under the weight. Two of the three men went down between the ships. I never saw them again. The third buddy landed on the ship."

Finally, the *Brilliant* had to leave. It had taken on about 750 soldiers and during the process had taken a pounding by the two ships smashing against each other. It was reputed to be taking on water itself. Men were still swarming down the side of the *Leopoldville,* trying to get on the destroyer before it left. The water around the ship was teeming with men. The destroyer had to pull away as men were bobbing in the waves and calling for help.

The event was recorded by a member of the *Brilliant's* crew, William E. Clark, Able Seaman Torpedo Man, 23 years old.

> My recollection of that terrible night, Christmas Eve, 1944, is still as clear as the actual happening. I was on watch at the time, being a Torpedo rating. Our other activities were to man the depth charges. We heard the report that the "Trooper" had been hit. The seas were rough, but our captain, Captain Pringle, brought the *Brilliant* alongside, which was no easy task, as we were rising up and down alongside only giving short periods for the troops to climb or jump on board. We tried to break the fall as they jumped by laying our hammocks on the deck, but quite a few damaged limbs when landing.
>
> The most horrifying sight was watching some of the guys sliding down ropes to our lower deck only to be squashed when both boats came together. Around 750 boarded that night, but I will always remember screams of those poor GIs who never had a chance of survival.[13]

From many accounts by survivors who were either left on the sinking ship or were already in the water, the situation at the site was utter chaos. All hope of rescue was vanishing. It was every man for himself. There were hundreds of men still clinging to the ship or bobbing around in the icy water. Hypothermia and exhaustion were beginning to take a toll. Men were praying to God, calling for their mothers, or just hollering in despair. It was now over two hours since the torpedo hit the *Leopoldville.* The ship was only three miles from Cherbourg and there was still no rescue effort from the port. The crew had deserted and there was no authority left to help the GIs. They tried desperately to free cables securing life rafts but could not do so. The situation could not have been worse.

Men began leaping into the sea to get away from the foundering ship. They clustered together in small groups, sometimes clinging to one another. With a frightening hiss of escaping air, the doomed vessel stood almost straight up in the water, stern down and bow up. Spotlights from a few remaining rescue vessels revealed many men still clinging to the ship as it slowly sank into the dark water. Five lifeboats and hundreds of life rafts were still secured to the ship, enough to have saved everyone. Captain Limbor was still on the bridge as the ship disappeared.

As the ship went down, General Donald MacWilliams, formerly First Lieutenant MacWilliams, was caught and started down with the ship. In his own words:

> The ship suddenly leaned and sank and I was taken down with it, having been caught by a stanchion of a life raft. I estimate that I went down 30 to 40 feet before freeing myself. I rose to the surface and credit my survival to the training on the cadet swimming team at West Point where I learned to use oxygen sparingly. I swam to a life raft and a harbor boat approached and threw a line to us. At this time, I spotted a man in trouble and got back into the water and managed to get him back to the raft. I was so weak I could barely climb on the boat. We were taken to hospitals, partially recovered, and then placed in French homes. They were wonderful to us. We were moved to homes because the next day another ship was sunk and the men, many of them badly burned, needed the hospital beds. Later, we were taken to a cemetery to try and identify bodies, very few of which were identified. It was a month before I got back to Company E, 262nd.

Another soldier who got caught and taken down a short distance when the boat began sinking was Frank Gray from Bakersfield, California. He decided not to try a jump to the destroyer, and after it left he soon realized that things were not going well. He related the following:

> The crew lowered lifeboats and departed. We were on our own. The end came suddenly when the starboard rail disappeared under water. I was trapped at first by the rail as the ship was sinking but after frantically struggling was free and in the water. After bobbing about in my life jacket, a large piece of wreckage came by and I was saved for the time being. All around, men were crying for mother and God. Just when I began to think there was no hope, a Coast Guard boat shined a light on me. A sailor threw me a line, which I caught and held onto. I was too weak to help myself and they hauled me on board. I was in the hospital for two weeks with a gash on my forehead and pneumonia. I was finally reunited with K Company.

Fred DeRibas of Summerfield, Florida, took to the water when the ship started down. He got on a lifeboat and was picked up by a navy ship and taken to Cherbourg and ended up in a hospital in England, later to join his company on the St. Nazaire sector. He sent a copy of a letter his company commander, Captain H. C. Orr, wrote to all surviving members of his company in memory of the 73 members of Company L, 262nd Regiment, who died. It is very meaningful and a portion is quoted as follows: "It is believed that numbers of men lost their lives by drowning, caused by the undertow of the sinking ship and ice cold water. Others were probably killed by debris and wreckage floating on the churning water. Literally hundreds of ships searched the area of the sinking for a radius of more than twenty miles. This search continued for more than a week. A total of 753 men and officers [later changed to 802] lost their lives. Seventy-three of these men were members of Company L, 262nd Regiment, of which bodies of 18 enlisted men and one officer were recovered and buried at Saint Mere Eglise, in Normandy, France. It was believed that the remainder went down with the ship."

First Sergeant C. P. Wood of Cathedral City, California, described the scene:

The ship began to settle by the stern. We threw a rope over and a couple of men started down the side of the ship. By the time my turn came, the water was at my feet and I just dove head first off the rail. Up until then, I thought I was a good swimmer, but I soon found that no matter where you want to go, the waves made the final decision. Funny thing about swimming, one boy in the company jumped overboard, swam to a tug, climbed aboard, and helped the crew. I know he had never been able to swim a stroke before. Others, good swimmers, were lost. I swam away from the ship as fast as I could. I wanted to get away from the crowd of men in the water. Some would grab onto anything near them, making it hard to stay afloat. I tried to get on a life raft one of the tugs had dropped, but again there were too many men. I finally found a hand-hold on a rubber raft, enough for one hand. We floated around a long time listening to the cries of men. The tugs were floating through the men, picking up everyone they could grab. One finally came near us. I was lucky and grabbed a line. I had myself halfway out of the water but could go no further. My hands were so cold I couldn't grip the line. A couple of men grabbed me, pulled me over the rail, and rolled me over out of the way on deck.

Meantime, the *Brilliant* was on its way in to Cherbourg and Colonel Richard Lee, Harbor Entrance Command, was on the shore watching. He reported that Captain John Pringle on the *Brilliant* signaled "coming in with survivors." Lee asked "Survivors of what?" Pringle then signaled the message "want assistance." Lee, thinking the *Leopoldville* might need a tow, sent out a tug and later a PT boat, one of which radioed back that the *Leopoldville* was sinking. This was the first news that anyone in Cherbourg had received about the disaster just three miles away; it was three hours after the attack. All available craft were sent, but the ship went down before they arrived. Darkness and choppy water made the rescue efforts very difficult. Some men had been clinging to debris for an hour before they were picked up, an inordinately long time in such cold water. Those who had drifted away had to wait even longer. For many, it was too late.

Lieutenant William Thompson from Marion, South Carolina, was in his room gathering his belongings and getting ready to disembark when the explosion occurred. He, like others, tried to rescue as many soldiers as possible. Two hours went by and no ship had appeared to tow them into the harbor. No instruction had been given to abandon ship. When he realized the ship was sinking, he moved to the starboard side near the middle where many soldiers were waiting. He encouraged them to get into the water and clear the ship, which many did. He swam out and held on to a hatch with several other men and later found a raft. He had a flashlight and shined it into the cockpit of a small rescue boat. The boat came over to them, but because of the tide and the current, they were almost swept into the propeller. They flagged the boat off to clear them and fortunately another came by, which he signaled with his flashlight. The boat had tires over the side, so they were able to climb up to the deck. Lt. Thompson was credited with saving approximately 15 men, who were hopelessly tossing in the sea, by pulling them on to the raft. He was awarded the Bronze Star for valor.

Kenneth Carr from Dowagiac, Michigan, like many others on the *Leopoldville,* was asleep in his hammock and abruptly awakened by the loud explosion of the torpedo. He landed on a table below him. He put on a life preserver and headed up to the deck. There was a dead man on the stairway, probably killed by the concussion. Carr says that there was no panic even though the crew could be seen heading for the lifeboats with suitcases. He decided not to try to jump to the destroyer, as he had seen some men try and miss. When the ship began sinking, he slid into the water and swam to a harbor tug, where he was pulled up to the deck.

Ray Clark from Buffalo, Wyoming, went into the water when the ship began sinking around 8:00 P.M. He was on a life raft for some time, but because of so many men being on it, he left for "open water" and floated and swam like a cork. He was very weak when picked up. A clock on the tug's wall showed 2:00 A.M. He had been in the water for six hours. His clothes were saturated with oil, possibly providing some insulation.

At this time, rescue boats of all kinds and descriptions began to show up to try to pick up survivors who were left in the water. But much was too little too late. The inordinately long time that it took for the news to reach

shore and help to arrive is a tragic blunder that cost the lives of many soldiers unnecessarily. The *History of Naval Operations* reported that over
1,000 men were left afloat (water temperature 48 degrees Fahrenheit)
without life jacket lights, which were on the ship but not issued. This made
the efforts of the rescue crews much more difficult in finding the men in
the water by spotlights and flashlights. For those left in the cold dark
Channel floating around on anything they could find to hold onto, the situation had become desperate. Time was running out, and another hour or
two was going to be too late.

The helplessness of so many men left alone to fend for themselves is
exemplified in a story told by Antonio Martinez from Grover Beach, California. He was on deck talking to a member of his platoon by the name of
Thibault. Thibault was very afraid and told Martinez that he couldn't
swim. They watched men jumping to the *Brilliant* and witnessed a few
falling short, so they decided to stay with the ship. Martinez said,

> I talked to him and told him what to do when he got into the water. I showed
> him how to "dog paddle" with long strokes with both arms and kick both legs
> up and down in rough ocean water. That's the only way I found out; I learned
> this when I was raised by the ocean. I was surprised that he made it that night.
> Later, he was hit on the knee with shrapnel at Lorient, France. I was on a road
> block when they had him and another soldier on a jeep. He did not recognize
> me; he was in shock. The other soldier was hit bad all over with shrapnel.
>
> After I went into the water, I got away from the ship as quickly as I
> could. When I looked back, there were still men on the bow as the ship was
> going down. There were a few life rafts but they were overloaded with men
> hanging on. I got away from the life rafts. I could hear everyone calling for
> their moms and God mostly. I, too, had words with mom and God. The
> water was cold and rough but I kept struggling. I only saw two tugs or res-
> cue boats. They would go right through the duffel bags and bodies, pushing
> them apart. I thought I would go under and get caught on the prop. But the
> boats would just knock you away as they kept moving. I finally got hold of
> a rope hanging on the side of one of the tugs. I tied my legs around and
> wrapped my arms around the rope. Finally a sailor saw me and called to
> another, "We got one more hanging on." They hooked me with a pole and
> both pulled me up and into the boat. I was shaking so bad I could hardly
> talk. I was in the hospital one night and then picked up a new weapon and
> was sent to St. Nazaire.

Keith L. Simmons of Loveland, Colorado, reported: "I took to the water
when the boat began to sink. Finally, after floating around a while, I was
pulled from the water by sailors on a boat. This boat stayed out in the

Channel until 4:00 A.M. Christmas morning looking for the submarine. I can remember being very cold and exhausted."

Walter Beran of Los Angeles, California, entered the water just before the ship sank. "The last thing that I remember was the buoyancy of my life jacket finally taking control because I was sucked into the water pretty badly. I got on top of the water, saw a lifeboat, and made for it. So many men were helpless in the water. There was the continuous moan over the water of men praying and calling for help. There was an amazing amount of noise. Men were trying to attract one another's attention, sometimes having to shout in order to be heard above the normal ocean sound of the wind and waves. Finally, I was pulled on board a small boat, utterly exhausted."

Don Gengler from St. Louis, Missouri, was another soldier who witnessed and reported that the crew lowered lifeboats for themselves and then took off. His statements about the promise of rescue are interesting.

> There were several announcements that a ship was coming out to get us all or tow the *Leopoldville* into Cherbourg. At 8:00 P.M. there was another announcement that everything was going to be okay and a ship to tow us to Cherbourg was on its way. Within 10 minutes, the *Leopoldville* began sinking very fast and it was every man for himself. I climbed over the rail and jumped. I was a nonswimmer and very scared. I grabbed a piece of lumber and held on to it. My life preserver and the piece of wood kept me up. You could hear soldiers crying and praying for help. There was a lot of panic now. Finally, a tugboat came close enough to see me. I was tired and the sailor who reached for me was also exhausted from pulling soldiers onto the boat. He grabbed my hand and said to pull myself up. I don't know how I managed to climb aboard and crawl down to the engine room. I became violently ill. A crew member wrapped me in a blanket. I guess I was in the water for an hour. My watch stopped at 8:15 P.M. I was in the hospital for eight days with pneumonia and cut legs. I was sent back to Company K. My platoon lost 21 of 42 men.

On the same night that the HMS *Leopoldville* and the SS *Cheshire* were approaching Cherbourg, there was heavy traffic to Cherbourg and Le Havre. The German submarine was in place waiting. *Slemish* (Convoy WEGI 14) and *Dumfries* (Convoy MUS71) were sunk by *U 772* close by on the same night. On Boxing Day, the frigate *Capel* was sunk and frigate *Afleck* damaged, both as a result of *U 486*'s torpedoes.

On December 28, 1944, *U 772* torpedoed and sank *Empire Javelin* (Southampton for Le Havre), carrying 1,448 United States infantry. Fortunately, only seven lives were lost. Torpedoed and damaged at the same time were the American Liberty vessels *Arthur Sewal* and *Black Hawk* (Convoy TBC21). The latter was beached and remained a total loss. Both submarines were later sunk; *U-772* by RCAF Squadron 407 on December 30, 1944, and *U-486* by HM *Tapir* off the west coast of Norway in April 1945. There were no survivors from either boat.

Investigation of the sinking of the *Leopoldville* was spotty and seemingly not very productive. The British admiralty's Board of Inquiry, in the secret report of April 1945, made note of the exemplary behavior of the United States troops but went on to say that the ship's officers and crew appeared to have carried out their duties in accordance with the best tradition of the Belgian marine. The only recommendation of consequence they made was to stress the importance of issuing life jacket lights. The whole report was less than three pages and remained classified until the late 1960s.

The United States inspector general, on November 23, 1959, 15 years after the sinking, declassified and released a summary of the report, which had been withheld from the public for "morale reasons." It read in part, "No Official 'Abandon Ship' order was given. If such an order had been given, it is reasonable to believe that fewer men would have been lost. The crew of the *Leopoldville* was negligent in performance of their duties. They were not at their posts instructing passengers, reporting the condition of the ship and launching lifeboats."

General George C. Marshall, when advised by a memo on January 6, 1945, of the details surrounding the sinking, responded in part, "Had this disaster occurred in peacetime, it would have been regarded as a shocking scandal. The loss of life to trained and equipped combat soldiers is all the greater reason for us to take appropriate action and follow through." *It never happened.*

Clive Cussler and his crew located the *Leopoldville* in 150 feet of water near the French coast in July, 1984. Cussler said, "It should be designated as a war memorial. It is still a tomb for hundreds of GIs just like Arlington Cemetery or any other resting place." Fortunately, the French government has made it one.

Arthur Nevala of Greendale, Wisconsin, cited a publication about the *Leopoldville* that punctuates the coverup of this tragic loss. The article was one that Nevala tore out of *Stars and Stripes* (a GI newspaper in the ETO) and tucked away in his prayer book, where it has been for 55 years. It was dated January 25, 1945.

Troop Carrier Sunk: 248 Die, Washington, D.C.

A troopship; carrying more than 2,000 United States soldiers was sunk recently in European waters as a result of "enemy action." Secretary of War Henry Stimson told his press conference today. He said that 248 men were killed and 517 are still listed as missing. He gave no further details. (Unofficial sources in New York said that this was the third troopship carrying American soldiers to the European Theater of Operations to be sunk since the war began.)

The loss of so many comrades delivered a serious, well-trained division to the ETO with a cadre of soldiers intent on revenge.

NOTES

1. Lawrence G. Byrnes, *History of the 94th Infantry Division in World War II* (Nashville: Battery Press, 1982).

2. This is another example of the organized defense that these pockets possessed. This attack ended, as did the German's stopping the advance of the 4th Armored Division at Pont Scorf at the beginning of the ground battle. There was just no way that a limited ground force without a substantial tank, air, and naval artillery force was going to proceed very far. Eventually, any attack without this support would be stopped in its tracks with numerous casualties. This occurred in my own company when an attack was attempted two weeks before the war ended. Fifteen minutes into the attack, our small force was not only stopped but sent into a hasty retreat with numerous members wounded and one of our officers killed. Our small-arms ammunition was expended quickly even though we were carrying extra bandoleers of rifle ammunition. In hindsight, the question was often brought up, "What were we trying to accomplish?" At the time, however, there was just no questioning orders. You just carried them out. There remained a bitterness about this seemingly unwise attack, as we all knew the capabilities of the German mortar and artillery fire that the Germans had banked in these heavily defended pockets.

3. "Dealer's choice." It is of no monumental importance.

4. Lieutenant Maurice Pollono was a sergeant major in the French air force during the battles of 1939–1940 and was decorated for his action against the enemy. He joined the Resistance in Pornic, which is near St. Nazaire; was arrested; and escaped. He became a member of the 1st GMR unit under Lt. Besnier and distinguished himself again in this battle south of the Loire. He is another example of the many brave Frenchmen who could have sat out the rest of the war but chose to re-enter for the honor of their country.

5. It must be realized that soldiers like Yves Bichan went into battle against the Germans with less than a fourth of the supplies, guns, ammunition, and vehi-

cles than the Germans had. Many had less than a week's military training and some of them took uniforms off Germans that they had killed, dyed them, and used them for their own. It was not unusual to see a group with a mixture of uniforms representing several different countries. The same is true for their weapons. They had one objective, and that was to kill as many Germans as they could.

6. The French had absolutely no artillery when they began to force the Germans into the pocket. It was men like Colonel Blanquefort who, through extraordinary effort, gained one gun at a time to persistently build up an effective artillery section.

7. The author had the pleasure of being a guest of the 8th Cuirassiers' 55-year anniversary celebration of the war's end. General Dumas-Delage from Lyon was their president. They have been most helpful in contributing material for this story.

8. Carol Coffee, *From Tragedy to Triumph: An Historical Memoir of the 66th Infantry Division in World War II* (Houston, Texas: Odyssey International, 1999). Company F, 262nd Regiment, was so decimated that each company in the regiment had to contribute men to make a new company.

9. E. P. "Bill" Everhard of Phoenix, Arizona, was a 21-year-old 2nd Lt. in Company B, 264th Regiment. He researched this tragedy exhaustively and his account was published in many newspapers 50 years later on the anniversary of this event after the official record had been declassified. His unedited account is published in *From Tragedy to Triumph* by Carol Coffee. Coffee states, "The accuracy of Everhard's story is attested to by the scores of still surviving veterans of the 66th Division who were on the vessel as the events of his recollection unfolded."

10. Carol Coffee, *From Tragedy to Triumph: An Historical Memoir of the 66th Infantry Division in World War II* (Houston, Texas: Odyssey International, 1999).

11. This same feeling, during the first hour or two following the torpedo explosion "that all was well," was prevalent among GIs. It was only later that those who stayed on the ship realized the grimness of their situation. They were essentially deserted and left on a sinking boat with no instructions.

12. Ben Thrailkill became a member of the South Carolina House of Representatives after the war. He was instrumental in getting Resolution H. 9517 passed April 19, 2000, by the House and concurred on by the South Carolina Senate in honor of the 15 South Carolina soldiers who lost their lives on the *Leopoldville*.

13. Bill Clark is an honorary member of the Panther (66th Division) Veterans Association.

Chapter 8

1945

ENTER THE 66TH INFANTRY (BLACK PANTHER) DIVISION

During the last days of December 1944, the 66th Infantry Division, recently devastated by the loss of many comrades, was undaunted and focused on the job ahead. The 66th relieved the 94th Division at the Lorient and St. Nazaire pockets quickly and efficiently. The transition was completed by January 1, 1945. The 66th Division had been brought to England in November and trained there several weeks in and around Dorchester. On December 23, around midday, orders were given to pack up and get ready to move out of camp and on to Southampton for the trip across the Channel. Most thought the Division was headed for "The Bulge," but to this day that remains questionable. The immediate events thereafter have been recorded. The division quickly regrouped at St. Jacques Airport in Rennes, France, in extremely cold weather and began moving to the St. Nazaire and Lorient pockets by truck. Many of the men who were plucked from the frigid waters of the Channel found themselves entering combat several days later. Many others were still in hospitals in France and England, some of whom rejoined their companies following recovery. It was ironic that they were pitted against the Germans who were defending the submarine bases from which the U-boat that sank their ship was probably based.

The situation that existed at St. Nazaire and Lorient when the 66th began to relieve the 94th during late December was a fairly static line, with

Table 8.1
66th Infantry Division

The division's insignia is a black panther's head on a circular orange background within a red border. The black panther was chosen to symbolize the attributes of a good infantryman: ability to kill, be aggressive, alert, stealthy, cunning, agile and strong.

Command and Staff

Commanding General	26 Nov 44	Maj. General Herman F. Kramer
Assistant Division Commander	26 Nov 44	Brig. Gen. George J. Forster
Artillery Commander	26 Nov 44	Brig. Gen. Francis Rollins
Chief of Staff	26 Nov 44	Col. John W. Keating
Assistant Chief of Staff G-1	26 Nov 44	Lt. Col. Elisha A. Crary
Assistant Chief of Staff G-2	26 Nov 44	Lt. Col. Edmond M. Rowan
Assistant Chief of Staff G-3	26 Nov 44	Lt. Col. Kelsie L. Reaves
	24 Jan 45	Capt. Frederick W. Gilbert (Acting)
	5 Feb 45	Lt. Col. Kelsie L. Reaves
Assistant Chief of Staff G-4	26 Nov 44	Lt. Col. Harold W. Browning
Assistant Chief of Staff G-5	23 Feb 45	Maj. James P. Brown
Adjutant General	26 Nov 44	Lt. Col. Henry C. Springer
Coommanding Officer, 262nd Infantry	26 Nov 44	Col. Leander D. Syme
Commanding Officer, 263rd Infantry	26 Nov 44	Col. Frederick L. Knudsen
Commanding Officer, 264th Infantry	26 Nov 44	Col. James R. Hamilton

Compostion

262nd Infantry	366th Medical Battalion
263rd Infantry	66th Division Artillery
264th Infantry	870th Field Artillery Battalion (105 Howitzer)
66th Reconnaissance Troop	871st Field Artillery Battalion (105 Howitzer)
(Mechanized)	872nd Field Artillery Battalion (105 Howitzer)
266th Engineer Combat Battalion	721st Field Artillery Battalion (105 Howitzer)

Special Troops

766th Ordinance Light Maintenance company	Military Police Platoon
66th Quartermaster Company	Headquarters Company
566th Signal Company	Band

Attachments

Antiaircraft Artillery

Fr 125th AAA Gp Forces Terrestres Anti-Aeriennes Cavalry	1 Jan 45–23 May 45
15th Cav Gp	1 Jan 45–17 Feb 45
15th Cav Rcn Sq	1 Jan 45–17 Feb 45
101st Gp	1 Jan 45–17 Feb 45
116th Cav Rcn Sq	1 Jan 45–17Feb 45
Fr 17th Bataillon de Chasserus Portes	1 Jan 23–May 45
Fr 19th Dragoons	1 Jan 45–23 May 45
Fr 1st Hussards	1 Jan 44–23 May 45
Fr 8th Cuirassiers	1 Jan 44–23 May 45
115th Cav Gp	10 Feb 45–24 Apr 45
104th Cav Rcn Sq (-Tr A)	21 March 45–29 Apr 45
107th Rcn Sq	31 Mar 45–24 Apr 45
106th Rcn Tr (106th Div)	15 Apr 45–15 May 45

Table 8.2
Twelfth Army Group Costal Sector Chain of Command

Headquarters, Twelfth Army Group Coastal Sector
Headquarters, 66th Infantry Division Chateaubriand, France
Major General Herman F. Kramer, Commanding

Lorient East Sector	St. Nazaire North Sector	Lorient West Sector	St. Nazaire S. Sector
Headquarters, Vannes, France	Headquarters, vic. Héric, France	Headquarters, vic. Plouay, France	Headquarters, Nantes, France
Brig. Gen. Borgnis-Desbordes (Fr.), Comdg.	Brig. Gen. George J. Forster, Commanding	Brig. Gen. Francis W. Rollins, Commanding	Brig. Gen. Chomel (Fr.), Commanding.
Vilaine Subsector	St. Etienne de Montluc Vilaine Subsector	Syme Subsector	Bourgneuf Subsector
South Subsector	Fay de Bretagna Subsector	Hamilton Subsector	Port St. Père Subsector
East Subsector	Blain Subsector	Jourteau Subsector	
Center Subsector	Fégréac Subsector	Leita Subsector	
Plesse Subsector			

both sides firmly entrenched in dugouts, foxholes, and bunkers—all of which were well fortified and protected by mines and booby traps. Both sides had formidable artillery units with many targets zeroed in, resulting in rapid delivery of fire when called for. The use of tanks was uncommon. Firefights and artillery duels were frequent. The St. Nazaire pocket spanned the mouth of the Loire River. When the 66th Division took over, there were some 28,000 Germans contained there who fought bitterly to protect the 14 submarine pens located there. They were commanded by General Werner Junck, who had supplied the port with large quantities of food, water, gasoline, and ammunition. Formidable reinforced concrete pillboxes had been built and extensive mine fields defended the pocket's perimeter. Hundreds of artillery pieces remained operational, although they had been used extensively against the prior divisions on that sector. The area defended was approximately 683 square miles and still contained 120,000 civilians.

Lorient had been more or less reduced to rubble. Although most of the civilian population evacuated as the bombing began in 1940, there remained 9,000 civilians. Approximately 22,000 Germans defended the city, which contained three newly constructed submarine pens. The area defended was 101 square miles. Lt. General Wilhelm Fahrmbacher, a 57-year-old artillery officer, remained as the commander of the Lorient garrison.

In addition, the Quiberon Peninsula, located between the two major pockets, was occupied with a battery of 340 mm cannon capable of firing a 700-pound shell 21 miles. These guns guarded the entrances to Lorient and St. Nazaire harbors, controlling the Gulf of Morbihan. Belle Isle and Ile de Groix were occupied islands off the coast with small civilian and German populations. Belle Isle had 3,000 civilians and Ile de Groix had 2,100. The German artillery units there helped guard the entrances to the ports. Toward the end of the war, a threatened breakout from Ile de Groix was silenced.

All of these garrisons continued to be well supplied by ships, U-boats, and planes. The U-boats remained operational and secured supplies from Spanish vessels and ports. Some war manufacturing continued in the sub pens—ammunition, cannon, and electric motors.

Operating under the control of the 12th Army Group, the 66th Division took over the mission of containing the German garrisons of Lorient and St. Nazaire and assumed operational command of the French forces in that sector. The Table of Organization as of January 1, 1945, is shown in Table 8.1.

Platoon or company command post, 66th Division. It is unusual to find a combat picture, as cameras were prohibited. Courtesy: The Grand Blockhaus Museum, Batz-sur-Mer, France.

The records show that the 12th Army Group Coastal Sector was divided into four subsections: Lorient West, St. Nazaire North, Lorient East, and St. Nazaire South. These were further subdivided for strategic purposes. The latter two sections employed only French troops and were commanded by French commanders. All French troops within the two American sectors were placed under the operational command of the sector commanders, and the entire area with approximately 44,000 French and American troops was under the command of General Herman F. Kramer, commanding general of the 66th Division. Brigadier General Francis Collins commanded the Lorient sector and Brigadier General George J. Forster commanded the St. Nazaire sector. Division headquarters was at Chateaubriand.

The soldiers of the 66th Infantry Division were ready to fight. They were well trained and fully confident. The tragedy in the Channel had turned them into veterans overnight, and when they went on line, they took their duties very seriously. Noncommissioned officers (non-coms) began patrolling immediately without orders to do so. There was no indiscriminate firing of weapons. Positions were well concealed. They would not be intimidated. It was "payback" time. As soon as the troops went on line, some squad leaders began to go out alone to familiarize themselves with their position or to check out something that worried them. Help was always available if needed. Frank Gray of Bakersfield, California, encountered a group of Germans in a small village that he was reconnoitering by himself. They did not see him, so he sneaked out with a patrol group. The patrol leader shot one of the Germans, but the rest of them opened up with an overwhelming barrage of automatic fire and the patrol had to withdraw. Lt. Colonel Martindale went back the following day with a large combat patrol to search the area for gun positions but encountered no enemy activity.

The Germans knew that a new division had taken over, and on New Year's Eve 1944, they opened up all of their guns, probably in an effort to draw fire, which would expose positions. With a lot of equanimity, the GIs of the 66th sat it out and let them shoot. However, it was notable the next morning that most soldiers were digging their positions a little deeper.

Early on, great respect was gained for the accuracy of the Germans' 88 millimeter cannon. It had a flat trajectory and was reputed to be aimed much like a rifle. Any exposure would invite a round or two within seconds. Norman Hohn from Holden, Massachusetts, was a combat jeep driver with multiple duties. He was charged with hauling ammunition from the Division Headquarters to the front lines and was also assigned to Company F, 262nd Regiment, as a driver for Captain Crane. The latter involved making reconnaissance (recon) runs to all areas of the company deployment, oftentimes having to cross an exposed area under enemy observation. This usually precipitated a few rounds from the German 88 quickly and with deadly accuracy. The drivers knew when to hit the gas and out run the 88. Charles MacCaskill, formerly from Camden, South Carolina, was also a jeep driver and gave a similar account. MacCaskill said he soon learned where the hot spots were and raced across them as fast as the jeep would go. These jeep drivers also faced the hazard of a thin wire stretched cross the road intended to severely injure or decapitate the driver. A vertical piece of angle iron welded to the front bumper did much to solve this problem.

Donald Katt from Springdale, Michigan, told of walking back for rations and having the 88s fire on him. This was a story often told. It was uncanny how individual soldiers would be observed even though they tried to keep cover. Eugene Rasmussen from Anaheim, California, related that a man in his company was killed by an 88 round in their mess area and it was believed that the Germans must have picked up the reflection of his mess gear in the sun, as he was a little apart from the group in a non-wooded area.

Maurice O'Donnell of Grand Blanc, Michigan, was giving covering fire with his squad along a hedgerow for a platoon-sized attack on some German gun positions. He was on the far end of the hedgerow firing his Browning Automatic Rifle (BAR). The German artillery fired on the group quickly and effectively. The squad was called in when their ammunition was depleted. O'Donnell had to run the length of the hedgerow and swore that a German 88 dropped shells right behind him all the way.

O'Donnell had another near miss when covering an advancing patrol sent out to capture a prisoner. He was positioned on a small ridge and could see several Germans with machine guns and another with a knee mortar. When a firefight started between his group and the Germans, he opened up with his BAR. The German with the knee mortar picked up his position and sent two rounds, which landed just over and just under him. He heard the "whump" of the third round and literally froze with fear, waiting for it to complete its trajectory. It landed only a few yards from him just on the downside of the ridge. Although he was showered with snow and dirt, he was not injured.

Keith Simmons from Loveland, Colorado, and his squad were on a patrol when fired upon and took cover in a cellar of a destroyed house. After 5 or 10 minutes, he went up to try to spot the German's position. An 88 fired at him, the shell coming close enough to explode behind him and wound him. It was his opinion that the Germans actually bore-sighted the gun and fired directly at him, as one would fire a rifle.

The Americans were not alone on this front. French troops totaled approximately 1,200 officers and 28,900 enlisted men. They were part of the FFI and FFO commanded by General Larminat, whose deputy, General Marchand, commanded all French forces in the 12th Army Group Coastal Sector. It was not unusual to see a combined combat patrol of American and French soldiers carry out a successful mission. The American commanders did everything possible to support these French units.

The fighting was very difficult against these German forces with their "hold or die" orders. First of all, the months of January and February 1944 were bitter cold, with much snow and sleet. It was the coldest winter in Europe in many years. Second, the Germans were well dug in with trenches and strong points surrounded by large mine fields, barbed wire, booby traps, and clear fields of fire. Most of their positions were in hedgerows, as were ours. Many of these German soldiers were seasoned veterans who had survived earlier campaigns. They were tough and not inclined to surrender. The terrain was crisscrossed with hedgerows and ditches. The German artillery and mortar fire was extremely accurate and their units had the Allied line zeroed in at all points. The hidden positions of the Germans posed a great threat, as a patrol could virtually encounter one with no telltale signs of its existence. Arthur Wagner of Ramon, California, was leading a squad raiding an enemy area. When the patrol encountered small-arms fire, the lead scout advanced to try to take out a machine gun holding up their advance. He fell seriously wounded five feet from the gun. The enemy flanked the patrol on both sides and Sergeant Wagner ordered the greater part of the patrol to withdraw so as to keep a corridor open. He placed two men to cover him and he moved forward to rescue the wounded scout. Despite much enemy fire, he reached the wounded soldier and with much difficulty dragged him back to the squad's position. He then stayed to cover the withdrawal of the patrol. He was awarded the Silver Star.

Stanley H. Reuter from Vancouver, Washington, related an experience often encountered. His platoon was sent deep into enemy territory and began to sustain intense small-arms and mortar fire. He said that even though he was flat on the ground, bullets were hitting leaves on a bush next to his head. He managed to crawl into a small trench where two of his patrol had already sought cover and succeeded in calling in three more of their platoon. After being pinned down for some time, they finally made it back, although they left two behind. Each platoon and company sent out patrols constantly, and, even though there was a price to pay, reconnaissance was so thorough that the enemy rendered few surprises.

The terrain was not well suited for tanks, and the mine fields were so extensive that they were not used very often for platoon or company strikes. Keith Simmons described one of the few times the tanks were used:

Company I, 262nd Regiment, was to stage a sneak attack on the Germans to our front. Technical Sergeant George Chun Fat, who was a Hawaiian and platoon sergeant for the First Platoon, was to lead the attack, which would be supported by my squad and Gene Stout's [Pennsylvania] squad from the Third Platoon. Sgt. Chun Fat was all man, weighed 135 lbs., but such an expert in hand-to-hand combat that he could subdue even the biggest man in our company.

The attack was to be supported by three Sherman tanks and was to jump off at dawn on a Sunday morning and was supposed to be a complete surprise to the Germans. As the tanks came up, all thoughts of a surprise attack went out the window as the screeching and squealing was ear splitting. Not only was there a lot of shouting back and forth between tanks, but also between tanks and infantry. The tanks led with the infantry behind them, one squad behind each tank. No sooner had they pulled out than the machine pistols ["burp guns"], machine guns, mortars, and artillery began to thwart their advance. The cannon fire and our own mortars joined in. A violent fight lasted for about 15 minutes.

Two of the three tanks made it back. The third tank fell through the roof of a German emplacement and the crew could not get it to budge, so set it on fire to deny it to the enemy and retreated. Sgt. Chun Fat brought back two prisoners. Three soldiers were killed and eight others wounded. The support squads were never committed, which was fortunate, for their men would have suffered the same fate in such a violent attack on a well-entrenched defensive position. Sgt. Chun Fat was awarded the Bronze Star for his bravery and heroism.[1]

During the research of this campaign, it was noted that the 104th Cavalry Squadron was attached to the 66th Division. What did a cavalry unit do in a static war of this kind? Reconnaissance was done by ground infantry patrols. Tanks operating in small numbers on this front were quickly eliminated by German artillery. Arnold Heinold of Hastings, Minnesota, and a member of the 104th Cavalry Squadron gave this report:

The 104th Cavalry Squadron relieved the 107th Cavalry Reconnaissance Squadron on April 2, 1945. The squadron was immediately dismounted and given an infantry mission to contain the Germans in the St. Nazaire pocket near Blain. All of the 250 armored and reconnaissance vehicles of the squadron were parked in a tactical motor park in Foret de Gavre, a large forest near Blain. Members of the squadron manned strong points, pillboxes, dugouts, and outposts along a 1,500-yard front, which in normal situations would be covered by a much larger force. The front extended along the Brest-Nantes Canal. The psychological adjustment that the troopers made was exemplary, as without training they were suddenly converted from fast moving cavalry "on wheels" to doughboys "digging in." They realized the necessity for holding each position, as the loss of one would jeopardize the whole squadron. Artillery and mortar fire was well organized. Constant liaison between a United States battalion on their left and a French battalion on their right was maintained.

Heinold related that on the night of April 10, 1945, an enemy patrol of 100 men with 40 in reserve crossed the canal and penetrated their line. At 0600, the morning of April 11, the Germans opened an intense artillery barrage against them and this was followed by an assault on the squadron's positions. The assault lasted until approximately 0800 when the German patrol became disorganized by Allied artillery. Approximately 700 rounds of enemy and friendly artillery had fallen in Troop C area.

The 104th sustained few casualties, as they stuck to their defensive positions and gained some valuable experience. They realized that although their mission was a defensive one, it was not going to be easy. On April 20, the Squadron Commanding Officer was informed that 107th Reconnaissance Squadron was being withdrawn; this stretched their line of defense immeasurably. Rear echelon personnel from all troops were brought forward and indoctrinated as infantry. The tank company was released from division reserve and helped to fill the gap.

During the remainder of April, there was a consistent daily shelling by the enemy. Patrol activity continued. Lt. Richard Bell was killed on April 28, 1945, by small-arms fire while leading a patrol along the canal in the Troop F area. During the month of April, the squadron fired 5,646 rounds of 75 mm Howitzer ammunition, 653 rounds of 60 mm mortar ammunition, and 531 rounds of 81 mm mortar shells.

Another unit that was quickly sent from England to join the 66th Division and converted to infantry was the 283rd Engineer Combat Battalion. It was originally headed for "The Bulge." Jack Kurtz from Charleston, South Carolina, was a member of the 283rd and furnished a copy of its history, from which the following was abstracted.

The unit was alerted suddenly while in England to head for France. Many of the men were on leave and all of them could not be found. The departure of the unit was so sudden that many were left behind to find transportation to Europe, usually in small groups. One truck convoy was headed to Southampton, and a truck from some other outfit going somewhere else slipped into the lead of their column during the darkness. The lead truck of the 283rd continued to follow this newcomer and the whole convoy found itself way off track the next morning. Other groups ran into problems in their odyssey to get to Europe and then find their outfit. One soldier, Swideriski, got in the line to wash his mess gear, followed those soldiers onto the wrong boat and ended up in Le Havre instead of Cherbourg where his unit had landed. A week later and after miles of hitchhiking in France, he finally found them. A small truck convoy went to Nancy instead of to Nantes and had to reverse its course and travel all the way back across France. Not much fun in cold snowy weather in the back of a truck. *C'est le guerre.*

The battalion was diverted to Brittany to aid the 66th Division and its members were to be converted to infantry. At first they were placed in reserve, and, after several weeks of accelerated infantry training, the trucks, air compressors, and tractors were left behind and they filed out of their bivouac area to relieve a battalion of the 262nd Infantry Regiment on the front line. They were infantry now. Their first position was around Caudan and Hennebont on the Lorient pocket. Their training as infantry continued while they were on the line—"On the job training." Officers from field artillery batteries came to their positions and instructed them in calling for artillery fire and how to adjust it to hit the target.

Immediately after taking their positions, patrolling began from platoon and company levels. Their experiences were the same—firefights, patrols pinned down, mortar and 88mm fire, and injured comrades—that other units had endured.

As engineers they were used to blowing up things, so at any time a building was suspected of being an observation point the explosives were loaded on their backs and off they went. The resulting explosions resounded all over the front. The history of their unit contains numerous stories of their patrols.

Finally, in April 1945, the 283rd was ordered to disengage and be replaced on the line. They were sent to Germany where they immediately began to build a pontoon bridge across the Rhine. They had performed magnificently as infantry on the Lorient pocket. (The conversion of these units to infantry was going on all over the ETO and documents the man-power shortage that the Allies were facing during the last months of the war.)

The defensive line of containment around the two pockets was a very thin line with a paucity of units in reserve. With any organized effort the Germans could have broken through, but, of course, without vehicles in number and a supply line, they would be stopped by the Allies bringing in other units, which were in reserve. The average battalion front for the 66th Division was three miles. Front-line infantry units were organized into strong points with four to eight men at each position. Usually, these were placed anywhere from 50–200 yards apart. A squad, if near full strength, ordinarily was responsible for two or three positions. Because of the loss of so many men in the Channel and general combat attrition, it was unusual to find a 12-man squad.

They usually dug into a hedgerow or into ground adjacent to the hedgerow. Outposts and listening posts were placed at intervals in front of the main line in an effort to detect any enemy infiltration, so that the main line could be alerted in case of an attack. Because of the thin line, a mobile reserve force was maintained to rush to any segment of the line threatened by an attack.

   The outposts were lonely duty. Some of them were only manned at night
with just two soldiers, while others were home for three or four soldiers
who had to maintain an extremely low profile with little or no movement
during the day. George Lizanich from Parma, Ohio, told of his and a platoon member's experience on an outpost one dark stormy night, which
shows how one's imagination, fear, and, finally, humor react in seemingly
the worst of situations. Actually, this same tale could be repeated by many
other GIs.

> On a cold snowy night in Brittany, Private Jonathan ("Lum") Edwards from
> Union, South Carolina, and Browning Automatic Rifleman George ("Zeke")
> Lizanich were paired for outpost duty. It was "no-man's land" between friend
> and enemy. The camouflaged outpost was in a corner of two hedgerows over-
> looking a valley of trees. The only tie with the front line was the sound phone.
> Throughout the night, we took turns listening through the phone's receiver for
> the low whistle from other outposts or from platoon headquarters. The snow
> was coming down pretty heavily and visibility was limited. During the day
> the area had received heavy artillery shelling, which caused a lot of damage
> to trees. We began to hear sounds of breaking branches. As the night went on
> it was harder to distinguish where the sounds were coming from and what
> they were. It could have been branches breaking, animals moving, or the Ger-
> mans.
>   Time passed slowly and the trees in the distance began changing shape
> as the snow and the tension mounted. Our minds started playing tricks. The
> sound power phone went completely silent. How long had it been before
> they had heard a signal? Had the line been cut? Was the next outpost intact?
> They decided to risk it and sent a signal. No response. They suddenly heard
> a very loud crash. Thinking the Germans were advancing, they fired a red
> flare to warn the front line that there was trouble and they were headed back,
> FAST!

   Later in the clear light of day, to their relief and amusement, they found
out a large tree branch had fallen very near their outpost. So many times at
night the tension was high, voices became shaky, and imaginations were at
their maximum. Dawn was always a welcomed event but sometimes
seemed it would never come.
   It was no wonder that tension increased during the dark hours. Germans
were very aggressive with patrols at night, when they would pinpoint a
position and then approach it by stealth to a distance of a few yards before
attacking it. They knew there was probably one man awake and on duty
and they could wreak havoc before the others could respond. Fred
Martschink of Charleston, South Carolina, had an unusual experience of

GI reconnaissance patrol on the outskirts of Lorient. Courtesy: Hotel de Ville, Lorient, France.

this kind while he was on duty at a four-man position on the line at about first light early in the morning. There was a hedgerow coming straight at his position, which was on the corner of two hedgerows coming together at a right angle. Coming down the hedgerow toward him was a very huge German who was moving slowly and standing straight up, which is unusual when on a patrol. When he was about 20 yards away, Martschink challenged him. The German seemed not to have heard him and slowly kept coming. Again, at about 15 yards, Martschink challenged him but to no avail. He seemed almost like a robot or under some kind of drug. One more time he was challenged, and, since he kept coming, he was shot and killed. On him was a diagram of all the positions on that segment of the line and numbers that were interpreted as the number of people in each position. He also was carrying a large number of grenades and some dynamite.

Elbert Nickells from Lateon, California, had a rude awakening at 0615 one morning when he was asleep in his dugout. He heard shooting just outside the entrance, grabbed a Browning Automatic Rifle, and ran out to find one of the men on guard killed and the other wounded. He was confronted by a raiding party of five Germans who opened fire on him from 25 yards. He killed one, wounded another, and caused the remaining three to flee. He then engaged another group with the help of the wounded comrade and they dispersed them also, thus aborting the German attack. He was awarded the Silver Star for his quick and valiant action.

Elmer Nicholson Jr. from Tucson, Arizona, says that his company was near a small abandoned village on the St. Nazaire sector with one of their machine guns set up in a partially destroyed house. The Germans discovered their position and one night tossed concussion grenades into the house and captured the lot of them with the exception of one man who crawled up the chimney and braced himself from slipping until they were gone.

The 66th Infantry Division thrived and stayed alert with frequent ambush patrols for prisoners to interrogate, reconnaissance patrols to learn more about gun positions, and combat patrols to knock out some fortified areas. The ambush patrols were always tough, as the German soldiers in the pockets had been indoctrinated in a no-surrender policy. It was uncommon for German soldiers to surrender voluntarily, but there were a few incidents where they did. Ray Clark of Buffalo, Wyoming, reported that late one afternoon while getting ready to go on patrol, he and other patrol members saw some movement in a wooded area in front of them. Four German soldiers with a white flag came out and advanced to Clark's position. They were blindfolded and taken back to the company command post for interrogation.

But voluntary surrender was very uncommon. Even when ambushed, most Germans fought back bitterly. Henry West (deceased) of Epping, New Hampshire, had such an experience when a firefight broke out at close quarters during an attempted ambush. Two squads went out to set up an ambush early one morning at an abandoned chateau that, according to G-2 (Army Intelligence), the Germans were using for an observation post. Shortly after daylight a German patrol came into the back of the chateau grounds. There was a break in the hedgerow, and the squad leader waited until the lead member of the patrol traversed this break and then stood up and challenged him at a distance of about five yards. There were several other members of the patrol behind him who West could see but who were hidden from the squad leader by brush. One of the Germans carefully raised his machine pistol and was going to shoot the squad leader through the hedgerow brush at a distance of about eight yards. West immediately shot the German with his Browning Automatic Rifle and a firefight erupted. West was shot in his hip. He had crossed the small road to get a better field of fire on the Germans. Mortar fire was called for by the squad leader. He signaled the remainder of the patrol to fall back as he, West, and Roy Davis were isolated and pinned down. The mortar was walked in on the Germans' position and Davis and the squad leader covered each other until Davis got close enough to run across the road and snatch West, who could not walk. The squad leader raked the top of the hedgerow to keep the Germans down. He then maintained a rear guard until West and Davis could go down the hedgerow leading back to their line, and then he, too, retreated. Both West and Davis were awarded the Silver Star.[2]

Bob Carroll from Rock Island, Illinois, saw a German patrol approach his position during first light on two consecutive mornings. They stopped short, stayed about 15 minutes, then retreated. He thought they were probably reconnoitering the area for American positions with the intent of coming back at night and destroying them. With the four men he had on his position, he set up on the corner of three hedgerows, placing himself on the one the Germans had approached, another squad member by himself on another, and two new replacements together on the other. Right on time, the Germans came but, unfortunately, down the hedgerow to the corner where the two new men were. The Germans got all the way to the corner, not five yards from his two men. He became very anxious and seeing what was going on, ran down toward them, keeping cover. The Germans saw him coming and took off. He got off a few shots and one fell but got up again and went on. He approached his two men (both just 18 with three months of basic training and one week on the line) and asked them, "What in the hell happened?" One of them, still pale with fear said, "Sergeant, we are really sorry but when they got real close, we just crawled up into our helmets." Carroll said that even though he was angry and bitterly disappointed, he could hardly keep a straight face.

The individual front-line soldier learned early to live as animals lived, to stay quiet and burrow into the ground or hedgerow. The object was to expose as little to the enemy as possible. An article that would reflect sunlight, such as a watch, dog tags, or insignia, was covered or removed. One reason that casualties remained reasonably light was due to the discipline of the troops in maintaining cover at all times.

Movement during daylight hours was kept to a minimum. On patrols, even at night, the men always followed hedgerows or ditches—never an open field. Small-arms fire was used only when essential, as the enemy could pinpoint this from their line by having different positions give the direction and approximate distance of fire. Allied units did the same. Also, no vehicles were allowed near the front line. All inspections were done on foot.

Wally Merza from Chicago, Illinois, gave a good example of the "costly mistake of exposure." Fortunately, it was committed by the Germans. Sergeant Merza and his squad were in a forward observation post in an abandoned German bunker. One day, just at dusk, they saw smoke coming from a German position. The Germans had started a fire to keep warm, but, unfortunately for them, they did it before it was completely dark. Sergeant Merza gave a good estimate of the position on a grid map and called for artillery. The first and second rounds were close but not on target. Adjustments were made and the third round was dead center on the target. Carelessness was costly. Merza added that the training and discipline of the 66th Division soldiers were such that he was impressed with the cleanliness around each position and the paucity of telltale signs. Surely, this saved many lives.

Any noise or light at night was prohibited, as they carried long distances and invited artillery and mortar fire. No one was allowed to posses a camera or write in a diary for fear of capture and possible information that a diary or photos might disclose.

Patrols were sent out in the evening after dark and early in the morning before daylight. Reconnaissance patrols were usually four to eight men with one radio. The mission was to avoid contact. The patrol was usually led by a squad leader or the platoon sergeant. Combat patrols usually numbered 20–30 men with at least one-third carrying automatic weapons. The mission was usually to capture prisoners or to eliminate an observation post or gun position. Radio contact was maintained with the company commander but kept to a minimum.

Night missions were usually reconnaissance patrols but less frequently a combat patrol was sent out to destroy some gun position after it had been well located. Darkness was good cover and surprise was much better executed than during daylight hours. But to avoid too much confusion and error, it was essential to know exactly where the position was located. Joseph Woodring from Poplar Bluff, Missouri, was a member of such a night combat patrol sent to destroy a German machine gun position. When arriving at a designated position near the machine gun, he and two other soldiers moved forward to reconnoiter the next hedgerow. The enemy opened fire and wounded his comrades. He purposefully drew fire to cause the machine gunner to expend his ammunition belt and have to reload. This allowed the two wounded to withdraw. Woodring remained as rear guard until they were safely to the rear, then crawled 125 yards under hostile fire. Although he escaped serious injury, he was struck in the forehead by shrapnel and later was awarded the Silver Star.

Company commanders seemed to have a lot of leeway in managing their sectors. Each company had its own unique way of fighting. Small offensives involving a company or platoon were carried out to advance segments of the company's line to a more advantageous position. The Germans opposed these moves with heavy artillery and mortar bombardment. Don Gengler from St. Louis, Missouri, was a platoon sergeant in Company K, 262nd Regiment, and was on the *Leopoldville*. Following his survival, he was given a new uniform and rifle and then sent back to his company, which was already on line. He remembers the constant artillery fire—night and day. His company sent out reconnaissance patrols, and each time a German position was located, they would regroup, organize a combat patrol (usually about 12 men), and try to take the position. Because of their stealth, these were usually successful but often sustained casualties.

Like many others, Gengler respected the 88mm cannon. There was a dangerous area that members of his platoon had to cross to get supplies and maintain contact with the platoons on the left. A huge camouflaged net was hung so that they could crawl behind it. The Germans had an 88mm set up to shoot anyone crossing the spot. This area was crossed at night, mostly, and the Germans shot at the net with the usual flat trajectory. No one was hit, but the net was constantly being repaired.

Donald Walter from Minerva, Ohio, reported that in his company they formed a group of BAR men and sent them out on seek-and-destroy missions as well as a unit to help rescue other patrols that were entrapped in a firefight. Acting as a secondary or backup squad, they were often successful.

The GIs on this front had a lot of respect for the medics, whose response was always immediate and dedicated. With only the Red Cross on their helmet to protect them, they rescued the wounded and gave them emergency care at the site. An example of their heroic deeds is that of Raoul Claude from Lowell, Massachusetts. On April 19, 1945, he was accompanying a tank-infantry team that attacked enemy positions near La Desertais. He was following behind some tanks when a machine gun opened fire. A soldier near him fell, wounded. At the same time, heavy artillery began to fall, and he covered the wounded man with his own body to keep him protected. While administering first aid, Claude was wounded with shrapnel in his hand and leg. He dragged the wounded man back to the litter bearers 150 yards to his rear. He then went forward again to retrieve another wounded man, again exposing himself to enemy artillery fire. He was awarded the Silver Star for his valiant efforts.

There were many instances when members of a patrol risked their lives to save comrades. Lloyd Haskins from Klamath Falls, Oregon, was on a night patrol in April 1945, when they encountered machine pistol and machine gun fire at close range from their right flank. Sergeant Haskins, realizing that the rear and flank of the patrol were in danger, crawled under machine gun fire to a position on the right. He saw Germans approaching and fired on them until his weapon jammed. At that moment, four more Germans approached him, but he calmly corrected the rifle jam and killed two of them at point-blank range. This dispersed the ambush, and the patrol was able to withdraw without further casualties. Haskins received the Silver Star.

The company command post was usually a half-mile to a mile behind the line, somewhat centrally located to the deployment of the company and sometimes in an abandoned house or in a bunker protected with sandbags. Rarely was it attacked by patrols or small-arms fire, but it did sustain artillery fire. Arthur Nevala from Greendale, Wisconsin, witnessed an unusual event at his company command post. It was typical of the randomness of casualties in combat but is sometimes referred to as the "luck of the draw." Nevala was the company clerk. One day while washing his socks in his steel helmet, he was called to see the company commander right away. While he was responding to the captain's request, a shell came in and hit exactly the spot where he'd been washing his socks. There was just one big hole where his helmet had been a few moments before.

The life of an infantry soldier was the same around the world. The young folks in the winter of 1945 were constantly exposed to the elements, vermin, and frostbite. There was a constant desire to have more food, get warm and dry, get some sleep, and stay alive. Everything else assumed lower priority. The desire to get home was always present, but that could wait. The big disappointments were no letters at mail call or that "Dear John" letter that many a soldier received. It took only a glance at a guy to know that he had received his. The signs were unmistakable and certainly compounded the existing loneliness.

So many things taken for granted before no longer exist in a soldier's world. Sunday dinner with the family, a drive to the drugstore for a cola, a fishing trip—all became dreams, or did they ever really exist? Even thoughts of an apple, an orange, an ice cream cone, and even a box of crackers were frequent, but the desire for such luxuries had to be put on the shelf. It was a situation of being reduced to a very basic existence way down on the totem pole of livability. Trying to get clean, wash some socks, and shave became major problems that could consume several hours.

Living huddled together in holes and bunkers created irritability, but it also produced courage, responsibility to others, unselfishness, and bonds between people that would be stronger than most they would make later in life. As intolerable as life seemed at times, most soldiers were glad to do their part. Morale remained high and humor was not abandoned. No matter how primitive the shelter, it was home, and the GI was imaginative and creative in making little improvements. Not the Ritz, perhaps, but a welcomed haven when coming in from patrol when it was cold or snowing, or as a safe harbor when enemy artillery started. It was a situation where the son of a president of some large corporation might become best buddies with an illiterate from a rural area. Background was out the window. It was what kind of person you were under those trying circumstances that was important. Former mayor of New York Edward I. Koch was assigned to Company F (rifle company), 415th Infantry Regiment, of the Timberwolf Division. He described how the experienced soldiers in his division looked down on the men from the Army Specialized Training Program, calling them "schoolboys," but how the distinction quickly became lost in combat. Koch's company was made up of soldiers from 47 states representing every major religion with IQs ranging from illiterate to near genius. The army homogenized them all. Mayor Koch summed it up all exceptionally well when he maintained that it made no difference what anyone thought at home. This was a new world with new standards. Whether you were handsome, had a lot of girlfriends, or played football counted for nothing. You were judged by one chief measure—whether you could be relied on when the chips were down.

Joseph Billodeau from El Paso, Texas, and Clare ("Willie") Williamson were fast foxhole buddies. After the war, Joe wrote a story on the experiences of "Willie" and "Joe," and on the cover was one of Bill Mauldin's (famous World War Two cartoonist) cartoons of the infamous Willie and Joe that the GIs enjoyed so much. It was well done. A few passages show that a GI doesn't lose his humor, even in combat. Billodeau related: "On alert one night, Willie and Joe heard and saw things that didn't really exist. Really shook up, Willie tossed a grenade that bounced off a tree limb and back into their position, exploded and damn near ended their 'heroic careers.' Joe said that one chance remark by Willie really humbled him on one occasion when they were huddled down in a hole with artillery shells going off nearby. As was usual, Joe was stating the fact that he didn't mind dying but he hated all the crap you had to go through to get there. Then he remarked, 'God you stink Billodeau.' I knew damn well I didn't stink worse than he did. After all, we only got two showers in five months on the line."

Artillery units attached to the 66th Division were especially effective against the German counterpart. The Germans had 240 mm guns on railroad mounts plus an assortment of other large-caliber cannon amassed in the early days of the war to protect their U-boat pens. On the Quiberon Peninsula, there were three 340 mm guns that could send a 700-pound shell 21 miles. Those were turned around from the sea to fire toward land.

The infantry soldier in the 66th was high in his praise of the artillery units. Many of them had been rescued by the units' accuracy and prompt delivery when pinned down on patrol or offensive attack. The artillery was great at laying down smoke to enable a patrol to withdraw from an untenable position.

Charles McWilliams of Danville, Pennsylvania, was on a patrol when they were ambushed and fired upon from a position not more than 15 yards from them. They hit the ground and hollered to the radioman to call back for artillery. A rain of bullets was hitting the hedgerow right above the radioman and they were sure that he was hit. Fortunately he wasn't and got the message off to the artillery, and the patrol got out. It was the radioman's last patrol, because when they were back at platoon headquarters during the critique, it came to light that he was only 15 years old.

At Lorient, forward observers were able to view ships in the harbor. At first their guns were out of range, but with constant maneuvering for better positions, the artillery finally sank 14 vessels. The final prize came when, after much maneuvering, a duel began for the purpose of knocking out the battery, and the guns were finally rendered useless. This was quite a relief for the soldiers who had experienced a barrage from these big guns. Norman Bullett, from Syracuse, New York, reported that one of his worst times was when the Germans turned their big coastal guns toward Allied lines and fired. The huge shells hit the line for 30 minutes and one hit 50 yards from Norman's position, moving the roof of his bunker.

In January 1945, an average of 450 artillery rounds were fired per day against strong points, gun emplacements, patrols, bridges, water purification plants, submarines, garages, and a bakery. Later, when enemy activity increased, over 1,000 rounds per day were fired. Because of the 140-mile front, artillery support could not be given simultaneously to all infantry units, so considerable artillery movement was required based on priorities.

Lorient was turned into a mass of rubble. All water systems were destroyed. A tanker bringing water from Port Louis was sunk. Electric

GIs shelling military targets in Lorient. Courtesy: Hotel de Ville, Lorient, France.

power lines were destroyed. Ammunition dumps were set on fire. The artillery observers had the whole city broken down into sections and could fire upon any location. All daylight movement in Lòrient stopped. Only the submarine pens offered any safe refuge.

On March 31, 1945, the 66th Division was placed under the Fifteenth Army, which took command of the coastal sector of France under the command of General Leonard Gerow. Remnants of the 106th Infantry Division, which had been overrun during the early days of "The Bulge," joined the 66th Division on April 15, 1945.

A German attack near St. Croix was repulsed April 15, 1945. Several strongly constructed enemy positions were taken April 19–29, 1945. The offensive action of the American and French troops escalated greatly that month. Numerous small attacks and combat patrols were launched with the intent of intimidating the Germans in an effort to coerce surrender.

Company E, 262nd Regiment, in early April, launched an assault against some German gun positions. Carl Miller from Barnegat, New Jersey; Willard Howland from Lisle, New York; and Paul Krinock from Latrobe, Pennsylvania, were sent on flank protection as the company began its advance. They carried a light machine gun and a Browning Automatic Rifle. As soon as they opened fire, the Germans discovered their position and bombarded them with artillery and mortar fire. Shrapnel shattered the cover latch on the machine gun, cut the chin strap on Krinock's helmet, and embedded a piece in his helmet. They got the machine gun going again and Krinock, although also wounded in the leg, moved forward and continued to spray in front of a squad that was trapped in a field, allowing them to move back. An officer was killed and about 20 men were wounded. Krinock was awarded the Silver Star for continuing to fire on the enemy, although exposed and wounded.

Another member of Company E was very bitter about this attack, thinking it entirely unnecessary, and did not believe it accomplished anything. He preferred to remain anonymous but said, "At the end of the war in late April, I was told that our mortar squad might be called upon to support some action in front of our position [He was a squad leader.] That was all—just be prepared. Early the next morning, I broke out a few rounds and we waited. During the night, unknown to us, an artillery piece had set up behind us. About three or four rounds were fired and the gun was so close that we felt the muzzle blast at the same time we heard it. After recovering from that surprise, about 30 or 40 minutes later, we received a firing order. I don't know how long we fired or how many rounds were used but the OD [olive drab] paint on our mortar tube turned dark brown, almost black, from the heat. I never learned the reason for the action or if anything was accomplished. I know that one of the platoon leaders, a 2nd Lt., was killed and numerous men were wounded." Another sergeant voiced his objections to this attack and protested its merit before the fact. However, he was a good soldier and carried out his orders. He was wounded during the attack.[3]

Seven days in May saw a decrease in activity, although some German patrols persisted. Around noon on May 7, the troops were notified that all firing would cease at 1300. The troops remained in position and on alert. That night the Germans began a general withdrawal with many explosions to their rear, which was probably ammunition and supplies being destroyed.

The official surrenders were held on May 10 and 11 for Lorient and St. Nazaire, respectively. Two rather unusual events happened to some GIs shortly after the cease-fire was announced. Stanley Ney from Atlanta, Georgia, and a buddy decided that since there was a cease-fire, they would go over and pay their respects to the German soldiers in front of them. They kept walking forward and suddenly they saw a German soldier waving to them to change their course a little to one side, and he hollered

"*Minen!*" It was then that they realized they had done something rather stupid but proceeded on anyway, thinking they were on a safe route, which, it turned out, they were. One of the first things the Germans asked them was whether or not they had any Glenn Miller records. The meeting was friendly and all agreed that it was good the war was over. They returned to their line without further incident.

The second story was more involved and showed that the Germans did have some compassion for their former enemy. When Bruce Newby from Columbia, South Carolina, took a patrol out, they passed through another company then made a turn back to travel parallel to their own company's segment of the line. Suddenly 88 mm rounds started falling 100 yards away toward the German lines. Newby thought this strange, as the gunners obviously saw his patrol and could have shelled them.

The war ended a day or two later and everyone was gathered in a field to celebrate the victory. Newby and some buddies decided to return to their former position. They heard three shots fired and, after a short interval, another three shots. They interpreted this as a distress signal and headed toward the area of the shots. Sure enough, there was a soldier lying in a field with a rifle. As they started toward him, some German soldiers on the edge of a woods hollered at them to go back and that the field was mined. They indicated that they would get the soldier out and bring him to them. They did so and it turned out to be their company commander and his arm had been severed by an exploding mine.

Reflecting back on the patrol, they deduced that the Germans saw them headed into the mine field and put down some rounds to try to keep them from going into it, knowing that the war was almost over.

By executive order, President John F. Kennedy awarded every soldier of the 66th Infantry Division who had earned the Combat Infantry Badge while fighting in Brittany the Bronze Star for Meritorious Service in ground combat.

FRENCH FORCES REORGANIZE AND STRONGLY HOLD THE LINE

During 1945, the French units made aggressive advances toward the Germans. The United States supplied them with food and other essentials but on a limited basis because of the demand by the United States troops. The 66th Division maintained a training program for them that was initiated by the 94th Division. They were delegated to a strong defensive position but were not encouraged to conduct any major offensive assaults. They continued to reconnoiter the German positions and strike when an opportunity presented itself and thus harass the Germans at every opportunity.

While fighting near Chauvé in February 1945, Lt. La Fayette, a descendant of General La Fayette of American Revolution fame, was killed when he and two fellow officers stepped on a mine. Many officers of the United States Army paid their respects when his body lay in view in the Presbytery. He is buried in Chauvé, and there is a monument there in memory of him and the two officers killed with him.

On February 21, 1945, a patrol from FFI unit IVa25 R.I. commanded by a young inexperienced lieutenant reconnoitered a German position at the village of La Montée near Sicaudais. The Germans had a position there commanded by Lieutenant Fritz Eitz. The French patrol followed a stream with hedges bordering it and got very close to the German post. Seizing the opportune moment, they opened fire and Lt. Eitz was seriously wounded. His men returned fire, killing French Corporal Alfred Bouchard. Corporal Guy Quéron turned back to help his fallen comrade and he, too, was killed. The patrol could not recover the bodies and the firefight was finally terminated by a French artillery barrage. Lt. Eitz survived. The Germans recovered the bodies of the two dead Frenchmen and took them to the college of La Montée. The German commandant arranged their funeral for the next Sunday morning, and, after a short church service, they were buried with military honors by a group of German soldiers.

At the end of February 1945, a transition began that converted FFI units into the regular French army and put regular officers in charge. For the most part, these regular officers had been inactive during the occupation and were referred to as "the Mothballs" by the soldiers, meaning that their uniforms had been hanging in the closet. Some of them, however, had taken part in the Organization de La Resistance Armee.

General Raymond Chomel, commander of the French 25th Infantry Division, redefined the role of the Resistance in the south pocket in March 1945. He requested that the Resistance not form armed groups, not cut German communication lines, not act as police, and not carry out guerrilla warfare. Instead, the Resistance began concentrating on gathering information and supplying it to the Allies, an invaluable service. The plans of the German positions that they furnished allowed the French Intelligence to establish precise maps about deployment of the German troops.

Members of the Resistance infiltrated the job forces of the Germans as administrative personnel and interpreters and thus were able to pass information to the French Intelligence. Information was also taken out of the pocket by Jeanette Lexteriaque, a midwife, who was allowed to cross the line. She was discovered but was able to escape to Nantes.

The Resistance monitored the radio constantly waiting to hear the phrase, "*L'etoile polaire vous verna dans deux semaines.*" ("The North Star will come to you in two weeks.") This was code for an all-out attack to take the pocket. The message never came.

OFFICIAL RECORD OF THE 66TH INFANTRY DIVISION

The following is the combat record of the 66th "Black Panther" Division as condensed from the record submitted to and maintained by the War Department Record Branch, S. G. O., Historical Records Section.

The 66th Infantry Division was training in Dorsetshire, England, on December 23, 1944, when orders were received to move to the European Theater immediately. An advance staff consisting of the commanding general, chief of staff, supply and intelligence sections, signal officer, quartermaster, and assistant ordnance officer left for London by military transport plane the next day, then flew directly to St. Jacques Airport near Rennes in Brittany.

In accordance with their assigned mission, they began planning with the staff of the 94th Infantry Division for the concentration of the 66th Division in Brittany and for the relief of the 94th Infantry Division in that region. (This would indicate that the plan was made prior to the sinking of the *Leopoldville* and that the 94th, and not the 66th, was to go to Germany and aid in the Battle of the Bulge.) The three infantry regiments and part of the artillery departed by boat on December 24, 1944. Other elements departed December 26, 27, and 29 from Weymouth, Portland, and Southampton.

The 66th Division had been attached to the United Kingdom Base on November 27, 1944, and now, on December 27, 1944, it was assigned to the 12th Army Group under General Omar Bradley. General Bradley directed the 66th Division to relieve the 94th Division in Brittany.

On January 1, 1945, the 12th Army Group Coastal Sector was divided into four areas of command called sectors. These were

Lorient West Sector—commanded by American Brigadier General Francis Rollins.

Lorient East Sector—commanded by French Brigadier General Borgnis Desbordes.

St. Nazaire North—commanded by American Brigadier General George Forster.

St. Nazaire South—commanded by French Brigadier General Raymond Chomel.

Total French troops in the two pockets—28,826

General Herman Kramer, commander of the 66th Infantry Division and of all Allied forces in the 12th Army Group Coastal Sector, approved a plan of subdividing each sector for greater tactical efficiency. (See Diagram 1.)

The French army forces were organized into the French 19th Infantry Division under General Borgnis Desbordes and the French 25th Infantry Division under General Raymond Chomel. Initially, these divisions consisted of elements of the Resistance and FFI. Gradually, there was a transition toward making these regular army units.

The French forces were supplied food, gas, and oil from United States Army stocks distributed to them by the 66th Quartermaster Company. Vehicles came through French channels. Maximum use was made of captured arms. The supply of ammunition to the French was difficult because of a lack of uniformity of weapons. Also, the front extended for 140 miles, with only one quartermaster truck company handling normal division as supply plus the regular provisions of rations, gas, and oil to the French forces.

The mission of the 12th Army Group Coastal Sector was one of containment. The defensive line consisted of a series of strong points connected behind a thin line of troops. Behind this line at intervals were reserves—some mobile, others dismounted. Automatic weapons fortified the strong points. Outposts were placed strategically in front of the main line.

HISTORY OF THE POCKETS

When the Allies broke away from the Normandy beaches, the German forces in St. Nazaire and Lorient proceeded north and intercepted them at Rennes. The Germans were badly defeated and withdrew back to St. Nazaire and Lorient. Some of the German units added to the two pockets at this time were

Two battalions of the 25th Fortress Base Regiment

Remnants of the 265th Infantry Division

Two naval antiaircraft brigades

Some German labor service units

Crews from several mine-sweeper and blockade-running flotillas

Other naval and shore personnel

Two paratrooper training units

When the 66th Division took over, the Lorient pocket covered 101 square miles, including Lorient proper, the Quiberon Peninsula, and the islands of Belle Isle and Ile de Groix. The pocket was bounded on the west by the Laita River and on the east by the Etel River. It was divided into three parts by the Scorf and Blavet Rivers.

The Lorient pocket was well organized in considerable depth. In some sectors there were as many as five prepared defense lines. The front line was a series of bunkers, barbed wire, and mine fields. Front-line companies were deployed in depth with one platoon in the front line and a second and sometimes a third posted behind the second line. The inner line was very strong with mutually supporting strong points, antitank weapons, tank obstacles, and extensive mine fields.

The St. Nazaire pocket was divided by the Loire River and commanded by Major General Werner Junck. He divided the territory into six sections. Two of the sectors, the one south of the Loire and the inner fortress, were under the command of Brigadier General Maximilan Huentin. The other four, north of the Loire River, were commanded by Colonel Deffner.

The defense of St. Nazaire was not as deep as that of Lorient. The second line of defense was approximately 10 kilometers behind the front line. The third and final line, known as the "Iron Ring," was very strong. The airfield was functioning and received about four flights a week from Germany.

CAMPAIGN OF THE POCKETS

During the month of January, there were many companies that had lost men on the *Leopoldville* and companies that had to furnish replacements. This put all of them in a state of reorganization. Members of the 66th continued to return after hospital stays in Cherbourg. This did not hinder the task at hand, and each company sent out day and night patrols on a regular basis. The French were very aggressive within the limits of their mission. French agents behind the lines brought in much-needed intelligence.

January was a period of becoming acquainted with the enemy and assessing his strengths and weaknesses. The Germans seemed to be creatures of habit and were repetitious in their activities. The Americans and

French sent out many patrols during January so as to locate German positions and intercept German patrols, which often repeated the same route each day. Allied casualties were light that month, but a large number of trench-foot cases were treated throughout both pockets.

During February, the 263rd sent out 297 reconnaissance patrols, of which 81 were at night. Seven combat patrols engaged the enemy, six captured prisoners, and one demolished a building used as an enemy observation post. (The number of patrols usually was many more than the official count indicated, as many were done on a company or platoon level on the spur of the moment for some reason and were not officially listed. A squad leader, for example, might send out three patrols during the day if he noted something suspicious and might not even let the platoon command post know that they were out. This was just part of due diligence.) One lesson learned was that small three- to four-man reconnaissance patrols were most effective, as this small number was less detectable.

Early in February, French agents inside the St. Nazaire pocket sent word that the Germans were preparing for an attack across the Brest-Nantes Canal. On February 8, two French patrols were sent to the two small communities of Le Thenot and Coisnauté on the north bank of the canal. They found that 150 Germans had crossed the canal and occupied both towns. Allied patrols were sent to these areas and supported by artillery. At 1200, Coisnauté was reoccupied by the French, and, at 1600, the French patrols took back Le Thenot. French losses were light.

Visibility increased during February, so more targets were engaged by Allied artillery. Allied patrols increased 38 percent, resulting in much more detailed knowledge of German front-line positions. Interrogation of prisoners revealed much about German life inside the pockets.

In March, the 262nd Infantry Regiment put all three battalions on the line when it occupied the Fay de Bretagne subsector. Increased enemy activity was experienced along the entire front line in this zone. The German patrols became more aggressive and would attack several Allied positions simultaneously with automatic weapons. At first, Americans withheld small-arms fire so as not to give away positions, but after eight front-line riflemen were captured, the policy changed. As soon as any Germans were seen, they were fired upon. Enemy patrols decreased, as did Allied casualties.

On March 9, one gun of the 194th Field Artillery Unit sank a 300-foot-long coastal freighter after hitting it 21 times while firing 71 rounds. On March 22, with one howitzer of the 721st Field Artillery, another ship, a 400-footer, was sunk. This same unit destroyed an ammunition dump after firing on it for two days.

In the St. Nazaire North and South Sectors, completion of the organization of the French 25th Infantry Division was accomplished by General Raymond Chomel, who announced its activation on April 1, 1945.

At the end of March 1945, troops in the two pockets numbered as follows:

Under French Brigadier General Borgnis Desbordes	20,647
Under French Brigadier General Raymond Chomel	17,940
United States troops assigned or attached to the 66th Division	17,582
Total	56,169

On March 31, the 66th Division, with attached troops, was assigned to the Fifteenth United States Army.

In April, the 262nd Infantry Regiment maintained all three of its battalions on the line in the Fay-de-Bretagne area and launched a three-pronged attack against the Germans after intensive reconnaissance. Before dawn, April 19, a heavily armed combat patrol, platoon sized, was launched from each battalion front. Five light tanks accompanied Company F. Two 75 mm assault guns of Troop E, 107th Cavalry, were associated with this party. The mission was to destroy enemy positions, take prisoners, and kill Germans. Bitter fights ensued. Artillery and mortar fire was heavy from both sides.

The 3rd Battalion patrol penetrated enemy lines, and, while the tanks fired on the German positions to the rear, the infantry flushed out German soldiers and brought out four prisoners. Five positions were encountered and four destroyed. Two tanks were lost. The other two patrols were prevented from penetrating the German defensive line. Both patrols were forced to disengage. Three Americans were killed and more than 20 were wounded. It was estimated that the enemy lost 33 men, killed or wounded. Complete surprise had been achieved, though enemy reaction was quite swift in some instances.

In the Lorient West Sector on April 11, 16, and 27, the 3rd Battalion of the 264th Regiment was the target of violent German attacks, first with artillery, then by infantry. The raids were repulsed with grenades, small-arms fire, and mortar fire. L Company received a second attack on April 16, carried out in the same manner as the first. It was repulsed, but these attacks by the Germans cost the Americans six dead or missing and 48 wounded.

On April 19, an outstanding infantry feat was accomplished by a mixed French and American patrol in the Lorient West Sector. Two officers and 88 men, including demolition experts from the French and American forces, were given the mission of destroying a huge stone tower used by the enemy as an observation post. It was 45 feet high and located 2,500 yards from the front lines. Two hundred and seventy pounds of explosives were carried in backpacks, 30 pounds to a man.

They left the friendly line at 0800, penetrated the enemy line without detection, and approached the tower from the rear. The demolition group was covered by security groups posted along the trail. Charges were implanted. The French captain and a United States Army lieutenant stayed at the tower until the patrol had departed. The tower was blown with a nine-minute fuse with complete success. The entire patrol returned without casualties. Careful planning, detailed reconnaissance, teamwork between the French and United States forces, skilled execution, and flawless cover and concealment made the mission a success.

In the Jouteau and Laita subsectors of the East Lorient Sector, from early April until firing ceased in May, the French 118th Infantry and the 19th Dragoons engaged in one bitter fight after another with the enemy. For some reason, the German patrols became more aggressive toward the French line and the French retaliated, precipitating vicious firefights. The French more than held their own and even advanced 700 yards in one section and 1,200 yards in another.

On the Atlantic Front, as on the Eastern Front, the final phase of the war was on and more and more pressure was placed on the enemy. Offensive activity was increased and deserters began to appear. They reported a low morale among the German troops and less desire to continue to fight. The Allies were dominating the fight in both pockets.

The addition of two artillery battalions, the 657th (8" howitzers) and the 540th (155 mm guns), both assigned to the Lorient West Sector, resulted in devastating fire into any section of Lorient and its harbor.

On April 16, the Fifteenth Army attached the remnants of the 106th Infantry Division to the 66th Division for training and reorganization. The 106th had been heavily battered and overrun during "The Bulge" and many of their soldiers had been killed or captured. They were held in reserve in Rennes.

During the first week of May, patrol and artillery activity was at its peak. The intense and unceasing artillery fire on all important enemy installations and troop concentrations in the Lorient pocket, contrasted with the ineffectiveness of the enemy's reaction there, made it apparent that surrender was imminent. Preparations were being made for concentrating the

263rd Regiment behind the 264th Regiment, which was holding the line in the Hamilton Subsector of the Lorient West Sector. Plans were drawn for a coordinated attack. Surrender came before the plans were approved. This spared many American lives.

EVACUATIONS

A series of evacuations were conducted under truce between the Germans and the 94th and 66th Divisions. These were planned and managed by the International Red Cross. Elderly people and children were the first priority followed by mothers-to-be and mothers of young children. Most evacuations were carried out at St. Nazaire through the railway station at Cordemais, which was on the perimeter of the St. Nazaire pocket. Mines were removed from the railway. American guards got off the train at Cordemais and German guards got on. Along with the train crew and guards was an International Red Cross representative and three French Red Cross girls who attended the sick and aged. These were the only personnel to enter the pocket.

After a night in St. Nazaire while evacuees were put aboard, the train returned through "no-man's land" the following day, the second day of the truce. The reverse routine was repeated at Cordemais. The German guards got off the train and the American guards got on.

After the 94th Division left, the 66th Division continued to support these evacuations and the first in 1945 took place on January 18. On this train were two Pullman cars for the children. At Chantenay, they disembarked. The children were placed in the hands of the Red Cross. Another train arrived at Nantes on January 19. More than 6,000 refugees were taken in at Maine-et-Loire, de la Mayene, and la Sarthe. On the 22nd, a third convoy arrived at Ancenis. On April 26, the last train of refugees left St. Nazaire for Ancenis. It was routine for our intelligence units to interrogate the evacuees.

Some truces were held at Lorient and along other sections of the long front of the 66th Division in compliance with urgent pleas from the Red Cross. South of the Loire River and along the Atlantic Coast was the German held city of Pornic, where a truce for evacuation of civilians was held.

Another truce for evacuation of civilians was held at the foot of the Quiberon Peninsula, where 150 Frenchmen were taken off the narrow strip of German-held territory.

NOTES

1. This attack was bound to fail. The noise of the tanks and shouting between parties alerted the Germans, and with their artillery and well-placed defensive positions, a patrol of this nature would precipitate a violent barrage quickly.

2. Thank God for soldiers like Henry West. The squad leader he saved wrote this book.

3. The greatest enemies of successful warfare are a lack of communication and confusion. Confusion will occur no matter how hard one tries to avoid it but a lack of communication is a correctable error. A few minutes of explanation to these two sergeants about the purpose and necessity of this mission would have done much to alleviate their objections. One man in a company could act as liaison between the planners and doers with remarkable results.

Chapter 9

SURRENDER

After the announcement of Hitler's death, the Germans at Lorient and St. Nazaire considered surrender. German Admiral Hans Mirow favored further resistance. General Werner Junck considered surrender but was not sure of his authority to do so. The Allies had recently flown 1,250 planes over St. Nazaire as a show of force. The Germans retaliated by firing the large railway guns at Savenay and Cordemais.

The Germans finally capitulated and met Allied representatives at Cordemais on May 8, 1945, under a flag of truce. Captain Hauptmann Mueller, representing General Werner Junck, met Colonel John Keating, who represented General Herman Kramer, commander of the 66th Infantry Division. Colonel Keating offered an unconditional surrender, which Mueller took back to General Junck.

A cease-fire began at 1:30 P.M., May 8, 1945, as ordered by General Kramer after General Junck had accepted the terms of the surrender. Captain Mueller was sent back to have the surrender document signed.

On May 9, 1945, the United States 66th Infantry used the captured transmitters in the chateau at Kerneval, Admiral Karl Donitz's former headquarters, to inform the long-suffering population that they were at last free again.

On May 10, 1945, an official announcement was made in Bouvron. General Raymond Chomel made the announcement at the Place Royal in Nantes, setting off an enthusiastic celebration. At Caudan, General Wilhelm Fahrmbacher surrendered to General Herman Kramer, commander

M. Hodges (Red Cross International) escorting German officers to surrender negotiation meeting. Courtesy: Hotel de Ville, Lorient, France.

of the 66th Infantry Division, and to French General Borgnis Desbordes, commander of the French forces in Morbihan at 4:00 P.M., May 10, 1945. With General Kramer was General Francis Rollins, commander of the Lorient Sector.

A brief ceremony was held and the 66th Division band played "The Star Spangled Banner" and the French national anthem. General Fahrmbacher arrived just before 4:00 P.M. with members of his staff. They were escorted to General Kramer who stood with Colonel John Keating. Colonel Keating presented General Fahrmbacher to General Kramer. General Fahrmbacher saluted General Kramer and held it until General Kramer returned it. General Fahrmbacher was presented to General Rollins and again salutes were exchanged. When introduced to General Borgnis Desbordes, General Fahrmbacher did not salute. He just looked straight head and finally broke the embarrassing silence by telling General Kramer that he had come to surrender unconditionally all German forces under his command. He then took out his pistol, which was still in the case, and presented it to General Kramer.

On May 11, 1945, Allied soldiers moved into St. Nazaire and again, as in Lorient, were met with flowers, bottles of wine, and many hugs, kisses, and tears. The streets were lined with appreciative civilians. While the ceremony of the surrender was held in Bouvron, the soldiers were immediately dispersed to seize all positions, collect prisoners, and confiscate all arms and ammunition. The Allied forces quickly took over the submarine pens. The Americans and elements of the French navy occupied the Forges de Trignac and all of the German naval installations at Marsac, La Baule, Saint-Marguerite, and Le Crosic.

At the official ceremony in Bouvron, representative French and American troops lined up in a large field. The French were represented by the 8th Cuirassiers, a famous regiment dating back to King Louis XIV. The distinguished American friend, General La Fayette, had been a member of this unit. Elements of the 66th Division, including five tanks, took their place in the formation. French and American national anthems were played. American Generals Kramer and George Forster and French General Chomel were present to accept surrender. Also present were the prefect of the Loire-Inferieure Vincent and the secretary of police, Monsieur Pontal. The Germans present were General Junck, Kriegsmarine Admiral Hans Mirow, two captains of the general staff, and a representative of the Luftwaffe.

All of the above were preceded by Colonel John Keating and Colonel Payhen, representing the Allies and in charge of the surrender arrangements.

General Junck handed over his pistol to General Kramer and saluted him. General Kramer returned the salute. All delegations returned to their cars. General Kramer handed over the civilian powers to Prefect Vincent, who returned to La Baule for a meeting of the town officials. At this meeting, Francois Blancho was reinstalled as mayor of St. Nazaire. By 10:30 A.M., May 11, 1945, the war was officially over. Le guerre est fini!

MONUMENTS

The French people were obviously very appreciative of the Allies for their liberation. There are four monuments dedicated specifically to the campaign that eventually liberated St. Nazaire and Lorient. There are other monuments dedicated to the Allied forces of both World War I and II.

At Caudan, located in a field by the side of the road on the outskirts, is a large stone monument with a bronze plate embedded in its surface that commemorates the site of the surrender of the German forces to the Allied forces on May 10, 1945. It states that at 1600 hours, May 10, 1945,

Beautiful monument in the Bay of St. Nazaire in memory of French and Allied soldiers killed in France in WWI and WWII. The Germans destroyed this monument and the French restored it post-war. Author's photo.

General Fahrmbacher, commandant of the German troops in Lorient, surrenders to General Kramer, commandant of the 66th Infantry Division and to General Borgnis Desbordes, commander of the French forces of Morbihan.

At Bouvron, which is on the outskirts of St. Nazaire, there is a tall granite monument with a large sword carved into the front. At its base, there is a large bronze plaque commemorating the surrender of the German forces at 10:00 A.M., May 11, 1945. There is also a display under glass showing actual photographs of the surrender.

Although not a monument, the railroad station at Cordemais has been restored as a historic landmark honoring the evacuation of hundreds of civilians from the St. Nazaire pocket accomplished by the Red Cross and members of the 94th and 66th Divisions under truces with the Germans.

A monument on the outskirts of Lorient at Pont Scorf commemorates the site at which the advance of the 4th Armored Division was finally stopped by the Germans. Engraved in the stone is "A La Memoire Des Soldats Francais et Americains." It goes on to list the 4th and 6th Armored Divisions and the 94th and 66th Infantry Divisions as well as units of French volunteers, FFI, Rangers, and other French units that fought the

Monument in Lorient, France, in memory of French and Allied soldiers killed in France during WWI and WWII. Author's photo.

Germans in the pocket surrounding Lorient from August 1944, until May 1945.

There is a large monument in Lorient dedicated to all French and Allied soldiers killed in World Wars I and II. Out in the water in the harbor at St. Nazaire is a beautiful monument with its silhouette against the sky that is dedicated to those French and Allied soldiers killed in World Wars I and II. On top of a tall granite column is the figure of a soldier with arms outstretched, holding a sword in one hand with the point downward. This figure is standing on a giant bird whose wings are outstretched.

Monument in Fort Benning, Georgia, dedicated to those soldiers of the 66th Infantry Division who lost their lives when the Leopoldville was sunk by U-486. Author's photo.

There are also magnificent monuments at Fort Rucker, Alabama, and at Fort Benning, Georgia, in memory of the soldiers of the 66th Division who lost their lives on the HMS Leopoldville. At Fort Benning is a black marble wall on which all of the names of those lost are engraved.

BIBLIOGRAPHY

Bertin, Francois. *Saint-Nazaire Sous l'Occupation.* France: Editions Ouest-France, 1999.

Bertrand, J. *Maquis et Liberation, 1944.* Batz-sur-Mer, France: Personal communication to The Grand Blockhaus Museum, 2000.

Bichan, Yves. *Memoirs December 21 and 22, 1944.* Batz-sur-Mer, France: Personal communication to The Grand Blockhaus Museum, 2000.

Bloyet, Dominique. *1939–1945 Saint-Nazaire la Poche.* Montreuil-Bellay, France: Éditions, C.M.D., 1998.

Blumenson, Martin. *United States Army in World War II: The European Theater of Operations. Breakout and Pursuit.* Washington: Office of the Chief of Military History. Department of the Army, 1961.

Bonn, Keith E. *When the Odds Were Even: The Vosges Mountains Campaign, October, 1944–January 1945.* Novato, California: Presidio, 1994.

Bourget-Maurice, Louis and Josyane Grand Colas. *Et la Tanniere Devint Le Village. Histoire De La Base Sour-Marins De Lorient-Keroman 1940–1947.* Rennes: Editions du Quantieme, 1997.

Braeuer, Luc. *La Base Sous-Marine de Saint-Nazaire.* La Baule, France: Imprimerie de Champagne, 2001.

———. *L'Incroyable Histoire de la Poche de Saint-Nazaire.* La Baule, France: Imprimerie de Champagne, 2000.

———. *La Poche de Saint-Nazaire Aout 1944–Mai 1945.* LaBaule, France: Imprimerie de Champagne, 1999.

———. *La Baule 1939–1945.* LaBaule, France: Imprimerie de Champagne, 1998.

Burrin, Phillipe. *France Under the Germans: Collaboration and Compromise.* New York: The New Press, 1996.

Byrnes, Lawrence G. *History of the 94th Infantry Division in World War II.* Nashville: Battery Press, 1982.

Calvocoressi, Peter, Guy Wint, and John Pritchard. *The Penguin History of the Second World War.* Middlesex, England: Penguin Books, 1999.

Churchill, Winston. *The Second World War: Tragedy and Triumph.* Boston: Houghton Mifflin, 1953.

———. *The Grand Alliance.* Boston: Houghton Mifflin, 1950.

———. *The Hinge of Fate.* Boston: Houghton Mifflin, 1950.

Coffee, Carol. *From Tragedy to Triumph: An Historical Memoir of the 66th Infantry Division in World War II.* Houston, Texas: Odyssey International, 1999.

Combat Chronicle. An Outline of U.S. Army Divisions Series: Order of Battle United States Army Military Institute. Historical Division, Department of the Army. Washington, D.C.

Combat History of the 6th Armored Division in the European Theatre of Operations 18 July 1944–8 May 1945. Yadkinville: Ripple Publishing Co., 1945.

Cussler, Clive and Craig Dirgo. *The Sea Hunters.* Boston: Wheeler Pub., 1997.

Dorian, James. *Storming St. Nazaire.* Annapolis: Naval Institute Press, 1998.

Dumas-Delage, General. Personal communication to the author of memoirs of World War II. France, 2001.

Fahrmbacher, General (German) Wilhelm. "Preparation for the Defense of Lorient." (This was a mandatory article demanded of him by the French while he was in prison post-war) National Archives, Washington, D.C. MS B-731.

Fleury, Robert. Personal communication to the author of *Memoirs of World War II.* France, 2001.

Francois, Lucien. Personal communication to the author of *Memoirs of World War II.* France, 2001.

Frankel, Nat and Larry Smith. *Patton's Best. An Informal History of the 4th Armored Division.* New York: Hawthorn Books, 1946.

Heinz, Karl and Michael Schmeelke. *German U-Boat Bunkers. Yesterday and Today.* Atglen, PA: Schiffer Publishing Ltd., 1999.

Hennebont, Morbihan. *Les Heures Tragiques De La Liberation.* Booklet in city archives. Hennebont, France: Imprimerie Artisanale (Pont Scorf, France), 1985.

Hoffman, George F. *The Super Sixth: History of the 6th Armored Division in World War II and its Post-War Association.* Louisville, 6th Armored Division Assn., 1975.

Infantry Tanks Assault Nazis. Black Panther Bulletin of the 66th Infantry Division, no. 2. France, May 8, 1945.

Keefer, Louis E. *Scholars in Foxholes: The Story of the Army Specialized Training Program in World War II.* Jefferson: McFarland, 1998.

Koyen, Kenneth. *The Fourth Armored Division: From the Beach to Bavaria: The Story of the Fourth Armored Division in Combat.* Germany, 1946.

Leroux, Roger. *The Resistance Movement in Saint Marcel.* Rennes, France: Editions Ouest-France, 1992.

Liddel-Hart, Sir Basil Henry. *History of the Second World War.* New York: Putnam, 1971.

Lugez, Michel. *Missions De Bombardements Americains Sur St. Nazaire: "Flak City" 1942–1943.* Rennes, France: Editions Ouest-France, 1998.

Magueres, Virginie. *Hennebont Pendant La Seconde Guerre Mondial.* Student Thesis. University of Rennes, 1995.

Maheo, Patrick. *Saint-Marcel: Haut lieu de la Resistance Bretonne.* Rue Des Scribes Editions, Ploërmel, 1997.

Mansoor, Peter R. *The G.I. Offensive in Europe: The Triumph of American Infantry Divisions, 1941–1945.* Lawrence: The University Press of Kansas, 1999.

Nazi 340's Damaged. Black Panther Bulletin of the 66th Infantry Division, no. 1. France, May 1, 1945.

O'Connor, Jerome M. *Into the Gray Wolves' Den.* Annapolis: United States Naval Institute: *Naval History* magazine, June 2000.

Official Record of the 66th Division. War Department Records Branch, S.G.O., Historical Records Section.

Pallud, Jean Paul. *U-Boote: La Base Sous-Marine de Lorient.* Bayeux, France: Editions Heimdal, 1997.

Palmer, R.R., B.I. Wiley, and W.R. Keast. *The Army Specialized Training Program and the Army Ground Forces.* Historical Division, Department of the Army. Washington, D.C., 1948.

Partridge, Colin. *Hitler's Atlantic Wall.* Guernsey: D.I. Publications, 1976.

Picaud, Pierre. *Memoires De Guerre.* Personal communication to The Grand Blockhaus Museum, Batz-sur-Mer, France, 2001.

Picture Tabloid of German Surrender at Lorient and St. Nazaire. Black Panther Bulletin of the 66th Infantry Division, no. 3. France, May 1945.

Pitt, Barrie, and editors of Time-Life Books. *The Battle of the Atlantic in World War II.* Alexandria, VA: Time-Life Books, 1977.

Queuille, Jean Paul. *1939–1945 Bretagne: Lorient dans la Guerre.* Mortreoill-Belay, France: Editions C.M.D., 1998.

Reconstrire Lorient: Brittany, France, Journal, Le Chasse-Maree/Ar Men, 1999.

Roberts, Ray. *The Leopoldville Trilogy.* Bridgman: Ray Roberts, 2001.

———. *Sequel to Survivors of the Leopoldville Disaster.* Bridgman: Ray Roberts, 1999.

———. *Survivors of the Leopoldville Disaster.* Bridgman: Ray Roberts, 1997.

Roberts, Ray, and Embree Reynolds. *A Tale of Two Panthers.* Bridgman: Ray
    Roberts, 2001.
Rondel, Eric. *Lorient et Saint-Nazaire. Les poches de l'Atlantique.* France: Edi-
    tions Club 35, 1944.
Roskill, S. W. *The War at Sea. 1939–1945,* vols. I and II: HMSO, 1954.
Ryan, Jack R. *History of the 283rd Engineer Combat Battalion.* Bavaria, 1945.
Sanders, Jacquin. *A Night before Christmas.* New York: Putnam, 1963.
Schoenbrun, David. *Soldiers of the Night. The Story of the French Resistance.*
    New York: E. D. Dutton, 1980.
Showell, Jak P. Hallman. *U-Boats Under the Swastika: An Introduction to Ger-
    man Submarines 1935–1945.* London: Allan, 1973.
Slader, John. *The Fourth Service: Merchantmen at War 1939–1945.* London:
    Robert Hale, 1993.
Standifer, Leon C. *Not in Vain: A Rifleman Remembers World War II.* Baton
    Rouge, Louisiana: State University Press, 1992.
Stanton, Shelby. *Order of Battle, U.S. Army, World War II.* Novato, Presidio, 1984.
Stimson, Henry Lewis. *On Active Service in Peace and War.* New York: Harper,
    1948.
Tardivel, Francois K. Personal communication to author of Memoirs of World
    War II, 2001.
Watson, William. First Class Privates. William Watson, 1994.
Wessman, Sintos. *The 66th Division in World War II.* Nashville: Battery Press,
    1946.
Wilson, J. B. *66th Infantry Division. Armies, Corps, Divisions and Separate
    Brigades.* Washington, D.C.: Center of Military History United States
    Army, 1987.

SOURCES: INSTITUTIONS

National Archives, Washington, D.C.
U.S. Army Military History Institute. Carlisle Barracks, Pennsylvania
Charleston County, South Carolina Public Library
Le Grand Blockhaus Musée 39/45 de poche de Saint-Nazaire, Batz-sur-Mer,
    France
Musée de la Resistance Bretonne, Malestroit-Morbihan, France
City archives of Hennebont, France
City archives of Lorient, France

INDEX

ABOUT THE AUTHOR

RANDOLPH BRADHAM is a retired thoracic and cardiovascular surgeon who practiced in Charleston, South Carolina, for 40 years. Formerly a staff-sergeant squad leader in Company E, 262nd Regiment, 66th Infantry Divison, he fought in Brittany against the Germans contained in St. Nazaire and Lorient.